Facilitator's Manual

On Course:
Strategies for Creating Success
in College and in Life

SEVENTH EDITION

and

STUDY SKILLS PLUS, SECOND EDITION

Skip Downing

WADSWORTH
CENGAGE Learning

Australia • Brazil • Japan • Korea • Mexico • Singapore • Spain • United Kingdom • United States

WADSWORTH
CENGAGE Learning·

ISBN-13: 978-1-133-60685-7

ISBN-10: 1-133-60685-7

Wadsworth
20 Channel Center Street
Boston, MA 02210
USA

Cengage Learning is a leading provider of customized learning solutions with office locations around the globe, including Singapore, the United Kingdom, Australia, Mexico, Brazil, and Japan. Locate your local office at: **www.cengage.com/global**

Cengage Learning products are represented in Canada by Nelson Education, Ltd.

To learn more about Brooks/Cole, visit **www.cengage.com/wadsworth**

Purchase any of our products at your local college store or at our preferred online store **www.cengagebrain.com**

Printed in the United States of America
3 4 5 6 7 16 15 14 13

Contents

Chapter 2: Accepting Personal Responsibility 71

Chapter 4: Mastering Self-Management 119

Chapter 5: Developing Interdependence 143

Chapter 7: Adopting Lifelong Learning   203

Chapter 8: Developing Emotional Intelligence   227

Chapter 9: Staying On Course to Your Success   249

Introduction

Purpose of *On Course*

On Course offers students the opportunity to learn essential skills for creating success in college and in life. The central premise of this text is that **success occurs from the inside out.** Although providing students with information about study skills and campus resources is helpful (and presented extensively in *On Course*), in my experience what most helps students achieve success (as they define it) is found at a deeper, more personal level that might best be called character.

The goal of *On Course*, then, is to empower students to develop inner qualities that will help them maximize their potential in college . . . and in life. At the center of the success skills addressed in *On Course* is the students' ability to make wise choices in every realm. *On Course* approaches the college experience as a laboratory where students practice making wise choices that support not only their academic success but their personal and professional success as well.

Teaching college students how to make wise choices is an extremely rewarding enterprise, one that generates benefits for all involved. Students benefit because they learn more effective ways to fashion the positive futures they have come to college to create. Colleges and universities benefit because retention, and therefore funding, improves. Instructors benefit because they have the gratifying experience of empowering students to live rich, personally fulfilling lives . . . and that, I suggest, is our greatest mission as educators, regardless of our specific discipline or job description.

Intended Courses for *On Course*

With its emphasis on making wise choices and on writing guided journals, *On Course* is appropriate for use in a variety of courses. It is ideal for use in student success courses that seek to help students write more effectively. And *On Course* is perfect for writing courses that seek to help students achieve greater success in college and in life. Let's look more closely at how *On Course* supports the goals of both student success and writing courses.

STUDENT SUCCESS COURSES

On Course is designed for use in first-year seminars, student success courses, personal growth classes, leadership courses, self-awareness courses, college orientations, and all courses intended to assist students with their personal, academic, and professional success. By reading and writing about proven success strategies, students discover many new options for improving all aspects of their lives. Specifically, *On Course* invites students to learn how they can . . .

- Accept greater personal responsibility
- Discover self-motivation
- Master self-management
- Employ interdependence
- Gain self-awareness
- Adopt lifelong learning
- Develop emotional intelligence
- Believe in themselves
- Learn effective study strategies*
- Develop critical and creative thinking skills*

*On Course provides extensive instruction in **study skills**, introducing these skills as part of the CORE Learning System. This natural learning system empowers students to design their own effective approach to learning, one that is adaptable to any subject across the curriculum. In the Study Skills Plus edition of the text, students learn study skills using a time-honored problem-solving method that causes them to experience and learn powerful critical thinking skills. **Thus, as they learn study skills, students are simultaneously learning to be effective problem solvers and critical thinkers.**

WRITING COURSES

On Course is also intended for use in developmental writing courses, first-year composition courses, and courses in personal or journal writing. (This emphasis on writing will come as no surprise to those who know that I taught writing for more than three decades, as well as coordinating my college's student success program.) As students write the 33 guided journal entries in *On Course*, they get extensive practice in the same composition skills that accomplished writers use to create effective prose. The directions of the guided journals guide novice writers through three essential elements of the writing process:

1. **Prewriting strategies:** choices for focusing on a topic and generating ideas about it through various heuristic devices.
2. **Drafting strategies:** choices for organizing, developing, and expressing the ideas gathered during the prewriting stage.
3. **Revising strategies:** choices for improving the writing done during the drafting stage.

By practicing this process in each journal entry, students are able to internalize the strategies and language skills necessary for college-level writing. In a community of fellow journal writers, students are motivated to write more effectively as they learn to live more effectively. Additionally, the journal entries in *On Course* give students compelling and motivating subject matter to explore in their formal writing assignments. Chapter 7 contains instruction in the writing process as well as specific writing skills; thus, writing instructors may wish to assign this content early in their course. At the end of each chapter in this Facilitator's Manual, you'll find suggested writing assignments that will enable students to turn their private journal writing into engaging public writing. These formal writings typically constitute the major part of their course grade.

Unique Benefits of the Text

Regardless of the course in which it is used, *On Course* provides students with the skills to achieve . . .

- **greater success in college and in life.** The success strategies that students learn and apply will improve the outcomes and experiences they create in all areas of their lives. Nearly two dozen colleges and universities have documented evidence showing the improved retention and academic success of students who completed an *On Course* class. The "One Student's Story" essays in the text illustrate how student-authors used *On Course* skills to dramatically improve their lives.
- **increased motivation and class participation.** Once students see improved results, they become more involved with their reading, writing, and classroom experiences. As students become personally involved, they learn first-hand the value of an active learning style.
- **improved written and oral communication skills.** Journal writing offers students extensive practice in effective writing skills. Class conversations and presentations stemming from activities in this Facilitator's Manual provide students with extensive practice in expressing their ideas orally to individuals, small groups, and the whole class.
- **stronger critical thinking and problem-solving skills.** Through reading about and practicing critical thinking skills, students become better at solving problems that interfere with their success, as well as constructing and deconstructing persuasive arguments.
- **a sense of empowerment.** By learning to make wise choices that can dramatically improve their lives, students learn to take control of their outcomes and experiences.

Changes in the Seventh Edition

The essence of the first six editions has been maintained:

1. **Short articles about proven success strategies**. These strategies—from innovators in higher education, psychology, business, sports, personal effectiveness, and more—provide practical ways for students to achieve success in college . . . and beyond.
2. **Guided journal entries.** These writing activities encourage students to become active, responsible learners as they apply the success strategies to their own lives.

3. **Case studies in critical thinking.** Each case study offers students an opportunity to apply their understanding of key success principles (such as self-responsibility, self-motivation, and self-management) to real-life situations.

4. **CORE Learning System.** Students read about the latest understanding of how the human brain learns, including three principles that maximize learning. They use these principles and the four components of the CORE Learning System (**C**ollecting, **O**rganizing, **R**ehearsing, and **E**valuating) to design their own personalized learning system, one that will improve their learning in any subject across the curriculum.

5. **Strong coverage of study skills.** *On Course* is offered in two editions—regular and Study Skills Plus. Both options offer students instruction in the essential study skills of reading, note-taking, studying, memorizing, test taking, and writing. The Study Skills Plus edition is different in two ways: (1) It provides a greater number of learning strategies and practice activities than the regular edition, and (2) study skills instruction is presented in a problem-solving format that turns learning study skills into a series of powerful **critical thinking exercises**. In learning to solve their own study problems, students learn a critical thinking process for solving any problem—academic, personal, or professional.

6. **On Course at Work articles**. These articles show students how each *On Course* principle affects their success in the work world. Because many students come to higher education to improve their career opportunities, these articles can motivate them to higher levels of effort.

7. **Money management and stress management strategies**. These sections provide students with ways to overcome two obstacles that keep many students from achieving academic success.

8. **Self-Assessments.** A pre-course self-assessment helps students identify areas for improvement and a post-course self-assessment provides evidence of their growth during the course. Another self-assessment helps students identify how they prefer to learn, helping them decide which learning strategies will help them maximize their learning and course grades.

9. **Learning college customs.** This feature, presented early in the text, helps first-year students learn and become comfortable with the unique customs and terminology of higher education.

10. **Online cartridge.** Complete resources are available for offering *On Course* in an online format.

11. **Embracing Change activities**. These activities provide students with a structure to experiment for a week with one new success strategy and evaluate its impact on their lives. This feature is now available in this Facilitator's Guide as well as online in the College Success CourseMate site for *On Course*, complete with downloadable Embracing Change forms. To access CourseMate, go to **www.cengagebrain.com**.

Enhancing this foundation from past editions are the following new or expanded features in the seventh edition:

1. **An article about "Understanding the Culture of Higher Education" and accompanying journal entry.** Students are introduced to the importance of culture on the choices they make and therefore the outcomes and experiences they create. The introduction of culture is designed to help students understand how colleges in general and their college in particular are different from educational cultures they have experienced previously. With this knowledge, they will more quickly feel at home in their new culture.

2. **An article about "Respecting Cultural Differences" and accompanying journal entry**. Having come to understand how culture shapes our lives and choices, students are introduced to the realities of a culturally diverse world and the importance of developing attitudes and skills to interact successfully with people who are different from themselves. The goal is to help students move from judging and fearing people who are different to respecting and interacting effectively with them. Throughout the text, students are presented with differing cultural perspectives on success principles and strategies.

3. **Additional "One Student's Story" essays.** A popular feature of previous editions, "One Student's Story" essays are authored by students who explain how they used *On Course* strategies to overcome obstacles and achieve academic success. By seeing the practical value that fellow students gained from *On Course* strategies, current students are motivated to implement new strategies themselves. With the addition of four new essays, there are now a total of 25 student stories illustrating the application of *On Course* strategies.

4. **New information about growth and fixed mindsets**. Revisions in Chapter 7 (Adopting Lifelong Learning) introduce students to the work of psychologist Carol Dweck and her colleagues, who have documented the importance of developing a growth mindset for success in academia and beyond. Students both learn about the theory and about strategies for developing this important way of perceiving themselves as lifelong learners.

5. **New information about academic integrity.** Additions to Chapter 7 present the issue of cheating and plagiarism, with a case made for both moral and pragmatic reasons to avoid such practices in the culture of higher education.

6. **A retrospective pre-assessment added to the self-assessment in Chapter 9.** Self-assessments have the built-in problem of accuracy caused by the natural urge to choose answers that make us "look good." A retrospective pre-assessment allows students to identify at the end of the course where they believe they were at both the beginning of the course (retrospectively) and at the end. Such an assessment tends to make a comparison of pre- and post-test scores more valid.

7. **New classroom activities.** Numerous new activities have been added to the Facilitator's Manual, offering new ways to create an active, learner-centered classroom. Some of these new activities have been submitted by experienced *On Course* instructors.

Using *On Course*

On Course allows instructors maximum flexibility in its use. It stimulates lively class activities, including discussions of the success strategies articles in the text, in-class readings of students' journal entries, exploration of the writing process, and experiential exercises that actively engage students in processing the concepts they have read and written about. These exercises are described in detail later in this manual. For distance learning, *On Course* now provides all of the materials needed for a valuable online educational experience.

Naturally, you will want to adapt *On Course* to your own style of teaching. In the sections that follow, I offer my thoughts on some of the issues you will certainly consider as you design and deliver your course.

ASSIGNING READINGS, STUDENT JOURNALS, AND OTHER FEATURES

As a guideline, I recommend assigning one article and its companion journal entry for each hour of class time. For the Study Skills Plus edition of *On Course*, I recommend spending two to three hours of class time on each study skills section you choose to assign. For the regular edition of *On Course*, I recommend devoting one to two hours of class time to each study skills section you choose to cover. Thus, in a course with 45 or more class hours, you will be able to cover most, if not all of the book. Later in this Facilitator's Manual, I provide guidelines for how to adapt *On Course* for classes that meet for fewer than 45 hours.

READING STUDENT JOURNALS

I recommend collecting journals early and often, weekly if possible. I first thumb through students' journals to verify completion of each assigned journal entry and give credit for a job thoroughly done (I call this "Diving Deep"). I skim all journal entries and read thoroughly those entries that catch my interest. This reading gives me a sense of some of the academic and personal issues that each student is facing. In a writing course, I also look for the writing problems with which each student needs help.

Whatever you decide in regard to reading journals, I recommend letting students know your intentions at the outset of the course.

RESPONDING TO STUDENT JOURNALS

Some instructors believe they must comment on everything their students write. Others believe just as strongly that journal writing is a private act and they have no business intruding upon this personal monologue.

I find myself falling somewhere in the middle of this debate. If I come across an idea that intrigues me, I write a response: encouragement, compliment, or question. The question I ask most often is "Can you dive deeper here?" Then I write a couple of questions that would assist the student to do just that, asking for examples, experiences, further explanation, and/or evidence. I begin many of my questions and requests with "I": I was wondering if . . . ? I would love to hear more about . . . I didn't understand . . . I wonder if this has gotten any better for you? When reading an electronic journal (now my preference), I insert my comments, highlighted in green, at the appropriate spot.

HELPING STUDENTS WITH PERSONAL PROBLEMS

On rare occasions, a student will reveal in his or her journal a serious personal problem that is beyond my expertise. I refer this student to an appropriate resource for assistance.

However, I suggest that you first talk with the student privately. Express both your caring concern and your lack of training in the area of concern. Ask if the student would like you to connect him or her with someone who is trained to assist with the problem. I have never had a student refuse such a referral. I believe the keys to getting the student to agree to accept help are to (1) demonstrate a genuine caring for the student's welfare and a candid concern about the problem, (2) explain fully why you are recommending the person you want the student to see, and (3) offer to go with the student and introduce him or her to the person.

One last point. Some instructors with no training in counseling feel uncomfortable upon encountering a student's personal problems. I felt this way in the past myself. I believed that the student's personal life was none of my business. Today I have a different view. I don't teach subjects; I teach students. I teach them strategies for living rich, personally fulfilling lives. Sometimes those strategies are how to write a compelling essay, and sometimes those strategies are how to be successful in college and in life. Anything that interferes with the success of my students is of concern to me. Some students won't be around to learn my academic subjects if I don't initiate an intervention into their personal problems. The problem will be there whether I read about it or not. But if I get to read about a problem in a student's journal, I have an opportunity to help that student transform a problem into an empowering learning experience.

GRADING

Without lowering my standards even an inch, my intention is to give students as much control over their final grade as possible. I want them to choose the grade they want and then perform the actions necessary to earn that grade. I believe this approach shows students that they are responsible both for what they learn and for the grades they earn. It is also consistent with theories of achievement motivation, which assert that students who expect to do well in a course and set personal goals to do so are more persistent in their academic efforts.

The sample syllabi that appear later in this Introduction offer specific examples of how you might put students in control of earning their grades. Meanwhile, here are some general suggestions for determining student grades:

Journal Entries

I don't believe that the spirit of writing a journal is compatible with grading students' ideas or writing styles, but I do believe in rewarding students for their efforts to explore a topic thoroughly. In my grading system (explained in greater detail later), I award up to 5 points for each journal entry. For entries that are lacking in completeness and/or quality of response I award a score between 1 and 4. I award 5 points for each entry that is complete and that demonstrates a commendable effort to explore in depth the issues at hand. For an extraordinary effort that goes above and beyond the expected, I have been known to lose my head and award a 6. After I check journals the first time, I invite students to revise any entries for a higher score; this one-time offer allows them to discover and adjust to my evaluation standards without a penalty to their final grade. It also encourages them to improve the quality of later work.

Quizzes

Occasional quizzes on readings have at least four benefits: (1) They can motivate students to stay up to date on their assignments. (2) They give students immediate feedback about whether they understand a concept that is being explored. (3) They are great practice for what students will face in other classes. (4) Studies have shown that frequent quizzes help students learn some material more thoroughly than students not quizzed. Short-answer quiz questions (true/false, multiple choice, and fill in the blank) appear in this manual at the end of each chapter. Practice quizzes are available for students in the College Success CourseMate site for *On Course*. To access CourseMate, go to **www.cengagebrain.com**.

Essays

In both a student success course and a writing course, I ask students to transform their personal journal writings into formal public writings. Formal writing assignment topics appear in this manual at the end of each chapter discussion.

You may also want to be on the alert for formal writing assignments that could be motivating for an individual student. For example, during a discussion about preferred ways of learning (Journal Entry 26), one of my students stated that some of her high school teachers had "made" her dislike school. She expressed such outrage at her experience that I encouraged her to write a formal letter to the superintendent of her school district and express her experience, her anger, and her suggestions. (I accepted this assignment as a substitute for another class assignment.) She took me up on my offer and produced her best piece of formal writing for the entire semester. She also demonstrated effective critical thinking and strong emotional intelligence in her letter.

Chapter Tests

A test bank is available online and in the instructor's CD. There is a test bank for each chapter that allows you to choose from a menu of questions, including true/false, multiple choice, fill in the blank, matching, and essay. In my courses, I also consider both journals and essays to be take-home tests. I believe that the most valuable examinations are those that not only evaluate a student's knowledge but also give the student an opportunity to apply his or her knowledge in a real-life situation. Whether you prefer giving tests in class or as homework, I recommend using essay questions as well as short answer.

SAMPLE SYLLABI

What follows is my syllabus for a 45-hour student success course conducted over a 15-week semester using the Study Skills Plus edition. Following that is a similar syllabus for use with the regular 7th edition of *On Course*. Next is my syllabus for a 45-hour writing class using the regular 7th edition of *On Course*. Some instructors use my syllabi exactly as they are; others adapt them to their particular needs. Others totally create their own. If you are reading this Facilitator's Manual in book form, please note that these syllabi are available in electronic format within the online version of this Facilitator's Manual on the Instructor's Companion Website.

I have collected syllabi from *On Course* classes being offered at many college and universities in North America. These syllabi are for courses that range in credits from one to four. To obtain an electronic copy of the *On Course* Syllabus Collection, send an email request to Info@OnCourseWorkshop.com. This is a large file and will take a bit longer than a usual email to download.

SYLLABUS FOR A STUDENT SUCCESS COURSE
(STUDY SKILLS PLUS EDITION)

Welcome! My goal in this course is to offer you one of the most valuable learning experiences of your entire life. And I need your full cooperation to make it work!

Course Purpose: This course is designed to help you create greater success in college and in life. In the coming weeks, you will learn many proven strategies for creating greater academic, professional, and personal success. We will use guided journal writings to explore these strategies, and as a bonus, you will learn to express yourself more effectively in writing. You may never again have an opportunity quite like this one to discover how to create a rich, personally fulfilling life. I urge you to make the most of this extraordinary opportunity! If you do, you will dramatically change the outcome of your life—for the better!

Course Objectives: In this course, you will learn how to . . .

1. **Take charge of your life.** You will learn how to take greater personal responsibility, gaining more control over the outcomes and experiences that you create both in college and in life.
2. **Increase self-motivation.** You will learn to create greater inner motivation by, among other things, discovering your own personally meaningful goals and dreams.
3. **Improve personal self-management.** You will learn numerous strategies for taking control of your time and energy, allowing you to move more effectively and efficiently toward the accomplishment of your goals and dreams.
4. **Develop interdependence.** You will learn how to develop mutually supportive relationships with people who will help you achieve your goals and dreams as you assist them to achieve theirs.
5. **Increase self-awareness.** You will learn how to understand and revise your self-defeating patterns of behavior, thought, and emotion as well as your unconscious limiting beliefs.
6. **Maximize your learning.** You will learn key research on how the human brain learns. You will apply this knowledge to develop your own learning system, giving you the keys to learning important course content in college as well as becoming a more effective lifelong learner.
7. **Develop emotional intelligence.** You will learn effective strategies for managing your emotional life, decreasing stress while increasing your inner sense of well-being.
8. **Raise your self-esteem.** You will learn how to develop self-acceptance, self-confidence, self-respect, self-love, and unconditional self-worth.
9. **Write more effectively.** You will learn how to improve your writing skills through the extensive writing practice offered by your guided journal entries.
10. **Improve creative and critical thinking skills.** You will learn how to enhance the thinking skills essential for analyzing and solving problems in your academic, professional, and personal lives. You will also develop reasoning skills that will help you both construct persuasive arguments and deconstruct illogical arguments intended to persuade you to think or act against your own best interest.
11. **Master effective study skills.** You will learn how to raise your grades in college by improving essential skills such as reading, taking notes, studying, memorizing, and taking tests.
12. **Manage your money.** You will learn helpful techniques for increasing your income (including gaining more financial aid for college) and decreasing your expenses.

Course Supplies:

1. *On Course*, Study Skills Plus 2nd edition, by Skip Downing
2. String-bound composition notebook, OR computer journal (with entries emailed to your instructor as attachments, then printed and stored in a three-ring binder)

Method: By reading *On Course* (our textbook), you'll learn empowering strategies that have helped others create great success. By keeping a guided journal, you'll discover how to apply these success strategies to achieve your own goals and dreams. By participating in class activities and focused conversations, and by completing a course project, you will further improve your ability to stay on course to your success. Once you make these new strategies your own through application, you'll have the ability to dramatically improve the outcome of your life—academically, professionally, and personally.

Course Grades:

	Points
A =	360–400
B =	320–359
C =	280–319
D =	240–279
F =	238 or below

Course Projects:

	Points
1. 15 Quizzes (5 points each)	75
2. 33 Success Journals (5 points each)	165
3. 6 Academic Skills Plans (15 points each)	90
4. 1 Final Essay	70
Total Possible Points	400

Each of these four components of your grade is explained below.

1. Quizzes (75 Possible Points)

This is a course for students who choose to be successful in college and in life. One of the most important factors of success in any endeavor is consistent and active participation. To encourage and reward your preparation for active participation at every class, 15 unannounced quizzes on the readings will be given. If you have read the assignment and completed your journal entry, you should have no trouble earning the maximum points (5) for each quiz. **No quiz may be made up.**

Great success is created one small step at a time. Each time that you earn your quiz points you take an important step toward your success in this course . . . and in life!

2. Success Journals (165 Possible Points)

Your Success Journal provides an opportunity to explore your thoughts and feelings as you experiment with the success strategies presented in *On Course*. By carefully examining each strategy in your journal, you will discover which ones will assist you to create a rich, personally fulfilling life. Although I will be collecting your journals and looking through them, **write your journal for yourself,** not for me. Your journal entries may occasionally be read by your classmates.

Journal Writings: During this semester, you will write 33 numbered journal entries from our textbook. These entries will be written outside of class. Additionally, you will write occasional lettered journal entries based on class activities. These journal entries will be written in class. At various times you may have an opportunity to read a journal entry to one or more classmates. **THEREFORE, PLEASE BRING YOUR TEXTBOOK AND JOURNAL TO EVERY CLASS.**

Note: If you wish, you may write the first draft of journal entries on loose sheets of paper, but all journal entries must be written in the composition notebook when it is handed in for evaluation. Or if you choose to write your journal on a computer, you will print hard copies of all entries and bring them to class neatly organized in a three-ring binder. This requirement will assure that none of your entries gets lost. At the end of this semester, you will have your entire journal to keep for years to come. Many students come to regard their personal journal as one of their most valued possessions.

Journal Evaluations: Journals are due weekly. It is not my intention to read every journal entry you write. Instead, I will look through your journal entries to verify the completion of each assignment and to give credit for a job well done. I read occasional journal entries to get a sense of the issues you are working on. With this knowledge I can be of greater assistance to you this semester. If you want my comment on a specific journal entry, please let me know with a note in your journal.

Journal Points: Each journal entry will be awarded up to 5 points. Thus, all 33 journal entries will be worth a possible total of 165 points. A journal entry will be awarded the maximum of 5 points if it fulfills the following two criteria:

1.   The entry is **complete** (all steps in the directions have been responded to), and
2.   The entry is **written with high standards** (an obvious attempt has been made to **Dive Deep**).

Grammar, spelling, and punctuation will NOT be factors in awarding points in this journal. You are free to express yourself without concern for Standard English conventions.

3. Academic Skills Plans (90 Possible Points)

You will complete a personal Academic Skills Plan for the following six topics:

Reading (Chapter 2)

Taking Notes (Chapter 3)

Organizing Study Materials (Chapter 4)

Rehearsing and Memorizing Study Materials (Chapter 5)

Taking Tests (Chapter 6)

Writing (Chapter 7)

The creation of each Academic Skills Plan will provide an opportunity for you to apply an effective problem-solving model to determine the most effective way for you to deepen your learning in college and beyond, not to mention raising your grades! In addition to improving your learning skills and grades, these activities will help you learn how to approach and solve virtually any problem you encounter, whether academic, personal, or professional.

Each of your personalized Academic Skills Plan can earn up to 15 points; thus, all six plans will be worth a possible total of 90 points. To complete each plan, simply follow the six-step process that you will find explained in each chapter, filling in your answer to the following questions:

1.   What's my present situation?
2.   How would I like my situation to be?
3.   What are my possible choices?
4.   What's the likely outcome of each possible choice?
5.   Which choice(s) will I commit to doing?
6.   When and how will I evaluate my plan?

4. Final Essay (70 Possible Points)

As your final project, you will choose one of the two following topics and write an essay.

OPTION 1: ONE STUDENT'S STORY

In this essay, you will relate the story of how you used a specific *On Course* strategy to overcome an obstacle to your success in college or in life. Use the "One Student's Story" essays in our textbook as models of how to write your story. If done well, your instructor may submit your story to the *On Course* Essay Contest. Winning entries will be published in the next edition of the *On Course* text to inspire future students. Winning entries will also be awarded a $100 prize. Full directions for writing this essay can be found at **http://oncourseworkshop.com/Contest.htm.**

An "A" paper will . . .

1. Explain a specific obstacle the writer faced.
2. Describe the specific *On Course* strategy used to overcome the specific obstacle.
3. Present the outcome of using the specific *On Course* strategy to overcome the specific obstacle the writer faced.
4. Show a commitment to excellence in preparation, including professional appearance and a command of Standard English.

OPTION 2: PERSONAL PHILOSOPHY OF SUCCESS ESSAY

In this essay, you will present your own Personal Philosophy of Success, identifying the *On Course* success principles and/or strategies that you will use for years to come. This essay is your opportunity to write the script that will keep you on course to a rich, personally fulfilling life!

An "A" paper will . . .

1. Offer the writer's personal definition of success.
2. Demonstrate the writer's careful consideration of three or more *On Course* success principles and/or strategies that he or she will use to achieve success.
3. Contain extensive support (examples, experiences, evidence, and/or explanation) for each strategy.
4. Show a commitment to excellence in preparation, including professional appearance and a command of Standard English.

Course Rules for Success

To create the very best environment for supporting your success and the success of your classmates, this course has three important rules. The more challenging these rules are for you, the more value you will experience by adopting them. By choosing to follow these three rules, you are choosing to be successful not only in this course but in your life. These rules will support your success in every goal you pursue!

1. **Show up!** To support my success, I choose to attend every scheduled class period in its entirety.
2. **Do the work!** To support my success, I choose to do my very best work in preparing all of my assignments and hand them in on time.
3. **Participate actively!** To support my success, I choose to stay focused and involved in every class session, offering my best comments, questions, and answers when appropriate.

Schedule of Assignments (15-Week Course)

REMINDER: Fifteen unannounced quizzes will be given. No quizzes may be made up.

The following assignments are due at the first class of the week in which they are due. Bring your textbook and journal to every class.

Week 1:   Read/Write Journal 1: Taking the First Step

                      Read/Write Journal 2: Understanding the Culture of Higher Education

Week 2:	Read/Write Journal 3: Becoming an Active Learner
	Read On Course Principles at Work
	Read/Write Journal 4: Believing in Yourself—Develop Self-Acceptance
	Read Wise Choices in College: College Customs
Week 3:	Read/Write Journal 5: Adopting a Creator Mindset
	Read/Write Journal 6: Mastering Creator Language
	Read/Write Journal 7: Making Wise Decisions
	Read Personal Responsibility at Work
Week 4:	Read/Write Journal 8: Believing in Yourself—Change Your Inner Conversation
	Read Wise Choices in College: Reading
	Write your personal Academic Skills Plan for Chapter 2: Reading
	Read/Write Journal 9: Creating Inner Motivation
Week 5:	Read/Write Journal 10: Designing a Compelling Life Plan
	Read/Write Journal 11: Committing to Your Goals and Dreams
	Read Self-Motivation at Work
	Read/Write Journal 12: Believing in Yourself—Write a Personal Affirmation
	Read Wise Choices in College: Taking Notes
	Write your personal Academic Skills Plan for Chapter 3: Taking Notes
Week 6:	Read/Write Journal 13: Acting on Purpose
	Read/Write Journal 14: Creating a Self-Management System
Week 7:	Read/Write Journal 15: Developing Self-Discipline
	Read Self-Management at Work
	Read/Write Journal 16: Believing in Yourself—Develop Self-Confidence
	Read Wise Choices in College: Organizing Study Materials
	Write your personal Academic Skills Plan for Chapter 4: Organizing Study Materials
	Read/Write Journal 17: Creating a Support System
Week 8:	Read/Write Journal 18: Strengthening Relationships with Active Listening
	Read/Write Journal 19: Respecting Cultural Differences
	Read Interdependence at Work
Week 9:	Read/Write Journal 20: Believing in Yourself—Be Assertive
	Read Wise Choices in College: Rehearsing and Memorizing Study Materials
	Write your personal Academic Skills Plan for Chapter 5: Rehearsing and Memorizing Study Materials
	Read/Write Journal 21: Recognizing When You Are Off Course
	Read/Write Journal 22: Identifying Your Scripts
Week 10:	Read/Write Journal 23: Rewriting Your Outdated Scripts
	Read Self-Awareness at Work
	Read/Write Journal 24: Believing in Yourself—Write Your Own Rules
	Read Wise Choices in College: Taking Tests
	Write your personal Academic Skills Plan for Chapter 6: Taking Tests

Week 11:	Read/Write Journal 25: Developing a Learning Orientation to Life
	Read/Write Journal 26: Discovering Your Preferred Ways of Learning
	Read/Write Journal 27: Employing Critical Thinking
	Read Lifelong Learning at Work
Week 12:	Read/Write Journal 28: Believing in Yourself—Develop Self-Respect
	Read Wise Choices in College: Writing
	Write your personal Academic Skills Plan for Chapter 7: Writing
	Read/Write Journal 29: Understanding Emotional Intelligence
Week 13:	Read/Write Journal 30: Reducing Stress
	Read/Write Journal 31: Creating Flow
	Read Emotional Intelligence at Work
Week 14:	Read/Write Journal 32: Believing in Yourself—Develop Self-Love
	Read Wise Choices in College: Managing Money
	Read/Write Journal 33: Staying on Course to Your Success
Week 15:	Final Essay Due

SYLLABUS FOR A STUDENT SUCCESS COURSE
(REGULAR EDITION)

Welcome! My goal in this course is to offer you one of the most valuable learning experiences of your entire life. And I need your full cooperation to make it work!

Course Purpose: This course is designed to help you create greater success in college and in life. In the coming weeks, you will learn many proven strategies for creating greater academic, professional, and personal success. We will use guided journal writings to explore these strategies, and, as a bonus, you will learn to express yourself more effectively in writing. You may never again have an opportunity quite like this one to discover how to create a rich, personally fulfilling life. I urge you to make the most of this extraordinary opportunity! If you do, you will dramatically change the outcome of your life—for the better!

Course Objectives: In this course, you will learn how to . . .

1. **Take charge of your life.** You will learn how to take greater personal responsibility, gaining more control over the outcomes and experiences that you create both in college and in life.
2. **Increase self-motivation.** You will learn to create greater inner motivation by, among other things, discovering your own personally meaningful goals and dreams.
3. **Improve personal self-management.** You will learn numerous strategies for taking control of your time and energy, allowing you to move more effectively and efficiently toward the accomplishment of your goals and dreams.
4. **Develop interdependence.** You will learn how to develop mutually supportive relationships with people who will help you achieve your goals and dreams as you assist them to achieve theirs.
5. **Increase self-awareness.** You will learn how to understand and revise your self-defeating patterns of behavior, thought, and emotion as well as your unconscious limiting beliefs.
6. **Maximize your learning.** You will learn key research on how the human brain learns. You will apply this knowledge to develop your own learning system, giving you the keys to learning important course content in college as well as becoming a more effective lifelong learner.
7. **Develop emotional intelligence.** You will learn effective strategies for managing your emotional life, decreasing stress while increasing your inner sense of well-being.
8. **Raise your self-esteem.** You will learn how to develop self-acceptance, self-confidence, self-respect, self-love, and unconditional self-worth.
9. **Write more effectively.** You will learn how to improve your writing skills through the extensive writing practice offered by your guided journal entries.
10. **Improve creative and critical thinking skills.** You will learn how to enhance the thinking skills essential for analyzing and solving problems in your academic, professional, and personal lives. You will also develop reasoning skills that will help you both construct persuasive arguments and deconstruct illogical arguments intended to persuade you to think or act against your own best interest.
11. **Master effective study skills.** You will learn how to raise your grades in college by improving essential skills such as reading, taking notes, studying, memorizing, and taking tests.
12. **Manage your money.** You will learn helpful techniques for increasing your income (including gaining more financial aid for college) and decreasing your expenses.

Course Supplies:

1. *On Course*, 7th edition, by Skip Downing
2. String-bound composition notebook OR computer journal (with entries emailed to your instructor as attachments, then printed and stored in a three-ring binder)

Method: By reading *On Course* (our textbook), you'll learn empowering strategies that have helped others create great success. By keeping a guided journal, you'll discover how to apply these success strategies to achieve your own goals and dreams. By participating in class activities and focused conversations, and by completing a course project, you will further improve your ability to stay on course to your success. Once you make these new strategies your own through application, you'll have the ability to dramatically improve the outcome of your life—academically, professionally, and personally.

Course Grades:

	Points
A =	270–300
B =	240–269
C =	210–239
D =	180–209
F =	179 or below

Course Projects:

	Points
1. 15 Quizzes (5 points each)	75
2. 33 Success Journals (5 points each)	165
3. 1 Final Essay	60
Total Possible Points	300

Each of these four components of your grade is explained below.

1. Quizzes (75 Possible Points)

This is a course for students who choose to be successful in college and in life. One of the most important factors of success in any endeavor is consistent and active participation. To encourage and reward your preparation for active participation at every class, 15 unannounced quizzes on the readings will be given. If you have read the assignment and completed your journal entry, you should have no trouble earning the maximum points (5) for each quiz. **No quiz may be made up.**

Great success is created one small step at a time. Each time that you earn your quiz points you take an important step toward your success in this course . . . and in life!

2. Success Journals (165 Possible Points)

Your Success Journal provides an opportunity to explore your thoughts and feelings as you experiment with the success strategies presented in *On Course*. By carefully examining each strategy in your journal, you will discover which ones will assist you to create a rich, personally fulfilling life. Although I will be collecting your journals and looking through them, **write your journal for yourself,** not for me. Your journal entries may occasionally be read by your classmates.

Journal Writings: During this semester, you will write 33 numbered journal entries from our textbook. These entries will be written outside of class. Additionally, you will write occasional lettered journal entries based on class exercises. These journal entries will be written in class. At various times you may have an opportunity to read a journal entry to one or more classmates. **THEREFORE, PLEASE BRING YOUR TEXTBOOK AND JOURNAL TO EVERY CLASS.**

Note: If you wish, you may write the first draft of journal entries on loose sheets of paper, but all journal entries must be written in the composition notebook when it is handed in for evaluation. Or if you choose to write your journal on a computer, you will print hard copies of all entries and bring them to class neatly organized in a three-ring binder. This requirement will assure that none of your entries gets lost. At the end of this semester, you will have your entire journal to keep for years to come. Many students come to regard their personal journal as one of their most valued possessions.

Journal Evaluations: Journals are due weekly. It is not my intention to read every journal entry you write. Instead, I will look through your journal entries to verify the completion of each assignment and to give credit for a job well done. I read occasional journal entries to get a sense of the issues you are working on. With this knowledge I can be of greater assistance to you this semester. If you want my comment on a specific journal entry, please let me know with a note in your journal.

Journal Points: Each journal entry will be awarded up to 5 points. Thus, all 33 journal entries will be worth a possible total of 165 points. A journal entry will be awarded the maximum of 5 points if it fulfills the following two criteria:

1. The entry is **complete** (all steps in the directions have been responded to), and
2. The entry is **written with high standards** (an obvious attempt has been made to **Dive Deep**).

Grammar, spelling, and punctuation will NOT be factors in awarding points in this journal. You are free to express yourself without concern for Standard English conventions.

3. Final Essay (60 Possible Points)

As your final project, you will choose one of the two following topics and write an essay.

OPTION 1: ONE STUDENT'S STORY

In this essay, you will relate the story of how you used a specific *On Course* strategy to overcome an obstacle to your success in college or in life. Use the "One Student's Story" essays in our textbook as models of how to write your story. If done well, your instructor may submit your story to the *On Course* Essay Contest. Winning entries will be published in the next edition of the *On Course* text to inspire future students. Winning entries will also be awarded a $100 prize. Full directions for writing this essay can be found at **http://oncourseworkshop.com/Contest.htm.**

An "A" paper will . . .

1. Explain a specific obstacle the writer faced.
2. Describe the specific *On Course* strategy used to overcome the specific obstacle.
3. Present the outcome of using the specific *On Course* strategy to overcome the specific obstacle the writer faced.
4. Show a commitment to excellence in preparation, including professional appearance and a command of Standard English.

OPTION 2: PERSONAL PHILOSOPHY OF SUCCESS ESSAY

In this essay, you will present your own Personal Philosophy of Success, identifying the *On Course* success strategies that you will use for years to come. This essay is your opportunity to write the script that will keep you on course to a rich, personally fulfilling life!

An "A" paper will . . .

1. Offer the writer's personal definition of success.
2. Demonstrate the writer's careful consideration of three or more *On Course* success strategies that he or she will use to achieve success.
3. Contain extensive support (examples, experiences, evidence, and/or explanation) for each strategy.
4. Show a commitment to excellence in preparation, including professional appearance and a command of Standard English.

Course Rules for Success

To create the very best environment for supporting your success and the success of your classmates, this course has three important rules. The more challenging these rules are for you, the more value you will experience by adopting them. By choosing to follow these three rules, you are choosing to be successful not only in this course but in your life. These rules will support your success in every goal you pursue!

1. **Show up!** To support my success, I choose to attend every scheduled class period in its entirety.
2. **Do the work!** To support my success, I choose to do my very best work in preparing all of my assignments and hand them in on time.
3. **Participate actively!** To support my success, I choose to stay focused and involved in every class session, offering my best comments, questions, and answers when appropriate.

Schedule of Assignments (15-Week Course)

REMINDER: Fifteen unannounced quizzes will be given. No quizzes may be made up.

The following assignments are due at the first class of the week in which they are due. Bring your textbook and journal to every class.

Week 1:	Read/Write Journal 1: Taking the First Step
	Read/Write Journal 2: Understanding the Culture of Higher Education
Week 2:	Read/Write Journal 3: Becoming an Active Learner
	Read On Course Principles at Work
	Read/Write Journal 4: Believing in Yourself—Develop Self-Acceptance
	Read Wise Choices in College: College Customs
Week 3:	Read/Write Journal 5: Adopting a Creator Mindset
	Read/Write Journal 6: Mastering Creator Language
	Read/Write Journal 7: Making Wise Decisions
	Read Personal Responsibility at Work
Week 4:	Read/Write Journal 8: Believing in Yourself—Change Your Inner Conversation
	Read Wise Choices in College: Reading
	Read/Write Journal 9: Creating Inner Motivation
Week 5:	Read/Write Journal 10: Designing a Compelling Life Plan
	Read/Write Journal 11: Committing to Your Goals and Dreams
	Read Self-Motivation at Work
	Read/Write Journal 12: Believing in Yourself—Write a Personal Affirmation
Week 6:	Read Wise Choices in College: Taking Notes
	Read/Write Journal 13: Acting on Purpose
	Read/Write Journal 14: Creating a Self-Management System
Week 7:	Read/Write Journal 15: Developing Self-Discipline
	Read Self-Management at Work
	Read/Write Journal 16: Believing in Yourself—Develop Self-Confidence
	Read Wise Choices in College: Organizing Study Materials
	Read/Write Journal 17: Creating a Support System

Week 8:	Read/Write Journal 18: Strengthening Relationships with Active Listening
	Read/Write Journal 19: Respecting Cultural Differences
	Read Interdependence at Work
Week 9:	Read/Write Journal 20: Believing in Yourself—Be Assertive
	Read Wise Choices in College: Rehearsing and Memorizing Study Materials
	Read/Write Journal 21: Recognizing When You Are Off Course
	Read/Write Journal 22: Identifying Your Scripts
Week 10:	Read/Write Journal 23: Rewriting Your Outdated Scripts
	Read Self-Awareness at Work
	Read/Write Journal 24: Believing in Yourself—Write Your Own Rules
	Read Wise Choices in College: Taking Tests
Week 11:	Read/Write Journal 25: Developing a Learning Orientation to Life
	Read/Write Journal 26: Discovering Your Preferred Ways of Learning
	Read/Write Journal 27: Employing Critical Thinking
	Read Lifelong Learning at Work
Week 12:	Read/Write Journal 28: Believing in Yourself—Develop Self-Respect
	Read Wise Choices in College: Writing
	Read/Write Journal 29: Understanding Emotional Intelligence
Week 13:	Read/Write Journal 30: Reducing Stress
	Read/Write Journal 31: Creating Flow
	Read Emotional Intelligence at Work
Week 14:	Read/Write Journal 32: Believing in Yourself—Develop Self-Love
	Read Wise Choices in College: Managing Money
	Read/Write Journal 33: Staying on Course to Your Success
Week 15:	Final Essay Due

SYLLABUS FOR A WRITING COURSE

Welcome! My goal in this course is to offer you one of the most valuable learning experiences of your entire life. And I need your full cooperation to make it work!

Course Purpose: The purpose of this course is to offer you the opportunity to learn powerful writing strategies. The theme of our class is **SUCCESS** . . . what success is for you and how you can achieve it. In the coming weeks, you will learn many proven strategies for living a rich, personally fulfilling life. We will use writing to explore these strategies, and through this practice you will learn to express yourself more effectively in writing.

Course Objectives: Specifically, by the end of this course, successful students (YOU!) will be able to write essays that

1. Are controlled by a clear **purpose**,
2. Develop that purpose with sufficient, well-organized **support**,
3. Adapt the purpose and support to a particular **audience**, and
4. Are written in a smooth, grammatically appropriate **style**.

Method: In this course, you will be reading, writing, and talking about how to create success (as you define it). You will keep a guided journal in which you will explore many strategies of success. Five times during the course you will write a formal essay based on the ideas you have been developing in your journal.

Once you make both these writing and success strategies your own, you will have the ability to dramatically improve the outcome of your life.

Course Supplies:

1. *On Course*, 7th edition, by Skip Downing
2. String-bound composition notebook OR computer journal (with entries emailed to your instructor as attachments, then printed and stored in a three-ring binder)

Course Grades:

		Points
A	=	666–740
B	=	591–665
C	=	516–590
D	=	441–515
F	=	440 or below

Course Projects:

	Points
1. 15 Quizzes (5 points each)	75
2. 33 Success Journals entries (5 points each)	165
3. 5 Essays (100 points each)	500
Total Possible Points	740

Each of these three components of your grade is explained below.

1. Quizzes (75 Possible Points)

This is a course for students who choose to be successful in college and in life. One of the most important factors of success in any endeavor is consistent and active participation. To encourage and reward your preparation for active participation at every class, 15 unannounced quizzes on the readings will be given. If you have read the assignment and completed your journal entry, you should have no trouble earning the maximum points (5) for each quiz. **No quiz may be made up.**

Great success is created one small step at a time. Each time that you earn your quiz points you take an important step toward your success in this course . . . and in life!

2. Success Journals (165 Possible Points)

Your Success Journal provides an opportunity to explore your thoughts and feelings as you experiment with the success strategies presented in *On Course*. By carefully examining each strategy in your journal, you will discover which ones will assist you to create a rich, personally fulfilling life. Although I will be collecting your journals and looking through them, **write your journal for yourself,** not for me. Your journal entries may occasionally be read by your classmates.

Journal Writings: During this semester, you will write 33 numbered journal entries from our textbook. These entries will be written outside of class. Additionally, you will occasionally write lettered journal entries based on class exercises. These journal entries will be written in class. At various times you may have an opportunity to read a journal entry to one or more classmates. **THEREFORE, PLEASE BRING YOUR TEXTBOOK AND JOURNAL TO EVERY CLASS.**

Note: If you wish, you may write the first draft of journal entries on loose sheets of paper, but all journal entries must be written in the composition notebook when it is handed in for evaluation. Or if you choose to write your journal on a computer, you will print hard copies of all entries and bring them to class neatly organized in a three-ring binder. This requirement will ensure that none of your entries gets lost. At the end of this semester, you will have your entire journal to keep for years to come. Many students come to regard their personal journal as one of their most valued possessions.

Journal Evaluations: Journals are due weekly. It is not my intention to read every journal entry you write. Instead, I will look through your journal entries to verify the completion of each assignment and to give credit for a job well done. I read occasional journal entries to get a sense of the issues you are working on. With this knowledge I can be of greater assistance to you this semester.

If you want my comment on a specific journal entry, please let me know with a note in your journal.

Journal Points: Each journal entry will be awarded up to 5 points. Thus, all 33 journal entries will be worth a possible total of 165 points. A journal entry will be awarded the maximum of 5 points if it fulfills the following two criteria:

1. The entry is **complete** (all steps in the directions have been responded to), and
2. The entry is **written with high standards** (an obvious attempt has been made to Dive Deep).

Grammar, spelling, and punctuation will NOT be factors in awarding points in this journal. You are free to express yourself without concern for Standard English conventions.

3. Formal Essays (500 Possible Points)

Purpose: Five times during the semester you will turn in a formal essay. In these essays, you will take ideas explored in your private journal and write them for a public audience. In this manner, you will practice and demonstrate the essay-writing skills that we will be learning in this course. Topics will be provided, but you are invited to offer alternative topics that appeal to you. Alternative topics must be approved before you write the essay. The minimum length of each essay is 750 words, and it must be prepared on a word processor. Each essay will be awarded up to 100 points. An essay earning 100 points will:

1. Be controlled by a clear purpose,
2. Develop that purpose with sufficient, well-organized support,
3. Adapt the purpose and support to a particular audience, and
4. Show a commitment to excellence in preparation, including professional appearance and use of Standard English.

OPTIONAL ESSAY: ONE STUDENT'S STORY

You may submit the following essay for any of the five assigned essays. In this essay, you will relate the story of how you used a specific *On Course* strategy to overcome an obstacle to your success in college or in life. Use the "One Student's Story" essays in our textbook as models of how to write your story. If done well, your essay may be entered in the *On Course* Essay Contest. Winning entries will be published in the next edition of the *On Course* text to inspire future students. Winning entries will also be awarded a $100 prize. Full directions for writing this essay can be found at **http://oncourseworkshop.com/Contest.htm.**

An "A" paper will . . .

1. Explain a specific obstacle the writer faced.
2. Describe the specific *On Course* strategy used to overcome the specific obstacle.
3. Present the outcome of using the specific *On Course* strategy to overcome the specific obstacle the writer faced.
4. Show a commitment to excellence in preparation, including professional appearance and a command of Standard English.

Essays will be penalized 5 points for each day late. You must complete all five essays to earn a passing grade in the course.

Course Rules for Success

To create the very best environment for supporting your success and the success of your classmates, this course has three important rules. The more challenging these rules are for you, the more value you will experience by adopting them. By choosing to follow these three rules, you are choosing to be successful not only in this course but in your life. These rules will support your success in every goal you pursue!

1. **Show up!** To support my success, I choose to attend every scheduled class period in its entirety.
2. **Do the work!** To support my success, I choose to do my very best work in preparing all of my assignments and hand them in on time.
3. **Participate actively!** To support my success, I choose to stay focused and involved in every class, offering my best comments, questions, and answers when appropriate.

Writing Course Schedule of Assignments (15-Week Course)

Note: Fifteen unannounced quizzes will be given. No quizzes may be made up. The following assignments are listed here on the day they are due in class. Bring your textbook and journal to every class.

Week 1:	*On Course*: Read/Write Journal 1	
	On Course: Read "Wise Choices in College: Writing" in Chapter 7	
Week 2:	*On Course*: Read/Write Journals 2 and 3	Essay 1 Due

Week 3:	*On Course*: Read/Write Journals 4, 5, and 6	
Week 4:	*On Course*: Read/Write Journals 7, 8, and 9	
Week 5:	*On Course*: Read/Write Journals 10 and 11	Essay 2 Due
Week 6:	*On Course*: Read/Write Journals 12, 13, and 14	
Week 7:	*On Course*: Read/Write Journals 15, 16, and 17	
Week 8:	*On Course*: Read/Write Journals 18 and 19	Essay 3 Due
Week 9:	*On Course*: Read/Write Journals 20 and 21	
Week 10:	*On Course*: Read/Write Journals 22, 23, and 24	
Week 11:	*On Course*: Read/Write Journals 25 and 26	Essay 4 Due
Week 12:	*On Course*: Read/Write Journals 27, 28, and 29	
Week 13:	*On Course*: Read/Write Journals 30 and 31	
Week 14:	*On Course*: Read/Write Journals 32 and 33.	
Week 15:		Essay 5 Due

[Reminder to writing instructors: Engaging topics for formal essays are offered in this manual at the end of every chapter.]

ADAPTING *ON COURSE* FOR CLASSES WITH FEWER THAN 45 CONTACT HOURS

Chapters 1, 2, and 3 present concepts and vocabulary that are foundational for all subsequent chapters. Chapter 6 presents concepts and vocabulary that are fundamental for work in Chapters 7 and 8. Chapter 9 offers students a second opportunity to take the self-assessment questionnaire that they took in Chapter 1. By comparing the results of these two questionnaires, students can see evidence of the changes in their behaviors, thoughts, emotions, and beliefs.

As a guideline, I recommend assigning one article and its companion journal entry for each hour of class time. For the Study Skills Plus edition of *On Course*, I recommend spending two to three hours of class time on each study skills section you choose to assign. For the regular edition of *On Course*, I recommend devoting one to two hours of class time to each study skills section you choose to cover. With this guideline in mind, I suggest that you follow one of three plans if you assign students fewer than all 33 journal entries and six Academic Skills Plans to complete.

Plan 1: Start with Chapter 1 and go as far into the book as time allows. Then assign Journal 33 (with the post-course questionnaire) in the final week. For example, if you have a 15-week course that meets 1 hour per week (15 hours), you might assign the following 15 journals:

Journals 1–14 and 33

You can assign other features (e.g., Wise Choices in College: Study Skills, Embracing Change, On Course at Work, One Student's Story) as you choose.

Plan 2: Assign foundational Chapters 1, 2, 3, and 6 and as many other chapters as time allows. For example, if you have a 15-week course that meets 2 hours per week (30 hours), you might assign the following 23 journals:

Chapters 1–4 (Journals 1–16)

Chapter 6 (Journals 21–23)

Chapter 7 (Journals 25–27)

Chapter 9 (Journal 33)

You can then assign other features (e.g., Wise Choices in College: Study Skills, Embracing Change, On Course at Work, One Student's Story) as you choose.

Plan 3: Assign foundational Chapters 1, 2, 3, and 6, and as many other individual journals as time allows. For example, if you have a 12-week course that meets 2.5 hours per week (30 hours), you might assign the following 27 journals:

Chapters 1–3 (Journals 1–12)

Journals 13, 14, 15

Chapter 6 (Journals 21–23)

Journals 25–33

You can assign other features (e.g., Wise Choices in College: Study Skills, Embracing Change, On Course at Work, One Student's Story) as you choose.

Creating a Learner-Centered Classroom

Within every class session, students will ideally experience three or more of the following activities:

1. An exercise that reinforces the reading and journal writing in the text.
2. A Quick-Write activity in response to an in-class exercise or prompt from the text (these Quick-Writes can be written in students' journals and lettered to contrast with the numbered journal entries from *On Course*).
3. A discussion (in pairs, trios, quartets, or with the entire class). For example, discussions could focus on one of the following features: "One Student's Story" or On Course at Work. The following directions suggest specific ways to generate these discussions.
4. Lecture/instruction (from the instructor, student[s], guest speaker, or video).
5. Exploration of study skills strategies, especially the Academic Skills Plans in the Study Skills Plus edition.
6. A quiz.

Let's take a look at each of these six activities:

1. **Exercises:** I recommend engaging students in active learning exercises in every class period. The exercises in this Facilitator's Manual (supplemented by the many additional exercises found at **www.OnCourseWorkshop.com**) provide you with more activities than you could possibly use in one semester. Each exercise is designed to engage your students as active, responsible learners, deepening their understanding of the success strategies they have been reading about in the text and writing about in their journals.

   This Facilitator's Manual provides you with two broad categories of activities. First are the All-Purpose Exercises that utilize the features present in most chapters in the text. Second are the Chapter-Specific Exercises that are paired with—and meant to reinforce—specific success strategies your students will be learning in *On Course*. Let's look at the options within these two categories of exercises.

   All-Purpose Exercises: Numerous features appear in most chapters (e.g., case studies) of *On Course*. The eight all-purpose strategies—described directly below—provide you with options for turning these textbook features into active learning strategies. If you find a strategy here that you like, you can repeat it with multiple chapters because the new content will make it fresh each time.

   A. Journal Entries: Thirty-three journal entries are provided, one after each article about a success strategy. Students sit in pairs with their journal entries in hand. (1) Student A reads a designated journal entry to Student B. (2) Student B responds to Student A, "What I hear you saying in this entry is . . . ." (3) Students now reverse roles and repeat Steps 1 and 2. (4) Students then take a few minutes to discuss or quick-write any thoughts or feelings that came up for them as they read or listened. (5) The class discusses what they experienced and learned during the entire process.

   This activity, as simple as it is, seldom fails to energize students' thinking, and it generates many benefits: (1) Readers hear their own ideas, often discovering how to take their thinking to deeper, more complex levels. (2) Readers hear their own voice, noting where their writing is clear and where it is muddy. As a result they improve as editors of their own writing. (3) Both readers and responders get to hear another person's thoughts on the same issue they have explored, an experience that often helps them develop critical and creative thinking (and also makes them more aware of the importance of audience in communication). (4) Responders learn to practice active listening, which allows them to more effectively discover the heart of any communication. This is especially valuable for reinforcing the listening skills that students will learn in Journal Entry 18. (5) The sharing of ideas by readers and responders creates community among class members, which often raises their level of commitment to the activities and learning available in the course.

B. Case Studies: Chapters 2–8 open with a case study that focuses on the topic of that chapter (e.g., personal responsibility, self-motivation, etc.). The goal of each case study is to get students actively engaged in thinking about the topic and its impact on real-life situations. The collateral benefit of this active engagement is the development of critical thinking skills as students express/defend their own positions and analyze/dispute the positions of others. Here are three different ways to debrief case studies:

- After students score the case study, ask a volunteer to explain his or her score ("Who did you choose as Number 1 and why?"). Then invite others with different opinions to voice their positions and reasons. Without revealing your own viewpoint, pit ideas (not students) against one another: "Who has a different point of view? Why do you think that? What experience have you had that influenced this view?" More important than students' viewpoints, explore their reasons, urging them to support their opinions as concretely as possible. Instead of pointing out a weakness in an argument (and thus appearing to be taking sides), ask, "How would you respond to a person who says . . . ?" Guide the discussion to explore the topic of the chapter by simply spending more time with points of view that focus on that topic.
- After students score the case study, have them get in groups with others whose top choice is the same. Have the groups choose a spokesperson and arm the spokesperson with arguments that will change the mind of others. Invite each spokesperson to present his or her group's argument, allowing others to change groups if their minds have changed. (Ask anyone whose mind is changed to explain what changed it.) Once again, avoid letting students know what you believe about the case study because they will often think that your opinion is the "correct" answer and all critical thinking (and debate) will cease.
- After students read the case study, have them rewrite it so that the characters model the quality of the chapter. For example, in the chapter on emotional intelligence, students would rewrite the case study so that each character in the story speaks and acts with emotional intelligence (as opposed to the lack of emotional intelligence they display in the present case study). You can have students either read or act out their revised case studies. Ask them to explain why they had their characters act and speak as they did (e.g., "How does that behavior illustrate emotional intelligence?")

C. One Student's Story: These brief essays, written by college students, explain how the authors applied *On Course* strategies to overcome an obstacle to their success in college or life. Following are three ways to debrief these essays. The goal is to get students to become more aware of (1) the many potential obstacles that can keep them from achieving success in college and (2) the importance of making wise choices to avoid or overcome these obstacles.

- Read the beginning of the essay to your students and stop after presenting the student's obstacle, problem, or challenge. Ask your students to identify any choices the student-author made to create the obstacle. Then discuss what they would do if they found themselves in the author's situation. Afterward, read the rest of the essay and have your students compare their options with what the student-author actually did.
- Have your students read the entire essay either in class or for homework. In class, ask them to discuss the choices that got the student into the predicament. Then have them propose additional ways the student-author could have overcome the obstacle.
- Ask students to identify a problem they are facing in college. Next, ask them to read a "One Student's Story" and find a way that they can use the same strategy for solving their own problem that the author of the essay used to solve his or her problem. Obviously, sometimes the strategy will not work for their problem. But more times than they might expect, the "forced-fit" approach leads to creative solutions they might never have thought of otherwise.

D. On Course at Work: These articles explain how the soft skills explored in each chapter of *On Course* are beneficial to career success. The goal is to get students to be more motivated to learn these personal skills by seeing their practical value in future careers. Here are three ways to debrief these articles:

- Ask students to identify their present career goal and talk about situations in which the chapter soft skill (e.g., personal responsibility) would be important in that career. For "undecided" students, ask them to imagine the importance of the soft skill in a particular career (perhaps their parents' careers).
- Ask students who have work experience to describe a time when someone at their workplace did or did not employ the soft skill under examination (e.g., interdependence) and the consequence. As a variation, this story could be turned into a case study.

- Ask students to find and bring in employment ads that list soft skills required of applicants. Discuss the various terms used to ask for soft skills. For example, the employment ad may ask for a "self-starter who is organized and able to work without direct supervision." Translation: the employer wants someone who is self-motivated and self-managing.

E. Quotations: Quotations in the margins of the text express what others (famous and not so famous) have said about the success strategies being considered. The objective is to get students to realize that many people place great importance on the ideas and strategies they are learning in the course. Here are three ways to use these quotations:

- Ask students to choose a quotation from the margins of *On Course* with which they strongly agree or disagree. They do a short (two- to four-minute) quick-write response to their chosen quote. Students then share their responses in pairs, small groups, or with the entire class.
- Have students identify a favorite quotation and do research to find out who the author is. They present their chosen quotation to the whole class, explain why they chose it, and share their findings about the author.
- Ask students to find and bring in a quotation that could be placed in the margin of the chapter they are reading. Students present their quotation to the class and explain how it fits into the topic under discussion. Alternative: Ask students to find and bring in lyrics of a song that could be placed in the chapter. A number of Internet sites provide song lyrics (e.g., www.lyrics.com and www.songlyrics.com/)

F. Cartoons: The goal of this feature is to help students to see the humor in serious topics, as well as the seriousness of humorous topics. And they're fun!

- Students read a cartoon and respond in a short writing to the question, "What does this cartoon say about being successful?" Or "Why is this cartoon funny . . . or not funny?" Students then share their responses in pairs (as in Exercise A), small groups, or with the entire class.
- Have students find and bring in their own cartoons that illuminate one of the strategies of success being considered.
- Provide students with a cartoon without any words. Have them add words to the cartoon to fit the topic they are studying (e.g., self-motivation). This is a fun creative thinking activity.

G. Focus Questions: One to three questions precede each of the 33 articles about success strategies. Discussing answers before they read the article enables students to preview the success strategies and discover what they already think and know about the topic. The point should also be made that reading the article through the filter of questions enables a reader to gain more valuable (usable) information. This exercise assists students to become better readers. It is wise to emphasize the focus questions early in the semester, so students get in the habit of thinking about them before beginning to read.

- Before they read the chapter, have students read the focus questions and write their best present answers to the questions. Students then share their responses in pairs (as in Exercise A), in small groups, or with the entire class.
- After they read the chapter, have students read the focus questions and write their best answers to the questions. Students then share their responses in pairs (as in Exercise A), in small groups, or with the entire class.

H. Chapter-Opening Charts (Successful Students/Struggling Students): Each chapter begins with a graphic organizer comparing successful and struggling students. Once again, make the point that previewing enables learners to gain more valuable (usable) information as they read.

- Have students read the chapter-opening chart and respond in a short writing to the questions, "Which of these choices do you think will be easiest for you? The most difficult?" Then have students share their responses in pairs (as in Exercise A), in small groups, or with the entire class.

Chapter-Specific Exercises: Most of the remainder of this Facilitator's Manual presents exercises that are paired with the specific success strategies your students will be reading and writing about in *On Course*. You'll find more exercises here than you could possibly use in a semester or quarter, so choose the ones that you believe will best help your students to understand the principles and strategies of success. Although each of these strategies is different, they all include the following six parts:

Purpose: Each exercise begins with a statement of the outcome(s) that the activity is intended to produce. This feature allows you to make a quick determination as to whether a particular activity is appropriate for your course.

Supplies and Setup: This information tells you what supplies (if any) are needed for the exercise; most of the supplies are common items that you probably already own or to which you have easy access. Setup instructions indicate anything that needs to be arranged before the exercise begins.

Directions: [Directions to the instructor are written in brackets—like this.] *Words of direction that you speak to the students are italicized—like this.* Directions labeled "Optional" may be dropped to save time.

One essential point about directions: The success of an exercise is dependent on whether students fully understand the directions. I recommend confirming that every student is clear on the directions before starting them on the activity. One way to clarify directions (especially complex directions) is to provide them on a handout or project them on a PowerPoint slide. Also helpful is giving a demonstration (DEMO) of exactly what you are asking the students to do. *So, here's what this would look like . . . What questions do you have? Okay, begin.*

Approximate Time: Each step in the directions has an approximate time indicated. These times are guidelines and can be adapted to your circumstances or time restraints. Most exercises have a step for conducting a class discussion. If the exercise is running long, you can shorten the discussion. If the exercise is running short, you can lengthen the discussion. In this way, you can always end right on time.

Instructor Notes: Sometimes there are special aspects of an exercise that are not part of the directions but that I have found make the activity more successful. I write these to myself after doing the activity so I'll remember them for next time. I have included my "Instructor Notes" here, and I suggest you add your own after you employ an exercise.

Source: Where appropriate, I have indicated my source for an exercise. In most cases, even if I have learned the idea from someone else, I have adapted it to my own style. I urge you to do the same. Make each exercise your own. Many exercises have been contributed by *On Course* instructors. Their names appear as the source.

2. **Quick-Writes:** Class discussions are usually improved when students first write about the issue under consideration. That is why Quick-Writes appear in many of the classroom exercises. This brief writing gives reflective learners time to gather and organize their thoughts for discussion. Such in-class writings can be lettered in students' journals to distinguish them from the numbered journal entries in *On Course*. I recommend timing these writings, starting with short sessions (one or two minutes) early in the semester and lengthening them to perhaps five to eight minutes toward the end of the semester. Typical directions to the students are as follows: *When I say, "Go," begin writing about ____ until I say, "Stop." There is no right or wrong thing to write. Simply follow your thoughts and feelings about this issue, wherever they lead. If your mind goes blank at any time, write, "My mind is blank. . . . I can't think of anything to write . . . What am I going to do? My mind is still blank. . . . Let's see—what am I supposed to write about here? Oh, yes, . . ." Eventually, your mind will usually return to the task at hand. If not, whatever you write is fine. Any questions? Ready, begin.* Students soon learn that quick writings of this nature are a powerful prewriting (or prediscussion) strategy for generating ideas.

3. **Discussions:** Discussions (in pairs, trios, quartets, or with the entire class) are usually quite lively when preceded by a stimulating exercise and/or journal writing. Before entertaining a discussion by the entire class, you may wish to put the students in smaller groups (two, three, or four) for a warm-up discussion. Introverted, shy, and English-as-a-Second-Language students are more likely to participate in these small groups and, after this dress rehearsal, may be ready to express their ideas to the whole class. Each exercise in this manual offers suggested debriefing questions for stimulating, meaningful class discussions. However, one all-purpose discussion technique is the PMI, suggested by Edward de Bono in his book *De Bono's Thinking Course*. P stands for Plus (the good points of an idea), M stands for Minus (the bad points of an idea), and I stands for Interesting (the intriguing points of an idea). To do a PMI discussion, simply explore these three elements of any idea, one at a time. De Bono argues that a PMI forces learners out of thinking ruts and promotes critical thinking (though, to be accurate, he calls it lateral thinking).

4. **Lecture/Instruction:** Once students' mental juices are flowing (after an exercise, journal writing, and/or discussions), they are ripe for further instruction. For some topics, you can assign students the role of instructor and let them instruct the class themselves. This approach gives students ultimate responsibility for their own education. (It is usually wise to have students do a dress rehearsal with you before they present to the class. In this way, you can exert some quality control.) Guest speakers or videos also add a nice change of pace.

5. **Study Skills Strategies:**

Regular Edition: At the end of each "Wise Choices in College" section in the regular edition of the text, you'll find an exercise that will help students practice the specific study skill they have been learning. You'll find additional strategies in this manual at the end of each chapter. Here, however, is a collaborative learning activity (a variation of a structure called the "Jigsaw") that can be used with any of the study skills sections.

A. Put students into "home" groups of three, each with a copy of *On Course* open to the study skill you are working on. You may have assigned the topic for homework, or you may have students seeing it for the first time.

B. Point out to students that the menu of study skills strategies is divided into three sections: Before, While, and After. Ask each student in a trio to choose one section.

C. Say to students, "Take 10 minutes to learn the one or two strategies in your section (Before, While, or After) that you think are the most valuable."

D. Have the students now move into three "expert" groups by the section they have chosen: Before, While, and After. Say to students, "In your expert group, you have 15 minutes to decide which are the two most helpful strategies in your section and prepare yourselves to return to your home groups and teach these strategies to your two partners."

E. Have the students return to their home groups. Say, "Now, going in order of Before, While, and After, teach your partners one strategy. After each of you has taught one strategy, continue going around, teaching additional strategies, until I call time. In this way, you will become familiar with six strategies."

F. As a final step, you can ask students, "What new strategies will you commit to experimenting with?" Because each of us has preferences for the way we like to learn, encourage students to experiment with various strategies, making those that improve their results in college part of their repertoire of study skills.

Study Skills Plus Edition: Each "Wise Choices in College" section in the Study Skills Plus edition is, itself, an extensive exercise that guides students to employ and strengthen personal responsibility and critical thinking along with learning academic skills. This exercise takes students through the six steps of the problem-solving method they will encounter in Chapter 2: The Wise Choice Process. The goals of the activity are twofold. First, students develop a personalized academic skills plan that addresses their self-identified learning problems. Second, by using a problem-based learning approach, they practice the process of critically thinking through a problem and making wise choices based on that thinking. Here are some ways to engage students in this activity during class. (Please familiarize yourself first with the six steps of the Wise Choice Process in Chapter 2 so these directions will make sense):

• After students identify their "situation" (the study problem they identify in Step 1 of the Wise Choice Process), put students in pairs and facilitate an "Eagles and Hawks" activity. In each pair, one student designates him- or herself as an Eagle and the other student becomes a Hawk. (This designation is to facilitate future movement of the students and has no other significance. If you live in Detroit and would prefer Fords and Chevys, that's fine.) One student in the pair shares his or her "situation" (study problem) and the other student offers suggestions for what that student could do about it. Then students switch roles, and they continue talking about the second student's "situation" and possible study options. After about four or five minutes, give a signal (such as ringing a chime) and announce either "Eagles Fly" or "Hawks Fly." The appropriate students in each pair fly off to find new partners, and all of the new pairs immediately continue their sharing of study problems and possible solutions.

• After students have identified their situation (problem) and academic skills plan (solution), have them meet in trios. Provide each student with time to present his or her "situation" (study problem) and academic skills plan. The other two students critique the academic skills plan and offer kudos and alternatives.

• After students have carried out their academic skills plan (the solution they devised for their study problem), have students report on what they learned or relearned. This report could be made in pairs, trios, quartets, or with the whole class. I like the option of having the conversation begin in a pair and then inviting students to nominate their partners to share success stories or lessons learned with the entire group.

Quizzes: Frequent quizzes motivate some students to come to class prepared, and quizzes act as a great review of the reading. I recommend having students exchange and grade quizzes in class so they receive immediate feedback. Quiz questions for every journal topic appear later in this manual. Practice quizzes are available for students in the College Success CourseMate site for *On Course*. To access CourseMate, go to **www.cengagebrain.com**.

On Course Newsletter

Subscribe to the *On Course* Newsletter and receive FREE monthly emails with innovative strategies for empowering your students to become active, responsible, and successful learners. This newsletter makes a great supplement to this Facilitator's Manual and is like a professional development workshop on your desktop. To subscribe, simply send an email request to Workshop@OnCourseWorkshop.com.

On Course Website

For additional classroom activities and out-of-class assignments, visit the *On Course* website at **www.OnCourseWorkshop.com**. Here you will find a large collection of student success strategies that work extremely well in the *On Course* classroom.

Ancillaries for *On Course*

Support for Students

- **College Success CourseMate.** *On Course* can include College Success CourseMate (9781133609865), a complement to your textbook. College Success CourseMate includes:
  - An interactive eBook
  - Interactive teaching and learning tools, including:
    - Self-Assessment *On Course*
    - Learning Preference Inventory
    - Quizzes
    - Flashcards
    - Videos
    - Wise Choices
    - Respecting Differences
    - and more!
  - Engagement Tracker, a first-of-its-kind tool that monitors student engagement in the course

Visit www.cengagebrain.com to access the CourseMate site for *On Course*, and look for this icon **CourseMate**, which denotes a resource available within CourseMate.

- **Aplia for *On Course*.** Aplia for *On Course* helps you thrive in the classroom and beyond. Engaging, interactive assignments ensure that you meet learning objectives, while automatically graded assignments offer immediate and constructive feedback. The problems and activities in Aplia for *On Course* teach you to develop the critical skills that you need to earn better grades, discover your potential, and chart a course for the future. For more information about Aplia for *On Course*, visit www.aplia.com/collegesuccess.
- **College Success Planner.** Package your *On Course* textbook with this 12-month, week-at-a-glance academic planner. The College Success Planner assists students in making the best use of their time both on and off campus, and includes additional reading about key learning strategies and life skills for success in college. Ask your Cengage Learning sales representative for more details.

Support for Instructors

- **Annotated Instructor's Edition**. To help guide instructors to the many ideas found within the Facilitator's Manual, the Annotated Instructor's Edition (9781133606833) provides specific cross-references directly in the margins to ideas and activities available in the Facilitator's Manual.

- **Newly Revised Facilitator's Manual**. The Facilitator's Manual, offered both in a printed version (9781133606857) and online at the Instructor Companion Site, offers educators specific suggestions for using *On Course* in various kinds of courses, and it endeavors to answer questions that educators might have about using the text. The Facilitator's Manual now includes tried-and-true activities provided by *On Course* instructors from across the country, additional study skills and diversity activities, sample student journal entry responses, and suggestions for teaching in an online environment.

- **Updated Instructor Companion Site.** This website, free to adopters, provides educators with many resources to offer a course that empowers their students to become active, responsible, and successful learners. Read or download the Facilitator's Manual, download PowerPoint slides, view content from the DVD *On Course: A Comprehensive Program for Promoting Student Academic Success and Retention,* and find a useful transition guide for educators who used previous editions of *On Course.* To access instructor digital resources, such as the Instructor Companion Site or instructor access for the College Success CourseMate for *On Course,* follow these steps:
  1. Visit **login.cengage.com**.
  2. If you have not previously created a faculty account, choose "Create a New Faculty Account" and follow the prompts.
  3. If you have created a faculty account previously, log in with your email address or user name and password.
  4. Search for *On Course* to add the available additional digital resources to your bookshelf.

  You will always need to return to **login.cengage.com** and enter your email address and password to sign in to access these resources. Use this space to write down your email address or user name and password below:

  Email Address:

  Password:

- **NEW! PowerLecture CD-ROM for *On Course*** (9781133606871). PowerLecture contains a brand new test bank in the ExamView test-generating software, enhanced instructor PowerPoint slides, and a PDF of the Facilitator's Manual. Use the dynamic software to create customized exams specific to your class!

- ***On Course*: A Comprehensive Program for Promoting Student Academic Success and Retention DVD** (9780547002170). This DVD provides instructors with an overview of the problems that keep today's capable students from being successful, complete with an explanation by author Skip Downing about how *On Course* differs from other student success approaches. Additional features on this DVD include a description of the extensive *On Course* learner-centered resources, videos of three students presenting their "One Student's Story" essays that appear in the text, and a sample *On Course* learner-centered activity, facilitated by Skip Downing. Following the activity, college and university educators discuss how this same activity positively affected their students. Presented in short chapters, parts of this DVD are intended for instructors and other parts are perfect for showing to students.

- **WebTutor™ on WebCT / WebTutor™ on Blackboard.** Jump-start your course with customizable, rich, text-specific content within your course management system, including interactive quizzes, videos, an eBook, and more.

- **Assessment Tools**. If you're looking for additional ways to assess your students, Cengage Learning has additional resources for you to consider. For more in-depth information on any of the following items, talk with your sales rep, or visit the publisher's *On Course* website.
  - **College Success Factors Index (CSFI) 2.0**, is an online survey that students complete to assess their patterns and behavior in ten factors that are specific to succeeding in the classroom/campus: Responsibility/Control, Competition, Task Planning, Expectations, Wellness, Time Management, College Involvement, Family Involvement, Precision, and Persistence. The CSFI is a perfect assessment tool for tracking your students' success in the course. For more information about this resource, visit http://www.cengage.com/success/csfi2.
  - **CL Assessment and Portfolio Builder:** This personal development tool engages students in self-assessment, critical thinking, and goal-setting activities to prepare them for college and the workplace. The access code for this item also provides students with access to the Career Resource Center.
  - **Noel-Levitz College Student Inventory:** The Retention Management System™ College Student Inventory (CSI; from Noel-Levitz) is an early-alert, early-intervention program that identifies students with tendencies that contribute to dropping out of school. Students can participate in an integrated, campus-wide program. Cengage Learning offers you three assessment options that evaluate students on 19 different scales: Form A (194 items), Form B (100 items), or an online etoken that provides access to Form A, B, or C (74 items).

Advisors are sent three interpretive reports: the Student's Report, the Advisor/Counselor Report, and the College Summary and Planning Report.

- **The Myers-Briggs Type Indicator® (MBTI®) Instrument and MBTI® Complete.**[1] The MBTI is the most widely used personality inventory in history—and it is also available for packaging with *On Course*. The standard Form M self-scorable instrument contains 93 items that determine preferences on four scales: Extraversion–Introversion, Sensing–Intuition, Thinking–Feeling, and Judging–Perceiving. MBTI® Complete is a one-stop, self-service online offering that combines the MBTI® assessment with a basic interpretation. Instructors are not required to be certified to administer MBTI Complete®. Students take the assessment on their own, participate in an interactive learning session, and automatically receive a three-page type description based on their results. Instructors will also have access to an instructor's guide, 16 Paths to Student Success, which includes lesson plans with PowerPoint® slides detailing the 16 MBTI types and how to incorporate MBTI personality styles into your instruction on time management, communication, learning styles, and study skills. These materials are available for download for instructors at www.cengage.com/login.

- **Cengage Learning's TeamUP Faculty Program Consultants**. An additional service available with this textbook is support from **TeamUP Faculty Program Consultants.** For more than a decade, our consultants have helped faculty reach and engage first-year students by offering peer-to-peer consulting on curriculum and assessment, faculty training, and workshops. Our consultants are higher education professionals who provide full-time support in helping educators establish and maintain effective student success programs. They are available to help you to establish or improve your student success program and provide training on the implementation of our textbooks and technology. To connect with your TeamUP Faculty Program Consultant, call 1-800-528-8323 or visit **www.cengage.com/teamup**.

- *On Course* **Workshops and Conference.** Skip Downing, author of *On Course*, offers faculty development workshops for all educators who want to learn innovative strategies for empowering students to become active, responsible, and successful learners. These highly regarded professional development workshops are offered at conference centers across North America, or you can host a one- to four-day event on your own campus. An online graduate course (3 credits) is available as a follow-up to two of the workshops. Additionally, you are invited to participate in the annual *On Course* National Conference, where hundreds of learner-centered educators gather to share their best practices. For information about these workshops, graduate courses, and the national conference (including testimonials galore), go to **www.OnCourseWorkshop.com**. Questions? Email Workshop@OnCourseWorkshop.com.

- *On Course* **Newsletter.** All college educators are invited to subscribe to the free *On Course* Newsletter. More than 50,000 educator-subscribers worldwide receive monthly emails with innovative, learner-centered strategies for engaging students in deep and lasting learning. To subscribe, simply go to **www.OnCourseWorkshop.com** and follow the easy, one-click directions. Or you can email a request to Workshop@OnCourseWorkshop.com.

Special note to instructors: If you have questions about or suggestions for improving either *On Course* or this manual, please email Info@OnCourseWorkshop.com. I will be happy to acknowledge you as the source of any exercises or suggestions that are included in subsequent editions. For your students, I thank you for helping them live rich, personally fulfilling lives. May you experience the same.

Skip Downing

---

[1] MBTI and Myers-Briggs Type Indicator are registered trademarks of Consulting Psychologists Press, Inc.

On Course Workshop

EMPOWER YOUR STUDENTS TO ACHIEVE THEIR GREATEST SUCCESS!

Learn practical strategies that engage your students in becoming active, responsible, and successful learners at this highly interactive faculty development retreat. Designed for educators across disciplines who want to help students achieve their greatest potential—academically, personally, and professionally—this workshop will inform and inspire you both professionally and personally.

You'll learn:

- How to use the seven domains available to educators to motivate and transform students.
- Best practices from innovators in education, psychology, business, sports, and personal effectiveness.
- New motivational strategies that appeal to a variety of learning preferences.
- How these strategies improve academic success and student retention.

These workshops are held at retreat centers in various parts of the United States and can be brought to your campus as well. Whether you use *On Course* as your course text or you simply want to revitalize your instruction techniques, this workshop is for you! **Graduate credits** are available with the completion of a follow-up online graduate course designed to help you master the learner-centered strategies learned in the workshop.

- Visit **www.OnCourseWorkshop.com**—for workshop dates, locations, and registration information, and to view a sampling of classroom strategies, or
- Email Workshop@OnCourseWorkshop.com for more information.

Getting Your Campus *On Course*

The following three articles explain the creative ways that colleges are using the On Course principles to create a culture of success on their campus.

Creating an On Course Campus

More and more colleges are creating an "On Course Campus." Their goal is greater student retention, academic success, and completion of certificates/degrees. They do so by infusing *On Course* principles and practices into many aspects of college life. The following describes such an effort at Asheville-Buncombe Technical Community College in North Carolina.

1. To adopt an On Course Infusion at your college, first determine who the decision makers are for this initiative. Determine the goals and outcomes for college-wide adoption. Define the focus, either narrowly or broadly.
2. To create an On Course Campus, identify the "reach" or extent of involvement (e.g., faculty, staff, students, advisors/ counselors, financial aid materials, policies, procedures, publicity, etc.).
3. Ensure that your college's executive leadership team/administration promotes an On Course Infusion. To do so:
   a. Facilitate a presentation to college administrators and/or the board of trustees that shares your own experiences with *On Course* along with data from On Course programs (http://oncourseworkshop.com/Data.htm).
   b. Encourage all administrators to attend an On Course I Workshop and/or the On Course National Conference.
   c. Make infusion of *On Course* principles a core component of the college's strategic plan.
4. Establish a taskforce or working group that reports to the chief academic officer and is charged with overseeing the implementation of an On Course Infusion.
5. Adopt the "best practices" of community colleges:
   a. Hold a mandatory New Student Orientation (NSO) session; infuse the language of *On Course* into the session and any printed materials/images.
   b. Do not allow late registration.
   c. Optional: focus additional efforts on your underperforming student group (as identified by college data).
   d. Require mandatory first-semester registration for your First Year (FY)/Student Success course; require re-registration the following semester for a grade of F in the first semester. Consider adding an FY course into each academic program's core course requirements, including transfer/associate degrees.
6. Add the "Eight Choices of Successful Students" from *On Course* into your college's general education core competencies.
7. Use the "Eight Choices of Successful Students" as a component of your college's quality enhancement plan (QEP), as part of the reaccreditation process.
8. If your college is a member of Achieving the Dream, choose the "Eight Choices of Successful Students" as an area of focus (initiative)—for example: "Infusing *On Course* into the Developmental Curriculum."
9. Seek funding to support your efforts, for example, the Perkins grant for infusing *On Course* into career/technical education (CTE) programs.

10. Hold "Lunch & Learn" sessions (for either faculty or On Course Ambassadors) around any of these topics:
    a. The "Eight Choices of Successful Students," throughout the academic year.
    b. *On Course* key topics such as the "Wise Choice Process," "Moving from Victim to Creator," "*On Course* Language for Frontline Staff," or an area particular to your college's needs/focus. Use the sessions as part of professional development.
    c. "Designing a Student Academic Skills Plan for ___ Using the Wise Choice Process" (reading, taking notes, taking tests, etc.). Note: See examples in *On Course, Study Skills Plus*.
11. Offer training to colleagues: On Course I Workshop, On Course II Workshop. Host training sessions on campus, provide lunch, and offer attendees professional development credits. As necessary, collaborate with area community colleges to share costs and benefits.
12. Offer training to frontline staff—from the offices of the registrar, bursar, financial aid, and admissions—on how to adopt practices consistent with *On Course* principles.
13. Fund attendance at On Course National Conferences.
14. Invite your college's president to speak in FY/College Success courses on an *On Course* topic. Consider capturing the session on video for use in online sections of your FY/College Success course.
15. Create *On Course* thematic posters, flyers, and so forth to display throughout your campus.
16. Add the "Eight Choices of Successful Students" to your college's student handbook/planner.
17. Mesh the "Eight Choices of Successful Students" with workplace readiness skills, activities, or initiatives.
18. Require mandatory completion of "Getting On Course to Academic Success," a one-hour session, for students receiving financial aid who are in jeopardy of losing aid due to academic warning/probation.
19. If your state is participating in the redesign of developmental math/reading/writing, begin now to include the *On Course* "language of success" into the curriculum and materials.
20. Include the *On Course* "language of success" in materials used in your college's math lab, language lab, tutoring center, writing center, and so forth.
21. Use the *On Course* "language of success" with initiatives such as a Minority Male Leadership Academy.

Source: Submitted by Sue Heath Olesiuk, Dean, Division of Academic Success; Shelly Blackburn, Chair of Academic Related Instruction; and Barbara Brownsmith Campbell, Associate Director, Faculty Development and Assessment, Asheville-Buncombe Technical CC, North Carolina.

Building a Strong College Success Program

The key to a fruitful college success program is having faculty who are the right fit for the course, and in fact, having the wrong instructors can do more harm than good when it comes to fostering student success. However, nobody holds a degree in college success, so how do we determine which instructors are well suited for the endeavor? At our college, we found that the essential ingredients are recruiting, hiring, and training. We started by brainstorming a list of qualities needed to teach the course:

1. We look for great instructors who:
   • hold a master's degree in order to qualify for teaching a 100-level course
   • embrace the course objectives
   • are both nurturing and empowering (helping to build student confidence while offering them the tools they need to succeed on their own)
   • possess energy, creativity, and enthusiasm
   • are willing to take an interactive, fun, and learner-centered approach in the classroom (as lecture is seldom used)
   • are open to specific training to develop/strengthen this teaching style and to deliver the course objectives using *On Course*
   • bring the qualities that make them good instructors in their discipline while being able to view and teach this course apart from that discipline
   • have a passion for (and preferably experience with) teaching developmental students
   • truly enjoy and care about students and their success

2. We conducted interviews of each candidate and selected those who met the criteria.
3. We then offered a full-day training session in which the faculty participated in the types of activities they would be using in the classroom. It was fun, festive, and well-received.
4. We also offered brown-bag lunch sessions to share best practices once a month throughout the semester and gave faculty access to a Blackboard site full of resources for grading, assignments, sample syllabi and schedules, multimedia, handy tips, and so forth.
5. Classroom observations of faculty hired and trained through this process have validated its effectiveness. It was well worth the time it took to lay a solid foundation to build the program.

The process for faculty development is ongoing, with a goal of continual improvement of instruction in the college success program.

Source: Submitted by Lisa Marks, Lead Instructor, Keys to College Success, Ozarks Technical Community College, Missouri.

On Course at Inver Hills Community College

During the 2005-2006 academic year, my colleague Brenda Landes attended the *On Course* I workshop and returned excited that the curriculum addressed the "inner qualities" essential to achieve success. Like so many colleges, our student success curriculum focused on the "how to's" of study skills instead of getting to the heart of whether students understand why they are here and whether they are committed to the sacrifices essential to achieve their goals and dreams. After piloting the curriculum in 2006-2007, two of my faculty counselor colleagues were able to get "INTS 1000 - *On Course*" approved as a new course, and it is listed as a recommended course on the student's placement report. We have grown from serving 125 students in 5 sections during our pilot year to serving 813 students in 33 sections during the 2009-2010 academic year!

While it is true that OC is a student success curriculum, that is only ½ the story. With teaching so many sections, we needed to enlist the support and assistance from others, in particular our content faculty. The result has been amazing. *On Course* is beginning to transform how we teach in the classroom in terms of instructional design and how we interact with students both formally via course design and informally by how we talk with students outside the classroom! The primary reason for this transformative experience for our instructors is that *On Course* is rooted in using active learning structures as a method. Our trained *On Course* faculty took these active learning structures and applied them to their course content! They found they were able to help engage students and "get through" to them using these methods!

On Course is becoming woven into the fabric of our campus. Here are some of the things we have done to integrate the curriculum and instructional principles across campus:

- Brought one-day and three-day *On Course* workshops to campus
- 104 *On Course* trained professionals on campus
- 7 educators are *On Course* Ambassadors
- 16 faculty disciplines have received training and have taught *On Course*
- *On Course* principles are incorporated into a one-day Success Day conference for students each semester
- *On Course* trained faculty utilize the active learning strategies in their work with students
- Creation of *On Course* identity by creating a logo with adaptations
- *On Course* is a component of several of our learning communities each term
- Enrollment Center incorporated *On Course* into orientation
- Campus publications & Web sites use *On Course* images (student bulletin, orientation, etc.)
- Student Academic Planner includes *On Course* "tip of the week"
- Student Bulletin publishes an *On Course* "tip of the week"
- College employee t-shirts worn for campus-wide events feature the *On Course* logo
- *On Course* active learning strategies have been presented during faculty development sessions
- Poster sessions promoting *On Course* for student and faculty events

- Training for Peer Tutors using the *On Course* principles
- Inver Hill CC co-sponsored with Anoka-Ramsey CC a statewide "*On Course* Across the Disciplines" mini-institute for campuses in the Minnesota State Colleges and Universities system
- Embedding *On Course* principles into the campus culture is one of the three priorities for our campus wide "student engagement" plan

Recently, our college was the recipient of the 2010 Minnesota State Colleges and Universities Innovative Student Affairs Award and a 2010 League of Innovation Award for Teaching and Learning for our use and incorporation of *On Course*.

Source: Submitted by Milissa J. Troen, M.S., Counselor, Inver Hills Community College, Minnesota.

Purpose of This Guide

Most schools now offer online courses using software platforms such as Blackboard, Angel, and Moodle. Although many people are familiar with sending email, paying bills electronically, and shopping online, teaching and learning via web-based classes is often a new experience. Conveying information and assessing student understanding of it can be challenging for online instructors. Online students face their own set of challenges. For example, being able to learn on their own schedule may be convenient, but it also requires more self-discipline and motivation. Teaching study skills to students is one way to help them overcome potential problems they may face in college, but it does little to develop self-discipline, motivation, and many other critical inner qualities that lead to success. The *On Course* textbook goes beyond study skills by focusing on the students themselves, which helps make the course content much more personal and approachable. Your goal for your online course should be the same—to make the content learner-focused and engaging.

This guide will help you, the online instructor, understand how to use the information presented in *On Course* by covering three important elements related to teaching an online student success course: the main features of the book, resources available online, and frequently asked questions. I will provide suggestions for using the textbook and other resources, and examples of assignments, activities, and grading rubrics. For more information about accessing any of the online resources I reference in the following pages, you can visit login.cengage.com or contact your Cengage Learning sales representative.

Main Features of *On Course*

On Course is different from many student success books in that it focuses on students' inner qualities and resulting choices rather than just study skills. As in any class, the textbook is the main source of information for a student taking an online course. Using the eBook is one way to link the online content with the book. The book or eBook can be used in much the same way as in a face-to-face setting, with students assigned a certain chapter or number of pages per week or class session, plus the associated journal entries. After students have read the textbook, present them with activities online. You can create activities, discussion board conversations, and assignments using the features within the book. These include the self-assessment, 33 success articles, journal entries, focus questions, case studies in critical thinking, *On Course* strategies at work, study skills, and 25 student essays about how they applied *On Course* strategies.

The self-assessment provided at the beginning of *On Course* can be completed online by accessing the College Success CourseMate site for *On Course*. A good way to use the self-assessment is to have students review the introduction to the self-assessment in Chapter 1 of *On Course*, take the assessment, get their scores, and use the assessment as a discussion board topic. You can also use Journal Entry 1 in Chapter 1 of *On Course* to encourage students to reflect on their scores; this will help set the tone for the rest of the course. Have students consider whether their scores reflect the way they see themselves and whether they would like their scores to change. At the end of the course, have them return to this self-assessment to retake it. Students can send you their responses to Journal Entry 1, and if students feel comfortable, have them share their experiences with the self-assessment in a discussion board. Some students might not yet feel confident enough to share their initial experience with the self-assessment, but consider making a discussion board topic mandatory after students have taken the self-assessment at the end of the course. At this point, students should be confident of the progress they have made and more willing to share their journey from their initial score to their final score.

The extensive use of journaling in *On Course* makes it adapt readily to an online environment. Students can write online journal entries just as they would in a traditional classroom, but submit them through the online course. As in a regular course, journal entries are used for reflection and to help students focus on and think through specific success strategies, such as "Becoming an Active Learner" (Journal Entry 3) and "Creating a Support Network" (Journal Entry 18), or inner qualities such as "Adopting a Creator Mindset" (Journal 5) and "Developing Self-Confidence" (Journal 15). Provide guidelines on length (this would vary depending upon the subject), and stress that the most important part of each entry is whether or not their writing is thoughtful and genuine—or in the author's words, are the students "Diving Deep"? Giving students a maximum of 5 points or so per entry provides motivation. I suggest you comment on at least some of the journals, not to point out errors, but instead to give the students further questions to consider (based on what they write) and let them know how they're doing (e.g., "Your insights on success really show that you've changed the way you think about choices."). Comments can be put into your online platform or directly on the files, depending on how your course is set up. The important thing is to make sure students can see the comments. For detailed suggestions from the author, please see the section titled "Using *On Course*" in the introduction to this Facilitator's Manual. Topics covered there include "Assigning Reading," "Student Journals, and Other Feature," "Reading Student Journals," "Responding to Student Journals," "Helping Students with Personal Problems," and "Grading."

There are Focus Questions throughout the book to help students prepare for the content that follows. These make good questions for online discussions. You can have students answer several of the questions in the chapter, or elaborate on just one. Make sure you provide guidelines for their responses. Here's a sample:

Focus Questions (from Chapter 1): What does "success" mean to you? When you achieve your greatest success, what will you **have**, what will you be **doing**, and what kind of person will you **be**?

Discussion: Post at least 3 times to this forum, based on the following:

1. Respond to the Focus Questions. Also explain whether you agree with the ideas about success and choices from Chapter 1 of *On Course*.

2. How will you know you've been successful in this course? In your personal life? At your job? How will these successes affect you?

3. Respond to other students, critiquing their definitions of success, with the goal of coming up with a definition useful to you and others.

Let students know how you'll be grading them. Here's a simple 15-point grading rubric for an online discussion. You would award students 3 points per category if they meet the guidelines, or 2, 1, or 0 depending on the degree to which they didn't.

Quality of Original Posts	Participation	Quality Replies to Classmates	Writing Mechanics	Timeliness
Posts demonstrate an understanding of course content and are supported by specific details, examples, and/or sources.	Responds to all questions. Exceeds requirement for minimum number of posts. Posts encourage further interaction within the group.	Replies to classmates' posts are relevant, offer constructive comments, and are respectful.	Posts are written in complete sentences and contain no spelling or grammatical errors.	First post written on or before required date; other posts done on separate days throughout the discussion period.

Online discussions should be graded to motivate students to participate. They are a good way for you and the students to get to know each other without face time, and they can help draw out students who might not speak up otherwise, especially in a regular face-to-face setting.

The Case Studies in Critical Thinking help relate the information in the book to real life. If you have the technology, you could get a group of people together to create video versions of the case studies for students to watch online. Giving students something other than written material is a great way to address different learning styles—those students who don't absorb information well through reading might prefer to watch the videos. The questions can then be presented on a document or in a discussion that students access online after watching the video. Even if you can't make videos, you can have students post short responses to the questions in a discussion board forum to get them thinking about the ideas in that chapter related to the case, or even have students create their own video versions of the case studies.

To create a learner-centered environment, any presentations should address various learning styles. In addition to text, consider including videos (e.g., the CourseMate site for *On Course* provides videos of students reading their *One Student's Story* from the text), audio clips, or visuals. By varying what you include in your online course, you have a greater chance of keeping students' interests while they are at the course web site. Written notes could expand upon important points from the chapter, such as providing more information about reading techniques. Another technique I use is to apply the concepts by describing how they might fit into a student's life (*you* know your students and the challenges they may face, so be specific), and offering personal anecdotes, similar to how author Skip Downing provides stories from his own life to explain concepts in *On Course*. Finally, I sometimes create graphics to provide a visual version of some information (something simple like the word "choices" shown as a puzzle piece linked to the word "success") and put those on my notes/lecture pages.

Resources Available Online

The resources provided with the textbook can help you reach students who don't easily learn just by reading. The Instructor Companion Site provides access to PowerPoint presentations, test banks, and an electronic version of the Facilitator's Manual, along with other items. The College Success CourseMate site for *On Course* provides student resources such as an interactive eBook and interactive teaching and learning tools, including the self-assessment, quizzes, videos, Wise Choices, *Respecting Differences*, and more. The CourseMate site also contains Engagement Tracker, a first-of-its-kind tool that monitors student engagement in the course. Using CourseMate, an instructor can assign activities, such as the self-assessment, and view the results for the entire class. Students receive immediate feedback when using CourseMate. To find out how to access CourseMate, see page 27.

There are additional resources available on CourseMate that can be incorporated into presentations and evaluations. For example, students can take the *self-test on locus of control* for Chapter 2, and students could write about their self-test results in an assignment or as part of a discussion board post. Another example is the *"Interactive Time Chart"* in the Chapter 4 Success Tools. After students do the activity, I have them submit a list of goals and a weekly schedule, along with a written description of their plans for incorporating study into their lives.

Another resource available with the book is *Aplia*. Aplia is an online, auto-graded homework system that improves learning by increasing student effort and engagement—without requiring more work from the instructor. Aplia provides even more interactivity, and allows for students to complete activities electronically. Aplia also allows students to complete activities related to each chapter and receive immediate feedback. For more information about Aplia for *On Course*, visit www.aplia.com/collegsuccess.

You can put links to any of these online resources within your course to allow students to easily access them. Links can all be posted in one area, such as a Web Resources page, or throughout the course within the relevant area. I also recommend you require that students complete at least some of these types of activities (self-tests, etc.) and build completion of them into graded evaluations. Seeing how students do on the evaluations helps you see whether they are engaging with and understanding the information in *On Course*.

Frequently Asked Questions

1. **How do I know whether students are really reading the book and learning anything?**

   This is where your evaluations come in—make sure your assignments and discussions incorporate ideas from *On Course*. Give your students very specific questions and require them to provide details and examples in their answers. I always try to incorporate a requirement about a situation or example from their lives as part of each assignment or discussion because such personal details are more difficult to copy from one paper to another.

2. How can I prevent students from cheating in an online course?

If you have students take tests online, make sure you use a test bank whenever possible. A test bank is available online and in the instructor's CD. There is a test bank for each chapter that allows you to choose from a menu of questions, including true/false, multiple choice, fill in the blank, matching, and essay. Keep tests at a minimum, however, and require students to describe their own experiences whenever possible.

On Course is well suited to an online student success course because it is much more learner-centered than many student success and study skills titles. Keeping this spirit in mind and incorporating it into your online course is the best way to help students succeed. Again, for more information about accessing any of these online resources, please visit the Cengage Learning website at login.cengage.com or contact your Cengage Learning sales representative.

CSFI & *On Course*: A Successful Combination

Gary J. Williams, Ed.D., Crafton Hills College

As an instructor who has adopted *On Course*, you have chosen a learning system that incorporates the best concepts of student development and student achievement. However, one of the most critical elements of ensuring that students put the concepts into practice is early assessment. Helping students identify their strengths and needs at the earliest opportunity, and connecting them to the best ideas and practices found in *On Course*, is the focus and the advantage of using the College Success Factors Index (CSFI), version 2.0, an online survey assessment tool available through Cengage Learning.

The CSFI shares a close affinity with the instructional principles of *On Course*. The central premise of *On Course* is that success occurs from inside out, and the CSFI provides an effective means of facilitating that inner transformation. The CSFI measures 10 affective factors or themes that are common among successful college students. These factors are:

Responsibility/Control	Wellness
Competition	College Involvement
Task Planning	Family Involvement
Expectations	Precision
Time Management	Persistence

The purpose of administering the CSFI is to help students understand the skills and habits they possess that contribute to being successful in college, and identify the areas where students can improve their chances for success. The goal is to empower students to become self-motivated, self-responsible, interdependent, and able to manage their own success in college. Students have the opportunity to link to transformative learning activities contained in *On Course*. Administering the CSFI and fully integrating the follow-up strategies will encourage your students to "Dive Deeper" into their lives, and acquire new ways of being and doing that will propel them toward success.

What Is the CSFI? How Can It Help My *On Course* Students?

The CSFI is a 100-item assessment instrument that students take online. (For more details about how students can access the CSFI, contact your Cengage Learning sales representative.) Once completed, the results are instantly available online to both student and instructor in an easy-to-understand, color-coded visual format:

Student View Sample of CSFI Results

RESULTS

Your results and related information are shown below for your review. In order to share your results with your instructor, you must click the "Submit Assignment for Grading" button above. When you do, this window will close, but you will be able to return here as long as your instructor has enabled return (which is typical).

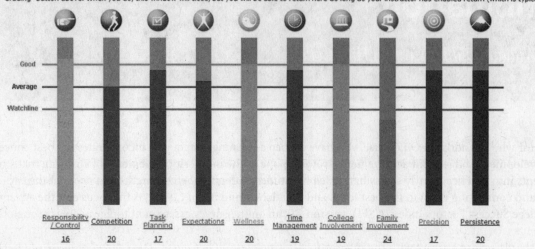

Responsibility / Control	Competition	Task Planning	Expectations	Wellness	Time Management	College Involvement	Family Involvement	Precision	Persistence
16	20	17	20	20	19	19	24	17	20

© Cengage Learning, 2013

The results for each of the ten factors are arranged in a bar graph format, as displayed in the figure above. Three ranges of scores are identified for each factor—Good, Average, and the Watchline.

When shown in full-color online, students can easily identify factors of strength (at or above the "Good" line and displayed in green), factors where they report an average awareness as compared with peers (displayed in blue), and factors identified as area(s) of need (flagged in red online). Clicking on the label below the bar graph of each factor provides the student with a detailed description of that particular factor, a list of strategies to build skills in that area, and also links that can direct the student to specific readings in the *On Course* text.

The CSFI presents the instructor and institution with additional benefits as well. As colleges and universities seek to address the growing numbers of students who arrive at college underprepared for the challenges that await them, the CSFI provides a powerful means for collecting and aggregating student learning data that can help focus attention and resources where they are most needed. This comes in the form of an Early Alert report built into the instructor's account that displays the overall results of a cohort of students and identifies the factors where students scored the highest as well as the lowest.

CSFI Aggregated Class Results, and Early Alert

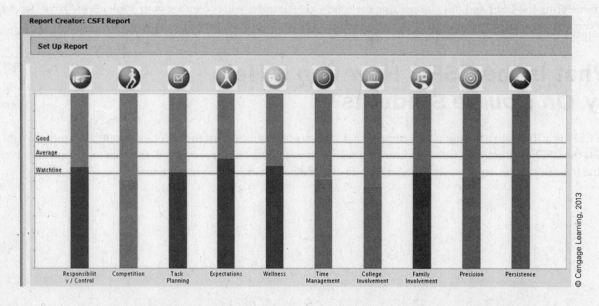

© Cengage Learning, 2013

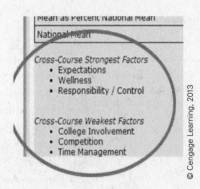

The CSFI instantly organizes student results, which benefits instructors and programs. This sample CSFI report displays the aggregated (combined) student results that easily identify the strongest as well as weakest factors, allowing instructors to focus their energies on the factors of greatest need.

The CSFI's Early Alert function also provides the ability to identify specific students at high risk based on their CSFI results. Students whose CSFI scores identify four or more factors at risk are flagged in red online, as illustrated in italics in the following screenshot. This feature provides the opportunity for instructors and institutions to follow up immediately with high-risk students before they fall into difficulty.

CSFI Student Results

(Early Alert Students Are Highlighted in red and italics)

Cross-Student Details	RESPONSIBILITY / CONTROL	COMPETITION	TASK PLANNING	EXPECTATIONS	WELLNESS	TIME MANAGEMENT	COLLEGE INVOLVEMENT	FAMILY INVOLVEMENT	PRECISION	PERSISTENCE
Brown, Robert										
Cuevas, Victor M										
Davis, Steven A										
Dekker, Amanda	*26.0*	*21.0*	*22.0*	*18.0*	*29.0*	*30.0*	*33.0*	*16.0*	*25.0*	*24.0*
Futch, Amora A	*29.0*	*29.0*	*27.0*	*22.0*	*27.0*	*29.0*	*26.0*	*19.0*	*22.0*	*28.0*
Gonzalez, Kerissa s										
Imming, Zacahary W	*17.0*	*27.0*	*26.0*	*23.0*	*25.0*	*29.0*	*25.0*	*21.0*	*21.0*	*31.0*
Lawson, Kaitlin K										
Martinez, Brant R	*22.0*	*34.0*	*23.0*	*23.0*	*35.0*	*33.0*	*32.0*	*16.0*	*33.0*	*32.0*
Menting, Nathan P	*28.0*	*32.0*	*27.0*	*22.0*	*23.0*	*28.0*	*35.0*	*21.0*	*30.0*	*22.0*

Paired with the skills and strategies contained in *On Course*, the CSFI can direct struggling students to the skills and strategies that can help them overcome challenges, help them make wiser choices, and put them on the road to success.

The CSFI is entirely congruent with the goals of *On Course*. As the following table indicates, the 10 CSFI factors provide numerous points of connection with *On Course* concepts and themes.

College Success Factors Index/ *On Course* Themes

CSFI Factor	*On Course* Concept(s)
Responsibility/Control: Students understand that they are responsible for their own success in college. They are in control of their education, make wise decisions, and take positive action to maintain a high academic standing.	Become an Active Learner (Ch. 1) Accept Personal Responsibility (Ch. 2) Adopt the Creator Role (Ch. 2) Master Creator Language (Ch. 2) The Wise Choice Process (Ch. 2) Being Assertive (Ch. 5) Gaining Self-Awareness (Ch. 6) Learning to Make Course Corrections (Ch. 7)
Competition: Students are motivated to perform at their highest level possible, by setting high standards for achievement, and by competing with themselves and/or their peers. They demonstrate a commitment to being successful in college.	Discovering Self-Motivation (Ch. 3) Committing to Your Goals and Dreams (Ch. 3) Creating a Success Identity (Ch. 4) Visualize Purposeful Actions (Ch. 4) Creating Flow (Ch. 8)
Task Planning: Students are task-oriented, and can break larger projects and expectations into smaller, more manageable tasks. They meet deadlines and commitments, and track progress toward completion of tasks.	Acting on Purpose (Ch. 4) Harnessing the Power of Quadrant II (Ch. 4) Creating a Self-Management System (Ch. 4)
Expectations: Students set high expectations for themselves, through challenging goals that are meaningful to them. They seek out learning opportunities, new experiences, and take risks. They articulate a strong desire for success in their chosen field or major. They demonstrate a high degree of commitment to their academic success.	Designing a Compelling Life Plan (Ch. 3) Committing to Your Goals and Dreams (Ch. 3) Change Your Inner Conversation (Ch. 2) Write a Personal Affirmation (Ch. 3) Discovering Your Preferred Learning Style (Ch. 7) Creating Flow (Ch. 8)
Time Management: Students practice sound skills in planning, calendaring, and prioritizing their tasks, commitments, and responsibilities. They exert control over the events in their lives, and can manage interruptions without losing sight of what is most important to them. They use a planning system that helps them keep track of their assignments, tests, papers, projects, and deadlines.	Mastering Self-Management (Ch. 4) Creating a Self-Management System (Ch. 4) Developing Self-Discipline (Ch. 4) Keeping Commitments (Ch. 7) Reducing Stress (Ch. 8) Creating Flow (Ch. 8)
Wellness: Students practice sound habits in personal health, nutrition, exercise, and stress management practices. They seek balance in their lives, their relationships, and the various roles they assume in addition to being a student. They understand what they need to perform at their best.	Developing Mutually Supportive Relationships (Ch. 5) Strengthening Relationships with Active Listening (Ch. 5) Identifying/Rewriting Your Outdated Scripts (Ch. 6) Developing Emotional Intelligence (Ch. 8) Reducing Stress (Ch. 8) Creating Flow (Ch. 8)
College Involvement: Students seek meaningful connections with the college, through formal as well as informal means. They develop a circle of support on campus that can assist them through times of challenge. They articulate a sense of satisfaction with their college experience.	College Customs (Ch. 1) Employing Interdependence (Ch. 5) Creating a Support Network (Ch. 5) Developing Emotional Intelligence (Ch. 8)
Family Involvement: Students have a circle of support that includes the people who are most important to them. Their circle of support provides advice and encouragement, and has a positive involvement in their lives that enables them to succeed in college.	Developing Mutually Supportive Relationships (Ch. 5) Creating a Support Network (Ch. 5) Strengthening Relationships with Active Listening (Ch. 5) Developing Emotional Intelligence (Ch. 8)

Precision: Students operate with a sense of exactness in all they do. They listen carefully, express themselves clearly, and read and recall with exactness. They clarify details as needed, and complete tasks with a high degree of precision.	Designing a Compelling Life Plan (Ch. 3) Mastering Self-Management (Ch .4) Acting on Purpose (Ch. 4) Creating a Self-Management System (Ch. 4) Developing Self-Discipline(Ch. 4) Active Listening (Ch. 5) Being Assertive (Ch.5)
Persistence: Students understand that overcoming obstacles is the key to success in college and in life. They display a sense of determination and urgency when facing obstacles and challenges. They possess a high level of commitment, doing "whatever it takes" to succeed.	Mastering Creator Language (Ch. 2) Developing Self-Discipline (Ch. 4) Changing Your Inner Conversation (Ch. 2) Rewriting Your Outdated Scripts (Ch. 6) Designing a Compelling Life Plan (Ch. 3) Committing to Your Goals and Dreams (Ch. 3) Creating Flow (Ch. 8)

Incorporating the CSFI can help greatly in advancing the *On Course* goal of encouraging success from within, by helping your students clarify their personal strengths and pinpoint the specific areas where they need the most help. It can be adapted to the demands of any course, orientation program, first-year experience, learning community, or other setting that is focused on student growth, development, and success. It can also provide a basis of documenting, measuring, and tracking the developmental learning outcomes of your course or program.

For more information about CSFI, visit our website at **www.cengage.com/success/csfi2** or contact your Cengage Learning sales representative.

Getting On Course to Your Success

Concept

By offering students an opportunity to assess their present strengths and weaknesses, we empower them with information that is essential to their success. Additionally, when we help students begin their academic journeys in an engaging and purposeful way, we motivate them to give their best effort. Students are more likely to commit to working hard in a course when they understand . . .

1. What the course is about
2. Why the course is of personal value to them academically and personally
3. How they can do well in the course
4. That they will enjoy the experience

It is as necessary for students to feel comfortable in this course as it is important for them to learn what this course is about and how it will benefit them. When students feel at ease in the classroom, they are more likely to stretch beyond their comfort zones and risk new behaviors, beliefs, and attitudes. As we begin our journey in this course, our first goal is to create a safe and motivating learning environment that encourages students to change.

Empowers Students to . . .

1. Begin thinking about what it means to be successful
2. Understand the value they can create for themselves in the course
3. Assess their strengths and weaknesses
4. Understand the culture of higher education
5. Understand how to maximize their learning

Remember also to use the all-purpose exercises mentioned in the introduction, actively engaging students in the exploration of JOURNAL ENTRIES, CASE STUDIES, ONE STUDENT'S STORY, ON COURSE AT WORK, QUOTATIONS, CARTOONS, FOCUS QUESTIONS, and CHAPTER-OPENING CHARTS. Remind students to use letters to label any in-class writing they do in their journals.

EXERCISE 0-1: Travel with Me

Purpose

To give an overview of the *On Course* text. Also, to raise student awareness of the choices successful students make in college. Once students are engaged in thinking about these choices, they become more motivated to value the course and have high expectations for being successful in college.

Supplies and Setup

Each student needs a copy of "Travel with Me," a message from author Skip Downing that appears at the end of the Preface to the *On Course* text (both editions). Post the following five questions at stations around the room:

Paragraph 1. What does being a successful college student mean to you?

Paragraph 2. List reasons why Downing always had some students who were successful and others who disappeared or failed.

Paragraph 3. Downing discusses struggling in his personal and professional life in his 20th year of teaching. He then chose to improve the quality of his life in various ways. Why do you think that Downing shared this information with us?

Paragraph 4. Why are successful people able to make wiser choices than people who struggle?

Paragraph 5. Discuss why Downing wrote this book and then answer the following question: Why is this book titled *On Course*?

At each station, place an easel and easel pad (or five large sheets of paper at least 11×14).

Directions

1. [Ask volunteers to stand and read one paragraph each of "Travel with Me." If you want to check students' comprehension, ask someone to explain the main idea of each paragraph.] [5 minutes]
2. [Have students form groups at each of the five stations.] *At your station, discuss the prompt and then write a response on the easel pad. You will have about 5 minutes at each station.* [5 minutes]
3. [Have students rotate to the other four stations and repeat what they did at the first station.] [20 minutes]
4. [Post all five sheets on the wall. Conduct a "gallery walk" in which students move to each sheet, reading what is posted on each.] [5–10 minutes]
5. [Class discussion] *What will you need to do to be successful this semester? What strategies will you need to learn about to become a successful student?* [List the strategies suggested on the board or easel pad. Discuss which ones they already use and which ones they will need to learn.] [5–15 minutes]

Approximate Time: 40–50 minutes

Instructor Notes

1. My original purpose for this activity was to introduce *On Course* to the students at my community college. I wanted to find an activity that would not only motivate them but would also give them an overview and deeper understanding of the outcomes and experiences they could achieve in this course. However, I've also used this activity as part of faculty training. For the final discussion with faculty, you might ask questions such as "What do you think are the reasons why students struggle in college? Does it appear that *On Course* will address these issues?"
2. "Travel with Me" does much more than summarize the book. It has given insight to both faculty and students on why *On Course* was written. Student engagement in this activity leads them into thinking about the strategies they can use to be successful. I find their motivation increases as well as their participation in class.

Source: Submitted by June Pomann, Union County College, NJ.

Journal Entry 1 Taking the First Step

EXERCISE 1-1: The Choices of Successful Students

Purpose

To identify the choices of successful students and have students see that they are capable of making these choices.

Supplies and Setup

Whiteboard (or blank overhead transparency or newsprint); students in groups of four or five

Directions

1. *In your group, create a list of the choices of successful students. In other words, what choices do successful students make that struggling students don't? Think about the choices you can see (outer behaviors) and the choices you can't see (inner attitudes or beliefs).* [5 minutes]
2. *Okay, let's hear what you came up with for the choices of successful students.* [Record the choices on the whiteboard.] [5 minutes]
3. *Which of these choices do you think are the most essential for success in college? Vote for three. As I call off a choice, raise your hand to cast your vote.* [Tally the votes each time, and record them next to the item on the list.] [5 minutes]
4. *Which of these choices are you willing to commit to so that you can be a successful student this semester? Make a list of them in your journal.* [5 minutes]
5. *Let's hear what you wrote.* [Invite students to stand and state the choices they commit to.] [5 minutes]

Approximate Time: 25 minutes

Instructor Notes

1. Encourage students to identify inner choices (attitudes or beliefs) as well as outer choices (behaviors). One way to distinguish them is to point out that behaviors are visible, so they can be recorded with a video camera. Attitudes or beliefs are invisible, so they cannot be recorded with a camera.
2. In faculty development workshops that I conduct, I've asked thousands of college instructors which behaviors and attitudes or beliefs they consistently see in their successful students. Here are the top vote-getters for behaviors: (1) attend class regularly, (2) do all assigned work and turn it in on time, and (3) participate actively. And instructors say the three crucial attitudes or beliefs are to (1) take personal responsibility, (2) be goal-directed, and (3) believe in yourself. Other beliefs high on the teachers' lists are to be self-disciplined, love learning, and have a positive attitude. You can inform students that all of these essential behaviors and attitudes are explored in *On Course*.
3. If there are any commitments that students choose unanimously, you could make these your course rules.

EXERCISE 1-2: Focus Questions

Purpose

To preview the course content and focus students' attention on finding answers to personally meaningful questions. Students also learn the power of using questions to find personally meaningful answers in readings, lectures, and class exercises or discussions.

Supplies and Setup

On Course, whiteboard (or blank overhead transparency), journal

Directions

1. *Thumb through* On Course. *Examine the table of contents. Check out the charts that precede each chapter. Look at the focus questions before each section of the text. Note the words in bold print in the text. Examine the diagrams, charts, and cartoons. Read some of the quotations in the margins. In your journal, jot down at least five questions that could affect your life for the better, if you discovered the answers to them during the semester.* [5–10 minutes]

2. *Now, let's hear the questions you want answered. If you hear a question you'd like an answer to, add it to your list.* [Call for questions, and record them for all to see. This process allows students to see the range of questions to which they could be finding answers during this semester.] [5–10 minutes]

3. *Put a star next to the five questions in your list that you most want answered. Your job this semester is to discover the answers to at least these five questions.*

Approximate Time: 10–20 minutes

Instructor Notes

1. I find it best to record questions exactly as students give them to me.

2. Point out to students that every reading section begins with focus questions and that reading for the answers is one way to get the most from every assignment.

3. An option is to publish a class question list. For example,
   1. How can I manage my time better?
   2. Why do I feel so nervous when I take tests?
   3. How can I feel more confident about asking questions in class?
   4. Why do I have to take this course?

When discussing questions in Journal Entry 27, you can return to these questions and analyze which of them are *probing* questions that promote critical thinking.

EXERCISE 1-3: Making Changes

Purpose

To identify specific changes students may wish to make in their lives.

Supplies and Setup

Students sitting in pairs (Student A and Student B). Students need their completed Journal Entry 1.

Directions

1. *Student A, read to your partner what you wrote for Step 2 in Journal Entry 1 about your highest scores. Student B, when your partner finishes, tell him or her what you heard. Say, "What I heard you say is. . . ." See how much you can remember. You'll have five minutes for reading and responding. Don't switch roles until I call time. If you finish early, take the time to get to know one another better.* [5 minutes]

2. *Now switch roles. B reads Step 2 to A. Then A responds, "What I heard you say is. . . ." Again, you'll have five minutes for reading and responding.* [5 minutes]

3. *Student A, read to your partner what you wrote in Step 3 about your lowest scores. Student B, when your partner finishes, you'll say, "What I heard you say is. . . ." Again, see how much you can remember. You'll have five minutes for reading and responding. Don't switch roles until I call time.* [5 minutes]

4. *Now switch roles. B reads Step 3 to A. Then A responds, "What I heard you say is. . . ." Again, you'll have five minutes.* [5 minutes]

5. [Quick-Write and/or Class Discussion] *As a result of what you learned in the self-assessment, are there any changes you'd like to make in yourself? What's the life lesson here for you?* [e.g., "It's amazing how much more I hear when I make a conscious effort to really listen."] [5–10 minutes]

Approximate Time: 30–50 minutes

Instructor Notes

1. This exercise is a powerful way to introduce the important issue of change. Points that might be made include: *If you keep doing what you've been doing, you'll keep getting what you've been getting . . . Improving our lives requires change . . . Change can be threatening . . . Change takes courage . . . One purpose of college is to help you change so you can improve your life.*

2. If time allows, you might introduce this question: *What might keep you from successfully making the changes you want to make?*

3. Many teachers report the value of having students complete the self-assessment during class time. In this way, you can better ensure that students understand the directions and complete the questionnaire with a serious and purposeful attitude.

Students can also take the self-assessment on the Internet, where they can immediately print out their results. To do so, visit the College Success CourseMate for *On Course*. To access CourseMate, go to www.cengagebrain.com.

EXERCISE 1-4: The Importance of Names!

Purpose

To begin creating a learner-centered classroom community where classmates and instructor learn how to pronounce and know each others' names.

Supplies and Setup

Black markers, table tents—cardstock or file folders cut in half, a sample with instructor's name and phonetic spelling underneath

Directions

1. [As the first three to five students enter the classroom on the first day of class, greet the students.] *Please take a table tent and marker, and then write your first and last name in large letters. Underneath write the phonetic spelling of your name.* [Display your table tent as a model for students. Then ask these three to five students to pass these same directions on to other classmates as they enter, using their own tents as a model. This allows you to focus your attention on welcoming students at they arrive.] [10 minutes]

> Gina Nguyen
>
> Geenuh Nu-when

[When everyone is in class and has completed their table tent.] *Welcome to the first day of class, I believe that learning each other's names is one of the most important things we can do to create a safe and welcoming classroom. We will now go around the room and I would like you to stand up and state your name and one thing you like to do or you value, etc.* [You can use any prompt you would like.] *I will go first, my name is . . . and I value. . . .* [10 minutes]

2. [Ask students to turn in the table tents at the end of class. Use the table tents to take attendance. Return the table tents at the beginning of the next class period. Have students use them until names are learned.]

Approximate Time: 20 minutes

Instructor Notes

1. This activity ensures the correct pronunciation of everyone's name and makes known the name the student wishes to be called by (i.e., this honors nicknames, speakers of other languages, and transgendered students, whose names may not be legally changed). Collecting the table tents allows instructors to practice pronouncing student names correctly before the next class.

2. One way to be green is to reuse file folders by cutting them on the fold. Then fold each side in half, top to bottom. You will have two table tents per file folder.

3. The website www.inogolo.com gives "English pronunciation to the names of people, places, and stuff."

Source: Submitted by Cris Davis and LuAnn Wood, Century College, MN; adapted from Dianne Del Giorno, Century College, MN.

EXERCISE 1-5: Mattering and Marginality

Purpose

(1) To help students understand their role in creating a community of learners who value and support each other; and (2) to help students identify actions they will commit to doing to show their classmates that they matter.

Supplies and Setup

Handout, "Marginalizing" (copied back-to-back), one for each student; 5 × 7 index cards, one for each student; blackboard/whiteboard/document camera or large white poster paper/marker

Directions

1. [Hand out "Mattering and Marginalizing." Inform students that they should look at only side 1, which says MATTERING.] *Today you are going to do an exercise called Mattering and Marginalizing. I am not going to say much in way of introduction. Together we will read the directions and then you will have time to answer the prompts. After each section you will be sharing your answers.*

2. [Read out loud to the students the text following the title MATTERING, including the Cues, Feelings, and Actions statements. You may need to illustrate an example for each. For example, Cues—the person looked me in the eye; Feelings—that made me feel happy; Actions—I wanted to work harder for that person.] *I will give you five minutes to think of a time you felt valued by someone. Once you have thought of the experience, please write down the cue(s), feeling(s), and action(s) related to the experience you are thinking of.* [5 minutes]

3. [Using the blackboard, whiteboard, document camera, or poster paper, write the word *Mattering* and then *Cues, Feelings*, and *Actions*. Ask the students to call out the cues they wrote down. Then repeat the process with feelings and actions.] [15 minutes]

4. [Next, have the students turn the paper over to side 2, which says MARGINALIZING. Repeat Steps 3 and 4 above with the word *Marginalizing*.] [15 minutes]

5. [Have the students form small groups.] *On the bottom of your handout you will find two questions. What are some ways we (can) show our peers they matter or are valued? and What are ways we (can) show our peers they are being marginalized or are not valued? In your small group, share your thoughts on these two questions with each other. One student from each group will need to write down your answers and then record those answers on the board.* [10 minutes]

6. [After having the students read the responses on the board, pass out one 5 × 7 index card to each student.] *You will be answering two more questions. What did you learn from this activity? and What one action will you commit to doing in this class/college to show your peers that they matter? Once you are done writing, I will ask you to share your commitment with the large group. I will collect your index cards at the end of the activity.* [10 minutes]

Approximate Time: 50–60 minutes

Instructor Notes

1. The Noel-Levitz Survey of Student Engagement has shown that students are more successful in their classes if they feel connected to part of a larger community. As student populations in colleges become increasingly diverse, educators need to find ways to ensure all students feel a sense of belonging.

2. Use this activity within the first six weeks of class to build a community of learners grounded in a mutual level of respect. When students feel that they matter to their classmates, they are more likely to stay in the course and participate with each other.

Source: Submitted by LuAnn Wood and Cris Davis, Century College, MN; adapted from Schlossberg, N. K. (1989). Marginality and mattering: Key issues in building community. In D. C. Roberts (Ed.), *Designing campus activities to foster a sense of community*. San Francisco: Jossey-Bass.

Mattering and Marginalizing

MATTERING

Please think of a time when you felt as if you really mattered; when who you are or what you did was valued. You do not need to disclose the circumstances of the particular event. Please write down the following:

Cues: What in the interaction let you know you were being valued?

Feelings: How did you feel as a result of this interaction?

Actions: What were your behaviors or actions that occurred as a result of this interaction?

CUES	FEELINGS	ACTIONS

MARGINALIZING

Please think of a time when you felt as if you did not really matter; when who you are or what you did was not valued. Sometimes marginalization in an interaction stems from identity characteristics, such as race, gender, perceived sexual orientation, ability status, age, and so on. Sometimes marginalization is influenced by our position within a group. Sometimes it is the result of an interpersonal dynamic in the absence of any other factor. You do not need to disclose the circumstances of the particular event. Please write down the following:

Cues: What in the interaction let you know you were not being valued?

Feelings: How did you feel as a result of this interaction?

Actions: What were your behaviors or actions that occurred as a result of this interaction?

CUES	FEELINGS	ACTIONS

What are some ways we (can) show our peers they matter or are valued?

What are ways we (can) show our peers they are being marginalized or not valued?

Source: Schlossberg, N. K. (1989). Marginality and mattering: Key issues in building community. In D. C. Roberts (Ed.), *Designing campus activities to foster a sense of community*. San Francisco: Jossey-Bass.

EXERCISE 1-6: Meet Your Classmates

Purpose

First- or second-day icebreaker to help students and instructor to get to know each other.

Supplies and Setup

None

Directions

1. One activity I use on the first day of class is a combination of icebreakers I've heard of over the years. I have each student come up with a descriptive adjective starting with the letter of his or her first name (e.g., "Lucky Lisa"). I then pair them up and have them introduce themselves with that moniker and tell one interesting, unusual, or surprising fact about themselves.

2. After the pairs have had a few minutes to talk, we come back together as a large group. Partner A then introduces the rest of the class to Partner B, using the descriptive name and telling us the fact learned about the partner. Partner B then introduces Partner A in the same fashion. (The only caveat is to make sure students share only ONE fact about their partners, though they may learn more than one fact in getting to know each other.)

3. I challenge myself to go back to the beginning and repeat all the names each time a pair finishes. It works fabulously to help me remember their names early on in the semester, and it lets the students know that I care enough to learn them.

4. I don't require them to stand up when giving the introductions. Even the shyest students seem more comfortable introducing someone other than themselves, and it gives them a chance to get to know other people, find commonalities, and develop a sense of community.

Approximate Time: Varies depending on class size.

Source: Submitted by Lisa Marks, Ozarks Technical Community College, MO

Journal Entry 2 Understanding the Culture of Higher Education

EXERCISE 2-1: What's Going on Around Here?

Purpose

To help students understand how deep-culture rules create confusion and frustration for people new to the culture. (This activity can also be used with Journal Entry 19: Respecting Cultural Differences.)

Supplies and Setup

This activity can be done either before or after students read/write Journal Entry 2: Understanding the Culture of Higher Education.

Directions

1. [Ask for three volunteers to play a game. Ask them to leave the room for a few minutes.] [2 minutes]
2. [Ask the remaining students to stand and form groups of five to seven.] *Each culture creates rules by which it operates. Some of these rules are visible, such as the appropriate clothing that people wear. Other rules are invisible to people who are unfamiliar with the culture, such as the proper way to talk to others. For the next few minutes, imagine that everyone here is in a culture that believes that people should always touch their face briefly before speaking. If someone does not do that, others will ignore that person. [Demonstrate what that would look like.] When I invite our three*

volunteers to return to the room, each group hold a conversation about what you've been experiencing so far in college. Keep the conversation going, and be sure you briefly touch your face each time before speaking. When the volunteers talk to you, unless they first touch their faces, ignore them. Keep talking to someone else . . . even turn your back to them. Of course, if they do briefly touch their faces, touch your own face and respond enthusiastically. However, if at any time they do not touch their faces before talking, go back to ignoring them. Do not explain the rule about touching your face before talking. [5 minutes]

3. [Retrieve the three volunteers. Before they enter the room, tell them,] *"Your classmates are having a discussion. Please join in."* [3 minutes]

4. [Observe the efforts of the volunteers to interact with the group. Note any behaviors that might illustrate the difficulties of people trying to learn the rules of a new culture. Use these to help propel the later discussion.] [5–10 minutes]

5. [Discussion with volunteers] *What was your experience? Why do you think people were responding to you as they did? How did you feel? Can you recall any time in your life when you ever felt like that before? What happened? Did you ever figure out why people were responding to you as they were? If so, how did you figure it out? How did you feel after you figured it out?* [5–10 minutes]

6. [Discussion with class members] *What was your experience? How do you think it made the volunteers feel? How did you feel? Can you recall any time in your life when you ever felt like that before? What happened?* [If the volunteers did not figure out the rule about touching faces:] *Who would like to explain to the volunteers why you were behaving as you were?* [5–10 minutes]

7. *What you've just experienced is what can happen when different cultures meet. Each culture has rules that dictate the "right" way to do something. In the experience we just had, the* right *way to talk with someone was to touch your face first. If you don't know a different culture's rules, you can feel awkward, embarrassed, ineffective, or even angry. Higher education has a culture, too. The culture of higher education has rules that the natives know but the people new to college don't know. What have you noticed already that makes college culture different from other educational cultures you have been in?* [e.g., "In college, instructors expect students to have read assignments before coming to class. College students are expected to find out where to get help with problems." For other examples, see the chart "A Dozen Differences Between High School and College Culture" in the text accompanying Journal Entry 2.] [5–10 minutes]

8. [Quick-Write and/or Class Discussion] *What's the life lesson here for you?* [e.g., "It's going to take a while for me to learn the culture of higher education. In the meanwhile when I don't understand something, I should ask questions."] [5–10 minutes]

Approximate Time: 35–60 minutes

Source: Adapted from Leeva Chung, University of San Diego, CA

EXERCISE 2-2: Culture Shock

Purpose

To help students identify and become more comfortable with aspects of college culture that they find upsetting and stressful.

Supplies and Setup

4 × 6 index cards, one for each student. Consider projecting a PowerPoint slide with the following: "Culture shock is the upset and stress we experience when confronted with behaviors and beliefs that differ significantly from our own."

Directions

1. *According to our* On Course *textbook, "Culture shock is the upset and stress we experience when confronted with behaviors and beliefs that differ significantly from our own." On your index card, write a brief description of something you've experienced here at [your college] that you have found to be confusing, upsetting, or stressful. For example, maybe an instructor used a word that you have never heard before and you didn't know what the instructor was talking*

about. Or maybe someone got upset with you because you didn't do something that you didn't even know you were supposed to do. Do not put your name on your card. As we read the cards later, no one will know who wrote it. [5–10 minutes]

2. [Collect the cards and shuffle them. Ask students to form groups of four to six. Give a card to each student.] [5 minutes]

3. *In your group, decide which card expresses the best example of culture shock in college. Remember, "Culture shock is the upset and stress we experience when confronted with behaviors and beliefs that differ significantly from our own." If your group happens to get your own card, do not reveal that it is your card. Just treat it as if it is someone else's card.* [5–10 minutes]

4. [One at a time, ask each group to read the card it chose. After each card is read, lead a discussion of the experience that led to culture shock. Help students understand what occurred. Start by asking students if they can clarify what happened. As a last resort, offer a clarification yourself.] [15–25 minutes]

5. [Quick-Write and/or Class Discussion] *What's the life lesson here for you?* [e.g., "It's natural to experience upset and stress when we find ourselves in a new culture."] [5–10 minutes]

Approximate Time: 40–60 minutes

EXERCISE 2-3: Get Connected!

Purpose

(1) To get students engaged in the college culture, and (2) to encourage students to explore cultures different from their own.

Supplies and Setup

"Get Connected!" handout; list of current events at your campus

Directions

1. *Research shows that students who are involved in college events are more likely to feel connected to their campus culture, enjoy their college experience, and, as a result, persist in higher education. In this assignment you will become aware of the many extracurricular activities our campus has to offer. "Extracurricular" activities are those that are not part of any courses you are taking. You will attend three different campus events over the course of the semester. One event must be multicultural, one must be a student success workshop, and one must be a club or organization meeting . . . (no need to join, but at least check one out.* [Adapt the three events to those available on your campus.] *After each visit, write a reflection for the event attended. Use the following questions to guide your reflection, and dive deep! Answer in paragraph form and be specific.* [Review the reflection questions on the "Get Connected!" handout.]

Approximate Time: 10 minutes to introduce assignment, brainstorm potential events, and answer student questions

Instructor Notes

1. Encourage students to attend events with a classmate, friend, or family member.
2. Scheduling due dates throughout the semester helps students get involved right away on campus as well as continue involvement throughout the semester.

Source: Submitted by LuAnn Wood based on a collaboration of many staff and faculty, Century College, MN.

Get Connected!

1. Attend three different campus events/resources over the semester.

   Choose an event that fits each of the following categories.
   a. Multi-cultural Event (for example, speakers and activities sponsored by the multicultural center, salsa dancing, etc.)
   b. Student Success Workshop
   c. Campus Club/Organization Meeting (you do not need to commit long-term, but at least check one out)

2. Write a reflection after each of the three campus events/resources attended. Use the following questions to guide your reflection of the activity/event attended—be specific and dive deep!

   a. List the event/resource; include title (name of activity or event), location, and date.
   b. **Why?** Explain the reason you were interested in this event/resource.
   c. **What?** Describe the event and what you learned. Especially note any similarities or differences you notice when comparing this event to the culture of the most recent school you attended.
   d. **So What?** Describe how this event impacted you or others. (What difference did it make—did this event change your thinking, was this event different than you expected?)
   e. **Now What?** Describe what you plan to do with the information learned. (How can you apply this new experience to your life, what would you like to learn more about, what follow-up is needed, what information can you share with others?)

3. Turn in each reflection by each due date listed below.
   #1 Get Connected Reflection: due <u>by the end of Week 5</u>
   #2 Get Connected Reflection: due <u>by the end of Week 9</u>
   #3 Get Connected Reflection: due <u>by the end of Week 14</u>

EXERCISE 2-4: Cultural Values and Expectations

Purpose

(1) To develop a sense of what different cultural groups value in home, school, and work lives; and (2) to understand the hidden rules/expectations that govern mainstream North American schools and workplaces.

Supplies and Setup

"Cultural Values and Expectations" handout

Directions

1. *People belong to many different cultural groups (for example, race, ethnicity, gender, socio-economic, religion, sexual orientation, etc.) and are shaped by the values, beliefs, and norms of those groups and thus engage in certain patterns of behavior. However, most schools and businesses in mainstream North America operate under their own set of hidden rules/expectations (values, beliefs, and norms) that we need to be aware of. This does not mean that you need to change your beliefs, views, and behaviors, but you need to know these hidden rules to be successful. To explore your multicultural self by identifying your cultural group and your group norms and values, you will have 10 minutes to complete the "Cultural Values and Expectations" handout.* [This handout could also be given to the class beforehand as an exercise or homework assignment]. [10 minutes]

2. *Now form groups of four or five students. Going around your group one at a time, share one of your cultural groups that may have many of the **same** values as the mainstream North American academic and work culture. Then share one of your cultural groups that may have **different** values from those of the mainstream North American academic and work culture.* [15 minutes]

3. [Journal Quick-Write and/or Class Discussion] *What did you learn from this discussion about what different cultures value? What did you learn about mainstream North American academic and workplace values/expectations? What value, belief, or behavior did you realize you may need to adapt in a college or work environment to be successful? What is the life lesson here for you?* [e.g., "Sometimes I used to think people of a different culture than mine were doing things wrong. Now I understand that I need to learn the hidden rules/values of mainstream North American academic and workplace culture, and I need to learn these hidden rules to be successful in college and work. For example, in my culture, it is OK to be late. However, in college, being on time is expected and valued by instructors. I need to leave my house five minutes earlier than I have been to be on time and earn class participation points."] [10 minutes]

Approximate Time: 50 minutes

Instructor Notes

It is important to remind students that these mainstream North American academic and cultural norms are generalizations and may change based on regions. Avoid using these generalizations to stereotype, "write off," or oversimplify your ideas about another person and his or her culture.

Source: Submitted by Cris Davis and LuAnn Wood, Century College, MN.

CULTURAL VALUES AND EXPECTATIONS

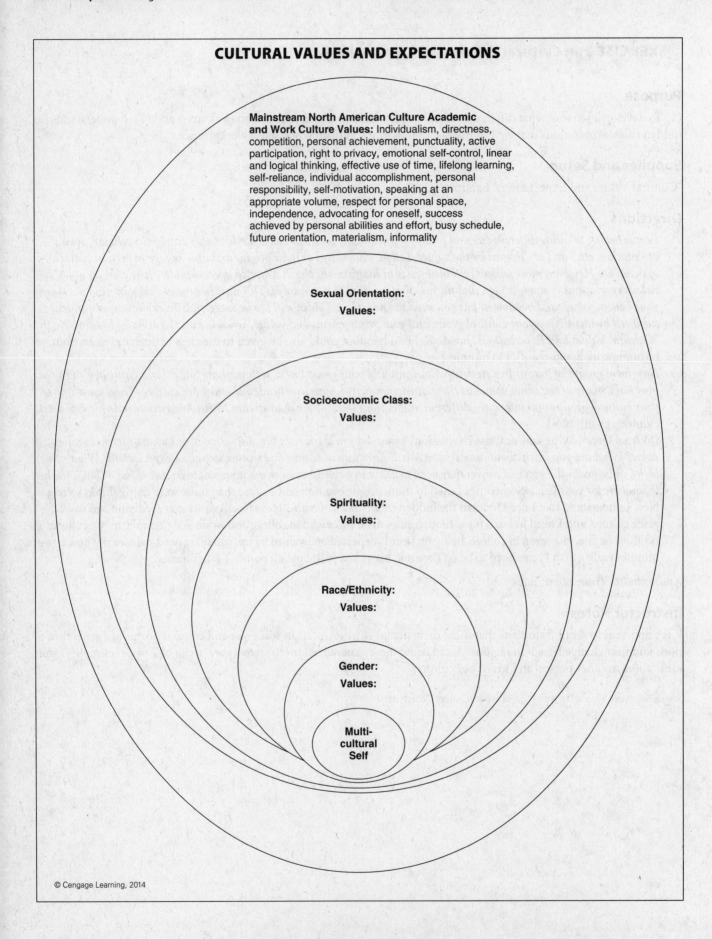

Mainstream North American Culture Academic and Work Culture Values: Individualism, directness, competition, personal achievement, punctuality, active participation, right to privacy, emotional self-control, linear and logical thinking, effective use of time, lifelong learning, self-reliance, individual accomplishment, personal responsibility, self-motivation, speaking at an appropriate volume, respect for personal space, independence, advocating for oneself, success achieved by personal abilities and effort, busy schedule, future orientation, materialism, informality

Sexual Orientation:

Values:

Socioeconomic Class:

Values:

Spirituality:

Values:

Race/Ethnicity:

Values:

Gender:

Values:

Multi-cultural Self

Journal Entry 3 Becoming an Active Learner

EXERCISE 3-1: The Learning Game

Purpose

To identify the value of being an active learner and paying close attention to feedback.

Supplies and Setup

A dollar bill folded into a very small square; one volunteer (A)

Directions

1. *Do you remember how you loved to learn as a child and how good you were at it? Many adults have lost both this love of learning and the effective way they went about learning when they were children. Today we're going to play a game to see if we can rediscover some of that lost love and the natural learning process we can use even today to maximize our learning.* [To Volunteer A:] *I'm going to ask you to go out of the room for a few minutes while we set up a learning game for you to play.*

2. [To the class after A has left the room:] *I'd like someone to hide this folded dollar bill somewhere in the room. It's important that everyone knows where the dollar is, so watch carefully where it's being hidden. When A returns, I'll tell her that her goal is to learn where the dollar is hidden. Notice how this situation is similar to coming into a new course. Whether the course is history, English, math, or another subject, your job as a student is to figure out where the valuable information is hidden. In this activity, your job is to be scientists and figure out some choices that enhance learning and those that diminish learning. To do that, watch and listen for everything that A does or says. See what she does that works to learn where the dollar is and what she does that doesn't work.*

   There are two parts to this activity. First, we'll just let A look for the dollar without any help. If she asks you a question, don't answer in any way. Second, after a couple of minutes, I'll fold my arms across my chest like this. That will be your signal to start giving A some feedback. Do you remember the kids' game called "Hot and Cold"? Well, as A gets closer to the dollar bill, we'll all start to hum like this: "Hmmm . . . ." If she gets closer to the dollar, we'll hum louder. If A stops or turns away from the dollar, we'll immediately stop humming. Watch very carefully what A does both before and after we give her feedback by humming. Write down everything she says or does. Remember, you're trying to figure out what behaviors help people learn something. [5 minutes]

3. [To A after returning to the room:] *We've hidden a dollar bill somewhere in this room. Your goal is to learn where it is as fast as possible. Please verbalize what you are thinking so we can understand how you learn where the dollar is. When you find the dollar, it's yours to keep. Any questions?* [No matter what the volunteer says, merely repeat these same directions. After a while, the volunteer will get the point and probably start looking.] [2 minutes]

4. [As the volunteer is looking for the dollar, you want to do two things: (1) Ask the volunteer to think out loud—explain what she is doing to learn where the dollar is. (2) Keep comparing what the volunteer is doing to what happens to many students in college. For example, if the volunteer gets frustrated because she is getting no answers to her questions, ask, "Have you ever had a teacher who didn't seem to give you helpful feedback? What did you do?" If the volunteer just stands and does nothing, ask, "Have you ever gotten stuck in a course and found it hard to do anything? Did doing *nothing* ever help you learn? What did help you learn?" If the volunteer says, "I quit. I just can't find it," ask, "Have you ever felt like quitting a difficult course?" The possibilities of the volunteer's actions and comments are many, so to facilitate this activity well, you need to stay alert.] [3–8 minutes] [Cut the activity shorter if the volunteer is getting too frustrated. Most volunteers will go as long as you wish, so you can gauge the duration on how long you think the class is getting value from observing the activity.]

5. [After a couple of minutes of A's searching, fold your arms to let the class members know it's time for them to give feedback to the volunteer by humming. Keep asking the volunteer to think out loud: "How are you now going about trying to learn where the dollar is?" Also keep relating the present events to the students' experiences in college:

"Is it possible that you had a teacher who was giving you great information and feedback about how to learn a subject, but you just didn't realize what he was doing?"] [3–8 minutes, again gauging the timing on the value present]

6. [After the volunteer has found the dollar and the class has given a huge round of applause—which is usually spontaneous in this activity—then comes a Quick-Write and/or Class Discussion. Lead students to identify one or more of the components of the CORE Learning System.] *What did you learn about learning? What actions help people learn?* [There are many "right" answers here, but a few you may want to highlight are (1) ask Creator questions, (2) collect relevant information, (3) organize information into empowering answers, (4) evaluate your present answers, (5) heed feedback, and (6) revise your answers when incorrect.] *What actions hinder learning? What thoughts help people learn? What thoughts hinder learning? What emotions help people learn? What emotions hinder learning? What beliefs help people learn? What beliefs hinder learning? Are there any changes you could make to become a better learner? What is the life lesson here for you?* [e.g., "Learning is a skill that requires my active engagement, and I can learn to learn better than I do now."] [10–25 minutes]

Approximate Time: 25–60 minutes

Instructor Notes

1. Don't let the lengthy directions scare you. This is one of my favorite classroom activities. Students love it, and it never fails to generate fascinating discoveries about learning and about life. The Learning Game has turned out somewhat differently every time I've done it. I find this unpredictability to be part of the magic of this activity. You just need to keep your goal (discovering how people learn) in mind and go with the flow. Let the learning be yours, too.

2. The directions here are very important. It is essential that the class members understand that they are to hum as the volunteer moves *toward* the dollar and to stay quiet when the volunteer *stops* or *moves away* from the dollar. If, during the game, it becomes apparent that the class is sending confusing feedback to the volunteer, ask the volunteer to leave the room again, and clarify the directions for the class.

3. The volunteer will likely get frustrated after a few minutes. That's usually OK, but be sensitive not to let the frustration go on too long. Keep giving the volunteer praise and support. Don't let the volunteer stop without the experience of success in finding the dollar bill—even if you have to virtually lead him or her to it (which isn't likely).

4. One of the most fascinating experiences I have had with this game occurred when the class was sitting in a circle and the dollar bill was hidden outside the circle. The volunteer came into the circle and, ignoring all feedback from the group, would not venture outside of the circle of chairs to look for the dollar. Afterward, students engaged in an insightful discussion about how we limit our learning because of mistaken beliefs that we hold—in this case that the dollar had to be hidden within the circle. Ultimately, the discussion led to a listing of limiting beliefs that students may hold: *I can't do math, I can't bother an instructor outside of class, I'm born with a certain writing ability and there's nothing I can do to improve it,* and so on. Identifying these beliefs laid a helpful foundation for a later discussion of beliefs and scripts in Chapter 6.

EXERCISE 3-2: Beautiful Questions

Purpose

(1) To offer practice in actively asking beautiful Creator questions, rekindling curiosity and wonderment; and (2) to have students identify the important questions for each academic course they are taking.

Supplies and Setup

Journals; five 3 × 5 index cards for each student; students in groups of four

Directions

1. *The poet e.e. cummings wrote, "Always the beautiful answer / Who asks a more beautiful question." Open your journal to a clean page, and title the page "BEAUTIFUL QUESTIONS." Now make a list of some of the beautiful questions that you'd like to find answers to during your life. You have five minutes to make your list of questions. To help yourself*

invent questions, think of your life roles. What do you want to know about being a student, a parent, a spouse, an employee, an athlete? Think of questions you'll need to answer in order to reach your goals and dreams. [5 minutes]

2. [Have volunteers share some of their questions with the class. Invite students to add to their lists when they hear questions they also want answered during their lives. When appropriate, ask. . .] *Can you think of a college class in which you might learn the answer to that question?* [10 minutes]

3. *Perhaps you never realized that what makes one college course different from another is its intention to answer different questions. A psychology course, for example, answers different questions from those a history course does. Turn to the next clean page in your journal, and title it "BEAUTIFUL ACADEMIC QUESTIONS." On that page, list the courses you're taking this semester, starting with this course. Leave five blank lines under each course. Beneath each course, write what you think are the three most important questions the course is designed to answer.* [10 minutes]

4. [Lead a discussion in which students share the questions they think various courses are designed to answer. Ask for students who are taking the same courses to compare their questions. Consider recording the questions by course on the whiteboard.] [15 minutes]

5. [Quick-Write and/or Class Discussion] *What advantage is it for you to know what the key questions are for all your courses? How would you go about determining what questions a teacher might ask on a test? What do you think makes one question more beautiful than another? What is the life lesson here for you?* [e.g., "If I ask the wrong question, I might get the 'right' answer but it won't be much help to me."] [10–20 minutes]

Approximate Time: 50–60 minutes

Instructor Notes

I like to point out that the root word of *question* is "quest," and a quest requires action. Additionally, the quality of any quest is determined by the quality of the question that starts it.

Journal Entry 4 Believing in Yourself: Develop Self-Acceptance

EXERCISE 4-1: What Is Self-Esteem?

Purpose

To identify the important contribution of self-esteem to success and to begin identifying choices for increasing self-esteem.

Supplies and Setup

Journals; students in groups of three. Optional: DVD of *Dead Poets Society*; DVD/TV monitor.

Directions

1. [Step 1 is optional but recommended: Show the scene from *Dead Poets Society* in which the teacher (played by Robin Williams) has his students read poems that they wrote for homework. Stop the video after the scene in which the teacher asks a student named Todd to read and Todd says he didn't write a poem.] *On a scale of 1–10 (with 10 high), how strong do you think Todd's self-esteem is? How can you tell? How successful do you think Todd will be in life if he doesn't increase his self-esteem? Why is strong self-esteem important to success?* [10 minutes]

2. *In your journal, write your personal definition of self-esteem. You'll have an opportunity to revise your definition later if you wish.* [5 minutes]

3. *Read your definition of self-esteem to your group. Also, see if you can identify someone you know who has high self-esteem according to your definition.* [4–6 minutes]

4. *In your group, decide on three things a person can do to raise his or her self-esteem. Pick a group reporter to share your ideas with the class.* [5–10 minutes]

5. [Invite group reporters to tell each group's suggestions for raising self-esteem. Record suggestions on the whiteboard or on an overhead transparency.] [5–10 minutes]

6. [Quick-Write and/or Class Discussion] *What is your definition of self-esteem? What do you think are good ways for a person to raise his or her self-esteem? What's the life lesson here for you?* [e.g., "I always thought that I was stuck with my self-esteem; now I feel hopeful that I can learn how to make it stronger."] [5–10 minutes]

Approximate Time: 35–45 minutes

Instructor Notes

Here are five definitions of self-esteem that you could share with students to promote conversation:

- *Self-esteem is the ability to value one's self and to treat oneself with dignity, love, and reality.* —Virginia Satir
- *Self-esteem is the experience of being capable of managing life's challenges and being worthy of happiness.* —National Council for Self-Esteem
- *Self-esteem is the capacity to experience maximal self-love and joy whether or not you are successful at any point in your life.* —David Burns
- *Self-esteem is the feeling that we are worthwhile in our personal, social, and work lives. It comes from feeling loved and respected as a child in our family, by friends, and at school.* —Jeffrey E. Young and Janet S. Klosko
- *Self-esteem is the reputation we have with ourselves.* —Nathaniel Brandon

EXERCISE 4-2: Overheard Praise

Purpose

To expose students to the positive perceptions others have of them and to encourage them to begin accepting these positive qualities.

Supplies and Setup

Journals and pens; chime; students sitting in groups of five to six in a circle, facing toward the center of the circle. In each group, one student turns his or her chair around so it is facing away from the center of the circle. All students have their journals open on their laps and pens in hand, ready to write.

Directions

1. *Turn to the next clean page in your journal, and title the page "Overheard Praise." Keep your journal and pen with you throughout this exercise.* [1 minute]
2. *Notice that one person has his or her back to your group. Imagine that this person isn't there. In his or her absence, your group is going to talk about all the things you like and admire about that person. Because it's early in the semester, you probably don't know this person well yet, but you have probably noticed some positive qualities already. Whenever possible, recall specific events to explain what you're saying about the person. For example, I might say, "I admire Joe because he comes to class prepared." Or, "I like Joanne because she has the ability to see the best in everyone. Last week I heard her telling Robert what a good writer he is." While this conversation is going on, the person who is "absent" writes everything the other people say about him or her. Don't choose; record everything. Each time I ring the chime, everyone moves one chair to the right. Then the group will begin talking about the new person whose back is to the group. Any questions? Okay, begin.* [4 minutes for directions; 2 minutes for the group to discuss each person] [15–20 minutes]
3. *Take a moment now to reread the overheard praise that you recorded in your journal. Let it sink in.* [2 minutes]
4. [Quick-Write and/or Class Discussion] *What was that experience like for you? What was it like to give praise and appreciation? Was it difficult or easy to decide what to say? What was it like to hear praise and appreciation of yourself? Is it difficult or easy for you to accept the praise? How do you feel right now? What can you do to feel like this more often? What's the life lesson here for you?* [e.g., "I'm going to be sure to give more praise to the people I love."] [10–20 minutes]

Approximate Time: 25–40 minutes

Instructor Notes

1. Consider repeating this activity later in the course when students are more familiar with each other and will have learned even more qualities they can praise in one another.
2. If you create success teams in your class, this is a good activity for creating a community within these teams.

EXERCISE 4-3: Using a Fish Story to Create Course Expectations

Purpose

To establish the classroom environment and expectations for the course. Once the activity is complete, the students identify what they have created. In conjunction with the syllabus, they have developed a student and instructor contract. Hopefully, they will also see that they will be transitioning from a "teacher-directed environment" to a more "learner-directed environment."

Supplies and Setup

"A Fish Story," five or more 15 × 20 pieces of paper, tape, two different colors of 3 × 3 Post-it notes—20 sheets of each color (you can add more if necessary)

Directions

1. After the very first class, the assignment is to read "A Fish Story," the case study that begins Chapter 7. In the second class, the instructor then reads "A Fish Story" to the class, with emphasis on certain parts of the story, such as "*PLEASE OBSERVE THE FISH, AND WRITE DOWN ALL YOUR OBSERVATIONS*." Then, briefly discuss and assign questions pertaining to the story that students are to include in a one- or two-page reflective paper.
   "A Fish Story"—questions to help you organize your essay:
   1. Why do think the professor did what he did in the story?
   2. Was the professor looking for something specific?
   3. In your opinion, what is the meaning behind this story?
   4. How would you feel if you were one of the students in this lab?
   5. What, if anything, did the students learn?
   6. Why did our instructor read us this story?
   7. What is our instructor's purpose? Is our instructor looking for something specific?
2. During the second class session, the students come into class and see five large pieces of paper taped on the board in the front of the classroom. Each page has a line dotted vertically down the middle with "Student" on one side and "Instructor" on the other. Each of the five pieces of paper has one of the following headings on the top:
   - Preparation for Class
   - Attitude and Behaviors in Class
   - Written Assignments Will Be
   - Quiz and Exam Preparation Will Be
   - Earning an A =, Earning a B =, Earning a C =, Earning a D =, How You Could Earn an F in This Course =
3. Split the class into four or five groups depending on the size of the class. Hand out the 3 × 3 Post-it notes (about 20 sheets of each color) to each group. Explain what each group will be doing—responding to what is written on each of the large papers hanging in the front of the classroom. For example:

   Preparation for Class—Student side = arrive on time, arrive with all your necessary materials, arrive to class prepared with assignments complete

   Preparation for Class—Instructor side = have a lesson plan with established goals and objectives (active learning practices also), using multiple visual aids and techniques, focusing on student engagement and less on lecturing

4. Each group must offer at least three ideas for each of the large papers. You can also elaborate and add more during the discussion. Type these up and hand them back in the next class session. In the third class session, relate this activity to "A Fish Story." How does it relate? Why does it relate? See if they "GET IT."

Instructor Notes

There are a lot of teachable concepts and lessons in "A Fish Story"—for example, motivation, locus of control, organization, neat written work, intellectual curiosity, and most of all "initiative." This ties in nicely with Chapter 1 and the self-assessment that students complete.

Approximate Time: Two 50-minute classes

Source: Submitted by Cynthia Thorp, Alfred State College–SUNY College of Technology, NY

Chapter 1: Quiz Questions

(Please visit the Instructor Companion website for *On Course* at login.cengage.com or contact your local Cengage Learning sales representative to find electronic versions of the Quiz Questions.)

1. Taking the First Step

1. The quality of our lives is determined by the quality of the _____ we make on a daily basis.

2. When we choose positive beliefs, these lead to positive behaviors. Positive behaviors often lead to positive results that reinforce our positive beliefs, and the cycle begins anew. This sequence describes the cycle of _____.

3. A time-tested tool for designing the life you want to lead is a _____, a written record of your thoughts and feelings about your past, present, and future.

4. People who are strong in the eight qualities shown in the *On Course* self-assessment tend to make wiser choices at forks in the road than do people who are weak in these qualities.   TRUE   FALSE

5. Five suggestions to help you create a meaningful journal are (1) be spontaneous; (2) write for yourself; (3) be honest; (4) be creative; and (5) _____.

2. Understanding the Culture of Higher Education

1. According to Geert Hofstede, a Danish psychologist and anthropologist, deep culture is

    A. the collective programming of the mind that distinguishes the members of one human group from another.

    B. a way of determining which group of people is more likely to be successful in college.

    C. the clothing and art that distinguish one group of people from another.

    D. a set of rules voted upon by a group of people, usually from the same country.

2. Surface culture consists of the shared beliefs, attitudes, norms, rules, opinions, expectations, and taboos of a group of people.   TRUE   FALSE

3. The unwritten rule in cultures such as the Middle East, Southern France, and Spain is that interruptions in a conversation are not tolerated. In fact, if someone interrupts a speaker, others are likely to leave the conversation.   TRUE   FALSE

4. Intellectual _____ is greatly prized in the deep culture of higher education.

5. Some cultures favor action over reflection, which may cause members of these cultures to have a negative judgment of reflective activities such a writing journal entries.   TRUE   FALSE

3. Becoming an Active Learner

1. To excel as a learner, you need to create as many strong neural networks (connections) in your brain as possible.   TRUE   FALSE

2. In order to create strong neural networks (connections) in your brain, you've got to _____ the learning process.

   A. participate actively in

   B. read about

   C. remember

   D. listen to a lecture about

3. Brain research reveals that when you connect what you are learning now to previously stored information (e.g., already-formed neural networks), you learn the information or skill more slowly and less deeply.   TRUE   FALSE

4. The human brain learns best when learning efforts are done in

   A. one long marathon session, using one method of deep processing.

   B. frequent sessions distributed over time using one method of deep processing.

   C. one long marathon session using a variety of deep-processing strategies.

   D. frequent sessions distributed over time using a variety of deep-processing strategies.

5. The four components of the CORE Learning System are <u>C</u>ollect, <u>O</u>rganize, <u>R</u>ehearse, and _____ .

4. *On Course* at Work: *On Course* Principles at Work

1. The *soft skills* you'll learn in *On Course* are ideal for succeeding in both college and your career.   TRUE   FALSE

2. *Soft skills* may be the skills that determine whether you will keep a job or lose it.   TRUE   FALSE

3. According to the SCANS report, *hard skills* are enough to help you get the job of your dreams and keep it.   TRUE   FALSE

4. About what percent of workers today are in jobs that did not exist a few decades ago?

   A. 10

   B. 25

   C. 50

   D. 75

5. According to the SCANS report, employers consider *soft skills*, like those taught in *On Course,* to be

   A. essential for work-world success.

   B. a nice complement to the truly important *hard skills*.

   C. unnecessary for continued job success.

   D. a thing of the past—no one worries about those any longer.

5. Believing in Yourself: Develop Self-Acceptance

1. Self-esteem is the reputation we have with others.   TRUE   FALSE

2. Self-esteem is strengthened by increased self-acceptance.   TRUE   FALSE

3. Accepting our weaknesses means

   A. we are content to stay as we are.

   B. we can now begin to strengthen the things about ourselves that can be changed.

   C. we are weak.

4. Successful people are usually willing to

   A. admit their personal weaknesses.

   B. set a goal to change.

   C. manage their actions to bring about change.

   D. look at feedback about their efforts to change.

   E. have the courage to change.

   F. do all of the above.

5. We are born with a certain level of self-esteem, and it remains that way throughout our lives.   TRUE   FALSE

6. *Wise Choices in College*: College Customs

1. The college catalog, available in the registrar's office, is your best source of information about your college's general education requirements.   TRUE   FALSE

2. Your college course load is determined by your GPA at the end of the semester.   TRUE   FALSE

3. The course syllabus given to you by your instructor is a contract for that class.   TRUE   FALSE

4. As you prepare to cross the border into college, you can use resources to assist you with your journey. Even before you begin classes, you can check out the lay of the land. Which of these sources provides the most reliable information about your college prior to the first day of classes?

   A. Your brother's girlfriend

   B. The college catalogue

   C. Your college roommate, who has attended four other institutions

   D. The members of your college social networking site

5. You are taking 15 credit hours in the spring semester at your college. Last semester, you successfully completed 9 credit hours with two C's and a B. However, you stopped attending six hours (two 3-credit courses) and did not officially withdraw. Which of the following statements is true of you?

   A. You have two F's on your transcript from the last semester.

   B. You are currently enrolled in a "full class load."

   C. Your GPA is below a 2.0.

   D. All of the above are true.

Chapter 1: Essay Topics

1. Many students come to college to be a "success," yet few have given great thought to what they mean by the term. In an essay written to your classmates in this course, offer your personal definition of success.

2. In a letter to a trusted friend, share with him or her what your self-assessment questionnaire revealed to be your greatest areas of strength and weakness.

3. Imagine that you have entered a writing contest for a college scholarship. The topic this year is to explain the changes that you want to make in yourself in order to be more successful in college and in life. Write this essay for the college scholarship committee.

4. Inform your teacher in this course about which of the Eight Choices of Successful Students will be the easiest for you to make and which will be the most difficult for you to make. Dive deep as you explain why.

5. Write an article for your college newspaper in which you describe the things you found most surprising, confusing, strange, and/or upsetting during your first week in your new college culture.

6. Inform your classmates about something you have learned well (information or a skill). Describe all of the steps you used in your learning process, noting wherever possible how you Collected, Organized, Rehearsed, and Evaluated your knowledge or ability.

7. Self-esteem is an important concept but one that is difficult to define. In an essay for a national magazine read by college students, write about a person you know who demonstrates high self-esteem. In this way, offer your readers your best definition of high self-esteem and how to achieve it.

8. Using the *One Student's Story* essays in *On Course* as a model, write an essay about how you used a strategy from Chapter 1 to overcome a problem in your life—academic, personal, or even at work. First explain the problem; then discuss the strategy you used and how; finally, identify what happened. Your instructor may submit your essay to the author for possible publication in the next edition of *On Course*. Additional directions for writing and submitting these essays can be found at http://oncourseworkshop.com.

Answer Key to Chapter 1 Quiz Questions

1. Taking the First Step

Answers: 1. choices   2. success   3. journal   4. TRUE   5. dive deep

2. Understanding the Culture of Higher Education

Answers: 1. A   2. False (Deep culture consists of the shared beliefs, attitudes, norms, rules, opinions, expectations, and taboos of a group of people.)   3. FALSE (In these cultures, interruptions are expected.)   4. curiosity   5. TRUE

3. Becoming an Active Learner

Answers: 1. True   2. A   3. FALSE   4. D   5. Evaluate

4. *On Course* at Work: *On Course* Principles at Work

Answers: 1. TRUE   2. TRUE   3. FALSE   4. B   5. A

5. Believing in Yourself: Develop Self-Acceptance

Answers: 1. FALSE (It is our reputation with ourselves.)   2. TRUE   3. B   4. F   5. FALSE (We can learn higher self-esteem just as we learned lower self-esteem.)

6. *Wise Choices in College*: College Customs

Answers: 1. TRUE   2. FALSE   3. TRUE   4. B   5. D

Accepting Personal Responsibility

Concept

There is great value in perceiving ourselves as the primary creators of the outcomes and experiences of our lives. At the very least, we are responsible for how we respond to any event, whether the event is of our creation or not. When academic outcomes and experiences are negative, many students blame others, often teachers. When academic outcomes and experiences are positive, many students credit others. Because the cause of their results is seen as existing outside of themselves, these students have no reason to evaluate and possibly change their own behaviors. Students like this typically wait for the world to change while they complain, blame, make excuses, and repeat ineffective behaviors. They may even blame themselves, all the while thinking there is nothing they can do to change their fate. By offering students the opportunity to see how their own choices contribute to their past, present, and future outcomes, we empower them to approach life with the beliefs and behaviors of a Creator mindset, thus giving up the passivity and bitterness of a Victim mindset.

EMPOWERS STUDENTS TO . . .

1. Accept a Creator mindset, taking responsibility for creating the outcomes and experiences of their lives (including their education), *and* reject a Victim mindset, giving up complaining, blaming, excusing, and paralyzing self-judgment.
2. Master Creator language, understanding that Creators and Victims choose different ways of thinking and speaking about their experiences, consequently changing both their perceptions of reality and the outcomes that they create.
3. Live more consciously, becoming more aware of their inner aspects—Inner Critic, Inner Defender, and Inner Guide, among others—and the corresponding inner dialogue that dictates students' subsequent actions.
4. Make wise choices by consciously recognizing important decision points in their lives, identifying all possible options at this point, and making decisions with awareness of their future consequences.
5. Make mature decisions, choosing to make long-term gain more important than immediate pleasure or immediate escape from discomfort.
6. Replace outer authority with inner authority, and resistance with cooperation.
7. Gain greater control over the outcomes of their lives.

Remember also to use the all-purpose exercises mentioned in the Introduction, actively engaging students in the exploration of JOURNAL ENTRIES, CASE STUDIES, ONE STUDENT'S STORY, ON COURSE AT WORK, QUOTATIONS, CARTOONS, FOCUS QUESTIONS, CHAPTER-OPENING CHARTS, and STUDY SKILLS. Remind students to use letters to label any in-class writing they do in their journals.

Case Study for Critical Thinking: The Late Paper

Purpose

To develop critical thinking skills by exploring a real-life situation concerning personal responsibility and the power of choices.

Supplies and Setup

"The Late Paper" in *On Course*

Directions

1. [Have students read "The Late Paper." One way to be sure everyone has read the selection before taking the next step is "Popcorn Reading." Have one volunteer read the first paragraph aloud, another volunteer read the second, and so on until the reading is complete. Then have students record their scores for the six characters.] [5 minutes]

2. [Find out by a show of hands how many students have picked each character as number one—that is, most responsible for Kim's failing grade. If two or more characters are chosen as number one, move on to Step 3. In the unlikely event that everyone chooses the same character as number one (or there is otherwise little diversity in opinion), ask how many students have picked each character as number six—that is, *least* responsible for Kim's failing grade. Often there is more diversity of opinion here.] [5 minutes]

3. [Create groups of like-minded students.] *Since you agree in your group about which character is most (or least) responsible for Kim's failing grade, decide how you are going to persuade other groups to agree with you.* [5–10 minutes]

4. [Have a spokesperson from each group present the group's position; then lead a debate on the issue by moving the discussion from group to group, allowing students to explain their positions in more detail and to rebut opposing views. Invite students to demonstrate a change in their opinions by getting up and going to the group with which they now agree.] [5–20 minutes]

5. [Journal Quick-Write and/or Class Discussion] *Did you change your mind? If so, why? What did you learn from this discussion about personal responsibility? What's the life lesson here for you?* [e.g., "Sometimes I used all of my energy blaming someone else for a problem rather than doing what I needed to do in order to reach my goal."] [5–10 minutes]

6. Additional debriefing questions:
   a. *Is there someone in the story who may also bear responsibility for Kim's failing grade?* [This is the Diving Deeper question.]
   b. *If Kim chose to strengthen the quality of personal responsibility, what different choices might she have made in this situation? How would those different choices have changed her outcomes and experiences?*
   c. *In what ways did Kim fail to understand the culture of Professor Freud's class?*

Approximate Time: 25–50 minutes

Instructor Notes

1. So as not to stifle discussion, I don't reveal my own opinion.
2. This class discussion is an excellent prewriting activity to be followed by students writing a persuasion essay supporting their choices for most or least responsible. Because students are now sharply aware of opposing views, they often write much more thorough and persuasive essays (including rebuttals) than would be the case without the debate.
3. An optional step for this activity is to ask students to do a Quick-Write and then a discussion about the Diving Deeper question: Is there someone not mentioned in the story who may also bear responsibility for Kim's failing grade?
4. After students have read the case study, another option is to have them get in groups and see if they can come to consensus about which person is **second** most responsible for Kim's failing grade in Psychology 101.

Journal Entry 5 Adopting a Creator Mindset

EXERCISE 5-1: Responsibility Circle

Purpose

To become more aware of how we create or contribute to many of the outcomes and experiences in our lives.

Supplies and Setup

Groups of five or six students sitting in a circle. Each student needs a pen and paper.

Directions

1. *Write four statements that are true about you as a student (or other roles). Alternate between facts that you are happy with and facts that you are not happy with; for example: (1) I have a great schedule this semester (fact about which I'm happy); (2) my math teacher is boring (fact about which I'm unhappy); (3) my history teacher seems like a nice guy (fact about which I'm happy); (4) I'm not very motivated this semester (fact about which I'm unhappy).* [5 minutes]

2. *Within each group, start with the person who lives farthest from this room. Go clockwise around your circle, with each person reading his or her first statement, then around the circle again with each person reading the second statement, then a third time around, and so forth, until everyone has read all four statements. As you read your statement, add the following words: "... and I am responsible." For example, "I have a great schedule this semester, and I am responsible." "My math teacher is boring, and I am responsible." Become aware of how it feels to say that you are responsible for the situation with which you are happy or unhappy. When you hear others, decide whether there is any truth in the statement that they are responsible.* [5 minutes]

3. [Quick-Write and/or Class Discussion] *Were there situations about which you said, "There's no way I'm responsible for this"? Were there situations about which you said, "Well, I guess I have to admit that I am at least partially responsible for that"? How do you decide what you are, in fact, responsible for in life? Would it be of any benefit to always assume that you are responsible for the results in your life? What's the life lesson here for you?* [e.g., "I have been blaming others for a situation in my life that I am actually more responsible for than I have wanted to admit. That awareness gives me the power to do something about it."] [10–20 minutes]

Approximate Time: 20–30 minutes

Instructor Notes

1. Scott Peck, author of *The Road Less Traveled*, says that one of the most difficult things for human beings to decide is what they are and are not responsible for. Someone else (I don't recall who) has said that people who are neurotic take too much responsibility for the results in their lives, whereas people who are psychotic take too little responsibility. The challenge of being a Creator, then, is taking responsibility for the appropriate results in your life and not taking responsibility for the results that belong to others. Help students see that although they are certainly not responsible for all the outcomes and experiences in their lives, they are, however, 100 percent responsible for how they respond to these outcomes and experiences. If they always act as if they are responsible for the results in their lives, they will often discover life-improving choices for which they would not otherwise have even looked, let alone discovered.

2. In this activity (and all that deal with the Victim/Creator mindset), acknowledge that some people truly *are* victims. For example, they may be unjustly treated by others because of their race, gender, religion, or sexual preference. Or they may have terrible things happen to them that were out of their control (such as a flood). The distinction is in the mindset and the way one responds to injustice or hardships. Victims typically complain, blame, make excuses, and fail to take action to improve their situation. In contrast, Creators consistently look for ways to take action with the goal of creating the outcomes and experiences they want. Creators aren't always successful, but they persevere in the face of adversity with a clear intention of creating a better life for themselves and others.

EXERCISE 5-2: Victim/Creator Role-Play

Purpose

(1) To become familiar with the difference between how those with a Creator mindset and those with a Victim mindset respond to life's stimuli; (2) to see that we often have more options than we realize; (3) to understand that each person responds sometimes as a Creator, sometimes as a Victim; and (4) to see the value of responding as often as possible as a Creator.

Supplies and Setup

Two student volunteers (A and B). Role-playing is enhanced if students have already completed reading and writing Journal Entry 5.

Directions

1. [To Student A] *Imagine that you work for B* [student's name]. *You're often late or absent. Today you arrived 10 minutes late, and B confronts you. Because you're a great Victim, whatever B says to you, respond by making excuses, blaming others, or complaining about something, like the employer's "unfair" rules. Whatever you do, don't accept any responsibility for your absence or lateness, and don't agree to try anything new.*
2. [To Student B] *You're the employer who has watched A often be late or absent. You're angry because A was 10 minutes late again today. Go ahead and role-play. As the angry employer, what would you say to A?*
3. *Let's repeat the same scene, except this time, A, you'll respond to your employer as a Creator instead of as a Victim.*
4. [Invite students to invent additional situations, especially in college, where some people respond as Victims. Repeat the role-play with as many situations as time allows.]
5. [Quick-Write and/or Class Discussion] *How do people with a Victim mindset typically respond to life? How about people with a Creator mindset? Can you think of a time when you responded as a Victim? A Creator? Can you imagine the same person acting like a Victim in one situation and a Creator in another situation? What's the life lesson here for you?* [e.g., "When I get upset, I tend to act more like a Victim than when I am feeling good."]

Approximate Time: About 10–12 minutes for each role-play and discussion

Instructor Notes

1. An important point to bring out here is that a person is not solely a Victim or a Creator. We each have the capacity in any moment to respond as either. One key to success is to begin responding to life more often with a Creator mindset.
2. After each role-play, you might say to the class, "Any suggestions on how the worker could be an even better Victim? An even better Creator?" Other students often want to try the same roles. Sometimes the original pair wishes a second take on the scene.

Journal Entry 6 Mastering Creator Language

EXERCISE 6-1: The Language of Responsibility

Purpose
To practice language that supports responsible choices and to have an opportunity to meet a classmate.

Supplies and Setup
"Language of Responsibility" handout (next page). It's best if students have completed Journal Entry 6 before doing this activity.

Directions

1. *Victims and Creators see the world very differently. As a result, they use different vocabularies to represent their respective realities. In other words, you can tell a Victim and a Creator by their choice of words. On the handout, translate the Victim language into Creator language. Keep in mind two qualities that characterize Creator Language. First, Creators accept ownership of their outcomes and experiences. Second, Creators plan and take specific actions to improve their outcomes and experiences. So, you can recognize Creators because they accept ownership and take action!* [5–10 minutes]

2. [Class Discussion] *Okay, let's see what you came up with. Read one of the Victim statements, and give us your translation into Creator language. Are there any statements you had trouble translating and you'd like to hear what someone else wrote?* [5–10 minutes]

3. [Quick-Write and/or Class Discussion] *Based on their different vocabularies, what would you say are the differences in the beliefs that Victims and Creators have about themselves? About other people? About the world? What do you think is the difference in the results created by Victims and Creators? What's the life lesson here for you?* [e.g., "If I want to create my goals and dreams, I better learn to think and act more like a Creator and less like a Victim."] [5–10 minutes]

Approximate Time: 15–30 minutes

Instructor Notes

1. Important concepts to come out in the discussion include the following: Victims believe that other people and bad luck are responsible for their problems. As a result, Victims seldom achieve their goals and dreams (though sometimes they get lucky and do). Creators often achieve their goals and dreams (though sometimes they get unlucky and don't). Acting as a Creator is a way to improve the odds of being successful, but (alas) it isn't a guarantee.

2. As you lead the discussion of the students' translations, reinforce the two qualities that characterize Creator language: (1) ownership and (2) a plan of action.

3. If you have 45 or more minutes for this activity, you can put students into groups of four to six. After they write their translations individually (Step 1), have them discuss their translations in these small groups. Then move on to a class discussion (Step 2).

Language of Responsibility

Victim Talk	Creator Talk
1. I would be doing a lot better at this college if the teachers were any good.	
2. They ought to do something about the food around here.	
3. I couldn't come to class because I had to go to the dentist for a checkup.	
4. You just can't pass a course when it's that hard.	
5. My boss makes me so angry.	
6. I can't help talking in class.	
7. I couldn't get the assignment because I was absent.	
8. I couldn't keep my appointment with you yesterday because my math teacher made me take a makeup test.	
9. People always get angry when they work hard and still fail a course.	
10. I couldn't attend class because I had to drive my mother to work.	
11. I would have called you, but my daughter got sick.	
12. They don't know what they're doing around here.	
13. I couldn't get to class on time because my last teacher kept us late.	
14. I tried calling him, but he's never home.	
15. I didn't have time to do my homework.	

EXERCISE 6-2: Have to/Choose to

Purpose

To demonstrate how language choices affect our attitude and our energy levels; to meet and interact with classmates.

Supplies and Setup

Journal

Directions

1. *In your journal, draw a vertical line down the middle of a page. On the left side of the line, make a list of five things you "have to" do. Example: "**I have to** go to college"; "**I have to** call my mother on Sundays"; "**I have to** eat . . ." [3 minutes]*

2. *[Milling] Everyone stand and choose a partner. Each partner reads from his or her list three things that he or she "has to" do. If you hear a new "have to" that is true for you, add it to your list. Then move on to a new partner and repeat the exchange of "have to's." Keep going until I call stop. As you do this activity, be aware of how you are feeling. [5 minutes]*

3. *Now, on the right side of the line, rewrite each of your sentences. Change "have to" to "choose to" and add a "because . . ." or "so . . ." clause to the sentence, one that gives a positive reason for your choice. Examples: "**I choose to** go to college because my degree will qualify me for the job I want"; "**I choose to** call my mother on Sundays so she will feel loved"; "**I choose to** eat because I want to be healthy." [7 minutes]*

4. *[Milling] Everyone stand and meet a partner as we did before. This time each of you will read three things that you "choose to" do. After you both read, move on to another partner. Keep going until I call stop. Notice if you feel any different this time. [5 minutes]*

5. *[Quick-Write and/or Class Discussion] Did you feel any different when you said "choose to" rather than "have to"? What does this experience suggest about how your language choices affect you? What is the life lesson here for you? [e.g., "I get myself upset by thinking I 'have to' do something when the truth is that I really don't have to do it. . . . I'm choosing to do it. Realizing this makes me feel a lot more calm and in control of my life."] [5–10 minutes]*

Approximate Time: About 20–30 minutes

Instructor Notes

1. A great way to clarify directions is to give a demonstration (DEMO). Steps 2 and 4 (above) will be most clear if you say, "So here's what that would look like . . ." and DEMO what you're asking for.

2. A point worth making in the discussion is that most people feel their energy level go up when they switch from "have to" to "choose to." That's because most people are depressed by Victim talk and energized by Creator talk.

EXERCISE 6-3: Choices and Ripples

Purpose

To explore how the choices students make now will have rippling effects in the near and distant future.

Supplies and Setup

Two student volunteers and one Slinky

Directions

1. Ask for two student volunteers. Each student takes an end of the Slinky and stretches it out. One student serves as the "choice" and the other as the "effect." Ask the student serving as the "choice" to shake the Slinky once. The class will see how by shaking the Slinky once, there are multiple and continuous effects on the other student. You could even have the other students time how long it takes for the Slinky to stop having these "effects."

Approximate Time: 25 minutes

Instructor Notes

Here are some guided questions to help with the discussion:

1. On a sheet of paper, please state a choice you have made that had and/or continues to have rippling effects.
2. Please make a list of the effects that the choice had. Also, don't forget that sometimes our choices can have effects on those around us. Please don't forget those!
3. After looking over your choice and the rippling effects it had, please reflect on how you could have prevented these rippling effects. What are some strategies from the *On Course* text that may have helped you prevent these effects?

Source: Submitted by Katy Goforth, Tri-County Technical College, SC

Journal Entry ▢7▢ Making Wise Decisions

EXERCISE 7-1: The Wise Choice Process

Purpose

To give students an opportunity to practice the Wise Choice Process, a powerful critical-thinking tool of Creators.

Supplies and Setup

Journal 7 in *On Course* (students will need to refer to the six steps of the Wise Choice Process); students in pairs

Directions

1. *In your journal, briefly write about a current problem or difficulty in your life. It doesn't have to be a major problem. Choose a problem that you are comfortable talking about with your partner.*
2. *Decide which partner will present a problem and which will be the Guide. The Guide will use the Wise Choice Process to assist the other person to discover his or her best options.*
3. *Guide, ask your partner the six questions of the Wise Choice Process. Your role is to guide your partner to discover his or her best options, without giving advice. If you come up with an option your partner doesn't think of, you can always tell him or her after class. For this dialogue, offer no advice. The easiest way to do this is simple:* **Stick to the six steps of the Wise Choice Process.** *Here's what that might look like.* [DEMO the Wise Choice Process.] *Any questions? When you're ready, begin.*
4. [Optional: If time allows, have partners switch roles and repeat Step 3.]
5. [Quick-Write and/or Class Discussion] *What was your experience as a Guide? How was it to avoid giving advice while helping your partner to solve his or her own problem? What was your experience as the person seeking a solution to a problem? Did you discover positive options for solving your problem? What's the life lesson here for you?* [e.g., "By not giving advice to my partner, she came up with a solution I never would have suggested. By answering the questions of the Wise Choice Process, I came up with options that I had never thought of before."]

Approximate Time: 15 minutes for each time through the Wise Choice Process; 5–15 minutes for discussion

Instructor Notes

1. An alternative format is to put students in trios instead of pairs. The third student acts as a silent observer during the Wise Choice Process. Afterward, the observer's role is to give feedback to the Guide about how well he or she followed the six steps of the Process. The observer's presence often causes the other two participants to focus more consciously on their purpose—coming up with positive options—raising the quality of the results they create. If time allows, you can rotate the trio so each person has a chance to experience all three roles.

2. This process is very powerful. Students often say, "I didn't think this process would really work, but now that I've tried it, I see that it's a great tool for helping someone find positive options to solve a problem."

3. Later in the semester, if a student asks you for advice (either privately or in class), ask if he or she would be willing to choose a classmate to act as a Guide though the Wise Choice Process. The class can observe and see the power of this decision-making process in action.

EXERCISE 7-2: The Road Not Taken

Purpose

To offer students an opportunity to see how their choices make all the difference in the outcomes of their lives.

Supplies and Setup

"The Road Not Taken" by Robert Frost (the text of this poem can be found in many literature books and on the Internet.) Project the poem on a PowerPoint slide or give as a handout.

Directions

1. *I'd like a volunteer to read "The Road Not Taken" by Robert Frost.*

2. *The narrator of this poem came to a fork in the road: "Two roads diverged in a yellow wood." He had to take one road or the other, and he made a choice "that has made all the difference." In your journal, make a list of the major choice points you've faced in your life. For example, you might put "Attend college after high school or get a job," "Get married or stay single," or "Have a child or not." [5 minutes]*

3. *Let's hear some of your choice points. Just tell us your options, not what you chose. If you hear someone else mention a choice that reminds you of one you've made, add it to your list. [2–5 minutes, depending on the energy. A way to pick up the energy is to ask after a choice has been called out, "How many of you have also made a choice like this?"]*

4. *In the poem, Frost says, "Knowing how way leads on to way, I doubted if I should ever come back." Now pick one of your choices and go back to the moment of decision. In your journal, quick-write about what your life would be like today if you'd chosen the road not taken. For example, if one of your choice points was to marry or not, and you did marry, write what you imagine your life would be like today if you had not gotten married back then. [5 minutes]*

5. *Who'd be willing to read aloud what you wrote? How do you feel about that choice now that you've looked down the other road? Did you make a wise choice back then? Why do you think so? What's the life lesson here for you? [e.g., "Once I've made a decision, it's going to affect my life for years to come, so I better think it through before I make an important choice."] [3–5 minutes for each volunteer]*

Approximate Time: 15 minutes for Steps 1–4; 3–5 minutes for each volunteer in Step 5

Instructor Notes

1. The point here is threefold: to assist students to examine the wisdom of the previous choices they have made, to help them see that every choice they make impacts the quality of their future, and to show that all experiences contain life lessons if we look for them.

2. Listen for the Inner Critic badgering a student about a "bad choice." If a student is critical of his or her past choice, you might ask, "Is that your Inner Guide speaking or your Inner Critic?" If the student says, "That's my Inner Critic," you might respond, "Remember, your Inner Critic likes to wallow in what you did wrong, whereas your Inner Guide takes ownership and then creates a plan to make things better. Which voice would be more helpful to listen to?" Most of all, resist giving advice to the student. Merely be a questioner and an active listener.

EXERCISE 7-3: Excuses and Reasons

Purpose

To consider the difference between mature reasons and immature excuses.

Supplies and Setup

Copies of the "Excuses/Reasons" handout (next page)

Directions

1. *Rank the statements on the "Excuses and Reasons" handout as explained in the **Directions.*** [5 minutes]
2. *Which statement did you rank #1 . . . as a Victim's excuse? Why?* [5 minutes]
3. *Which statement did you rank #9 . . . as a Creator's reason? Why?* [5 minutes]
4. [Discuss the Diving Deeper questions on the handout.]
5. [Quick-Write and/or Class Discussion] *What differences do you see that distinguish Victims' excuses from Creators' reasons? What's the life lesson here for you?* [e.g., "People love to pretend that their excuses are actually reasons, but pretending doesn't make it so."] [5–10 minutes]

Approximate Time: 20–25 minutes

Instructor Notes

1. Important points to make in the discussion:
   - Payoff of excuses for Victims: They minimize present discomfort or maximize present pleasure.
   - Price of excuses for Victims: They seldom achieve their desired outcomes and experiences.
   - Price of reasons for Creators: They sometimes experience present discomfort.
   - Payoff of reasons for Creators: They often achieve their desired future outcomes and experiences.
2. An alternative is to choose one statement and have students line up by the score they gave that statement from 1 to 9. This structure is called a "Value Line." (You may want to make a horseshoe so that the two ends of the line are closer to each other.) Going from one end of the line to the other, have students say their score out loud to make sure everyone is in the right place. (In a large group, you may have students at every number.) Now ask students at each end of the line to explain their choice. A point that often arises is that we see "reasons" when we've had a similar experience and see "excuses" when we have not.

Excuses and Reasons

Here are some choices that students have made more important than turning in a college assignment on time. Rank them from 1 through 9. Put a *1* next to the decision you consider to be the weakest Victim's excuse. Put a *9* next to the decision you consider to be the strongest Creator's reason. Rank the other decisions in order from 2 through 8, giving a different number to each statement. You may assume that all nine students believe they are telling the truth (which is why this activity is not called "Lies and Reasons").

Victim's Excuse 1 2 3 4 5 6 7 8 9 Creator's Reason

I didn't turn in my assignment on time because . . .

_____ I helped my aunt move to a new apartment.

_____ I rushed my daughter to the hospital because she was having an asthma attack.

_____ I stayed home to wait for the telephone repair man.

_____ I visited my boyfriend because he's having problems at home, and I felt like he needed me.

_____ I didn't look at my schedule carefully, so I totally forgot when the assignment was due.

_____ I had a headache and stayed home.

_____ I decided I could improve the assignment if I worked on it for a few more days.

_____ I started the assignment last night, and I didn't have time to finish it.

_____ I went to an appointment with another teacher instead of coming to class.

Diving Deeper:

What criteria do VICTIMS use to make their choices? What's the payoff? What's the price?

What criteria do CREATORS use to make their choices? What's the payoff? What's the price?

Educator John Holt wrote, "Caring teachers accept no excuses." What do you think of this belief?

Journal Entry 8 Believing in Yourself: Change Your Inner Conversation

EXERCISE 8-1: Inner Dialogue Role-Play

Purpose

To dramatize the impact of the ongoing inner dialogue among the Inner Critic, Inner Defender, and Inner Guide.

Supplies and Setup

Four volunteers (A, B, C, and D) for a role-play. Have student A sit in a chair.

Directions

1. *Student A, you're going to speak to the class about your thoughts and feelings about college. There's no right or wrong thing to say, so just tell us whatever you want about your experience so far in college. After you speak, pause to hear what your inner voices have to say. When they are finished, make another statement about college.*

2. *Student B, you'll position yourself at Student A's right side and be his or her Inner Critic. This means that whatever Student A says, you'll find some way to criticize him or her for it. For example, if Student A says, "I like college," you might say, "You're a lousy math student; you can't even get to your classes on time . . .."*

3. *Student C, you'll position yourself at Student A's left side and be his or her Inner Defender. This means that whatever the Inner Critic says, you'll find some way to defend against the accusations by blaming problems on other people or circumstances. For example, you might say, "No one could be a good math student with such a lousy teacher. And with the terrible parking around here, of course you're late to your classes . . .."* [5–10 minutes for Steps 1–3]

4. *[After the scene has played out] So, Student A, what's on your mind right now? Did you recognize any of those voices? Do you think those voices have any effect on your success?* [Ask Inner Critic, Inner Defender, and class to add their observations.] [3–5 minutes]

5. *Now, Student D, you'll position yourself behind Student A and be his or her Inner Guide. Your job is to offer a more objective view on Student A's life. For example, if the Inner Critic says, "You're a lousy math student," you might say, "You can improve your math skills by spending more time studying." If the Inner Defender says, "You have a lousy math teacher," you might say, "You can always go to the math lab to get additional help."* [3–5 minutes]

6. *[Quick-Write and/or Class Discussion] So, what did you learn from this role-play? What's the life lesson here for you?* [e.g., "I've got a lot of voices chattering in my head, and some of them won't help me achieve my goals. That's why it's really important that I am careful about which one I listen to."] [5–15 minutes]

Approximate Time: 25–40 minutes

Instructor Notes

1. Let the role-play go for as long as it's entertaining and making a point. You'll probably have to slow down the dialogue, especially so that the Inner Guide has time to respond to the comments of the Inner Critic and Inner Defender. An important point to make is that the Inner Critic and the Inner Defender are both inner voices of the Victim. The difference is whether the finger of judgment is pointed inward (Inner Critic) or outward (Inner Defender). The Inner Guide is the inner voice of the Creator. Our choice about which voices to listen to affects how we feel and what we do, and therefore determines our results in life.

EXERCISE 8-2: Revising Stinkin' Thinkin'

Purpose

To practice identifying irrational beliefs that tear away at our self-esteem.

Supplies and Setup

Students should have completed Journal Entry 8. Copies of the "Revise Stinkin' Thinkin'" handout (p. 85).

Directions

1. *Fill in all the empty spaces in the A + B = C chart. Some items give you "A" (the Activating event) and "C" (the Consequence), and you must fill in "B" (the Belief). Others give you "A" and "B," and you must fill in "C." Still others give you only "A" and ask you to fill in both "B" and "C." Go ahead and do that now.* [10 minutes]

2. [Lead a discussion about the Beliefs and Consequences the students have filled in for each event. For each item, ask:] *Is this belief wise thinkin' or stinkin' thinkin'? Is this event likely to raise or lower the person's self-esteem? What is the life lesson here for you?* [e.g., "How I feel about myself depends more on what I think and believe than on what I accomplish."] [15–20 minutes]

Approximate Time: 25–30 minutes

Instructor Notes

1. Remind students of psychologist Albert Ellis's belief that much of the world's emotional misery is caused by stinkin' thinkin' and that stinkin' thinkin' leads not only to poor outcomes and experiences but also to lowered self-esteem.

2. The important point to be made here is that any activating event allows for many possible responses. How we respond is a result of the core beliefs we hold about ourselves, other people, and the world, and it is these same core beliefs that powerfully affect our self-esteem.

Revising Stinkin' Thinkin'

Activating Event (What happened)	+	Belief(s) (What I think)	=	Consequence (Emotions and behaviors)
1. I fail a midterm test.		1.		1. I get depressed and stop attending the course.
2. A friend doesn't meet me at the time we agreed upon.		2. My friend is usually very reliable and keeps his agreements.		2.
3. A speeding car cuts across two lanes of highway, just missing my car, then rockets off the next exit ramp.		3.		3.
4. Shortly after I hand in an essay, my instructor tells me, "I need to see you right away."		4.		4. I get very nervous and put off making an appointment to see my instructor.
5. I get an application for financial aid.		5. This form is very complicated, and I'm sure to make a mistake filling it out. I don't want anyone to know I'm confused.		5.
6. I'm going to be late for work for the third time this week. I've had one unexpected problem after another this week, but my employer doesn't know this, and she's bound to be furious when I get there.		6.		6.

Reading

READING EXERCISE 1: ACADEMIC COACHES (OPTION 1)

Purpose

To help students identify reading challenges in college and possible solutions to those problems.

Supplies and Setup

4 × 6 index cards (one for each student); students have read the "Wise Choices in College: Reading" section in *On Course*, Chapter 2.

Directions

Note—this activity can be repeated with each study skill.

1. [Students in pairs] *The purpose of most reading assignments in a college class is to inform you about three things: (A) a key concept, (B) main ideas about that concept, and (C) supporting details about the main ideas. Brainstorm with your partner and list possible challenges that could keep you from fully understanding a reading assignment. For example, one problem might be that your mind keeps wandering when you read. After you together come up with five reading challenges, each of you choose one of the problems (not the same one) and write it on a 4 × 6 card. You'll get the most value from this activity if you choose a reading problem that has been a challenge for you.* [10 minutes]

2. *Decide which of you will be a "coach" and which will be a "client."* [Make sure that every pair of students has one coach and one client, and encourage them to recall which they are.] *In a few moments, I'm going to say, "Clients, get a coach," and everyone who has chosen to be a client, stand up and move to a new partner. Coaches, you stay seated and wave your hand in the air to let clients know that you need a partner. When a new partner joins you, put your hand down. You'll be with each partner for a five-minute conversation, and then I'll say "Clients, get a new coach." Clients will move to a new partner, and coaches will stay seated, waving their hands to let clients know they need a new partner.* [It helps to demonstrate exactly what this way of changing partners will look like.] *So, what will you talk about with your partners? When clients get to their coach, share the reading challenge on your card. Your partner will then coach you on how you might overcome this problem. Coaches, you may refer to the reading strategies in* On Course *if you wish. Clients, take notes on the suggestions.* [It helps to demonstrate exactly what the conversation might sound like, with the client stating the reading problem and the coach offering a suggested solution from the text or personal experience.] *What questions do you have? Ready . . . Clients get a coach!* [10–25 minutes, depending on how many times you have students move to a new partner.]

3. [Have students reverse roles: Coaches become clients and clients become coaches. Continue the process of changing partners as in Step 2.] [10–25 minutes]

4. [Discussion] *What's a reading challenge that you or one of your partners identified? What is one way to overcome this challenge? Can anyone think of another way to overcome this challenge?* [10–20 minutes]

Approximate Time: 40–80 minutes

Instructor Notes

1. If you have participated in an *On Course* Workshop, you will recognize that this activity is an adaptation of a structure called "Eagles and Hawks."
2. Give directions carefully (including a physical demonstration of how students change partners).
3. If you have an uneven number of students, you can designate one student as an "observer." This student joins any pair that he or she chooses.
4. This activity could be spread over two class periods by dropping Step 3 in Day 1. In Day 2, start with Step 3 and finish, as previously, with Step 4.

READING EXERCISE 2: MARKING AND ANNOTATING

Purpose

To provide students with an opportunity to practice marking and annotating a reading assignment.

Supplies and Setup

Handout: Copy a page from *On Course* (or another text) that students have not yet read. Make three copies for every two students. In a previous class, assign students to bring with them the note-taking tools that they use when they read class assignments (e.g., pencils, pens, highlighters). Students should have previously read "Wise Choices in College: Reading" section in *On Course*, Chapter 2.

Directions

1. [Discussion] *When you read an assignment for one of your classes, what is your purpose?* [To accurately and completely identify the key concepts, main ideas, secondary ideas, major supporting details, and minor supporting details. This allows you to return later and <u>C</u>ollect the key concepts, important ideas, and supporting details without rereading the whole assignment.] [5 minutes]
2. *Marking and annotating what you read will help you do just that. Let's brainstorm a list of helpful ways to mark or annotate your reading assignments.* [Record a list on the whiteboard: for instance, circle key concepts, underline or highlight main ideas, write comments in the margin, write questions in the margin alongside their answers in the text, use different-color highlighters for ideas of different levels of importance, write questions in the margin that you will ask in class, underline or highlight examples, put stars next to very important ideas.] [5 minutes]
3. [Distribute the handout, one to each student; hold the additional handouts for later.] *Read this text and do the best job you know how to mark and annotate it so that the key concepts, important ideas, and supporting ideas are easily seen.* [10 minutes]
4. *Now pair up with a partner.* [If there is an extra student, create one trio. Give each pair/trio a third unmarked copy of the handout.] *With your partner(s), mark and annotate this new handout by combining the best from what each of you did earlier. Remember, your goal is to mark and annotate it so that the key concepts, important ideas, and supporting ideas are easily seen.* [10 minutes]
5. *Now, each pair join another pair.* [If there is an extra pair, create one sextet.] [Collect the just-completed handouts from each group. Mix up the handouts, and redistribute two handouts to each group, making sure that no group gets a handout created by any of its members.] *Choose a group spokesperson. The spokesperson's job will be to tell us which handout you think has the better marking and annotating . . . and why. That means you'll be explaining specific examples of effective marking and annotating. And, if there's something that you think would improve the marking and annotating, tell us that as well.* [10 minutes]
6. [Call on team spokespersons to present the positive marking and annotating features their groups found in their chosen handout. Urge each presenter to be specific about what positive techniques were used and what concepts, ideas, or details were highlighted. Ask the presenter if there is anything the group thought would improve the marking and highlighting.] [10–20 minutes]

Approximate Time: 50–60 minutes

Instructor Notes

1. In my experience, some students are initially reluctant to write in their college books. Sometimes this is a carryover from high school where they were forbidden to write in their school-owned books. Sometimes it is because students plan to sell their books after the course and don't want to lower their value by writing in them. If you face such reluctance, consider reminding students that now they (not the school) own their books and should use them for maximum learning and high grades. Additionally, they will receive only a small fraction of their purchase price back, and it would be a false economy to trade deep and lasting learning for a few extra dollars in used book sales, especially when the cost of books is such a small percentage of their investment of money and time to earn their education.
2. If you mix up the handouts well in Step 5, no student or group will know who created the handouts not chosen. Thus, no student should experience being the "loser" of a competition.

Embracing Change: Do One Different Thing This Week

Many people resist change. It's easier to complain, blame, and make excuses. More challenging is experimenting with new beliefs and behaviors, evaluating your results, and then adopting the more helpful ones permanently. And that is exactly what Creators do. Creators crave new methods for lifting the quality of their lives up a notch. And then up another notch. And another. Creators embrace change because it's a great way—maybe the *only* way—to maximize their potential to live a rich, full life.

   In this chapter, you have encountered a number of empowering beliefs and behaviors related to personal responsibility and self-esteem. Here's an opportunity to experiment with one of them. First, from the following list, choose one belief or behavior you think will make the greatest positive impact on your outcomes and experiences.

1. Think: "I accept responsibility for creating my life as I want it."
2. Write a list of Victim statements used by other people and translate the statements into Creator language.
3. Catch myself thinking or speaking Victim language, write a list of these statements, and translate them into Creator language.
4. Use the Wise Choice Process to make a decision.
5. Catch myself using stinkin' thinkin' and dispute it.
6. Demonstrate personal responsibility at my workplace.
7. Your choice: A different belief or behavior you learned in this chapter with which you would like to experiment.

   Now, write the belief or behavior you chose under "My Commitment" in the following chart. Then, track yourself for one week, putting a check in the appropriate box each day that you keep your commitment. After seven days, assess your results. If your outcomes and experiences improve, you now have a tool you can use for the rest of your life.

My Commitment						
Day 1	Day 2	Day 3	Day 4	Day 5	Day 6	Day 7

During my seven-day experiment, what happened?

As a result of what happened, what did I learn or relearn?

Chapter 2: Quiz Questions

(Please visit the Instructor Companion website for *On Course* website at **login.cengage.com or contact your local Cengage Learning sales representative** to find electronic versions of the Quiz Questions.)

7. Adopting a Creator Mindset

1. When people create the best life possible given their circumstances, they are employing a _____ mindset.

    A. Creator

    B. Victim

    C. student

    D. all of the above

2. When people allow life to happen to them, they are employing a _____ mindset.

    A. Creator

    B. Victim

    C. student

    D. none of the above

3. When we respond to a stimulus as a Creator we are most likely to

    A. seek solutions.

    B. take action.

    C. try something new.

    D. all of the above.

4. When we respond to a stimulus as a Victim, we are most likely to

    A. blame.

    B. complain.

    C. excuse.

    D. all of the above.

5. The key ingredient of personal responsibility is choice.   TRUE   FALSE

8. Mastering Creator Language

1. "I failed because my instructor is terrible" is something that would probably be said by your Inner

    A. Critic.

    B. Defender.

    C. Guide.

    D. Creator.

2. "I'm so stupid, it's no surprise I failed math" is something that would probably be said by your Inner

    A. Critic.

    B. Defender.

    C. Guide.

    D. Creator.

3. When you hear ownership and an action plan, you know you are talking to a Victim.   TRUE   FALSE

4. "I was late because I chose to sleep 30 minutes later this morning" is something that would probably be said by your Inner

    A. Critic.

    B. Defender.

    C. Guide.

    D. Victim.

5. "I don't think I'm smart enough to make it in college" is something that would probably be said by your Inner

    A. Critic.

    B. Defender.

    C. Guide.

    D. Creator.

9. Making Wise Decisions

1. What we will experience in 5 or 10 years is greatly affected by the choices we make from here on.   TRUE   FALSE

2. Your Inner Defender will be of great help as you take the first step of the Wise Choice Process, which is objectively identifying "What's my situation?"   TRUE   FALSE

3. In Step 4 of the Wise Choice Process, the ideal is to come up with how many possible choices?

    A. one

    B. two

    C. three

    D. as many as possible

4. If you can't predict the outcome of one of your possible choices, you should stop and gather more information before making any decisions.   TRUE   FALSE

5. After implementing your plan, the final step of the Wise Choice Process is to evaluate the success of your plan. One good way to do this is to compare your new situation with how you would like it to be (as you defined it in Step 2). TRUE   FALSE

10. On Course at Work: Personal Responsibility at Work

1. As long as I believe my career success belongs to someone else (like "lousy" bosses), I'm being a Victim, and my success is unlikely.   TRUE   FALSE

2. Creators know that the foundation of success at work (as in college) is accepting this truth: By our choices, we are each the primary creators of the outcomes and experiences of our lives.   TRUE   FALSE

3. Victims usually don't explore their career options thoroughly or match career requirements with their own talents and interests, and they make uninformed choices.   TRUE   FALSE

4. What are the advantages of being a Creator in the workplace?

    A. Creators bring a positive and productive attitude to the workplace.

    B. Absenteeism and poor working habits are not problems for Creators.

    C. These employees get the job and then excel at the job.

    D. All of the above are advantages.

    E. None of the above are advantages.

5. Taking responsibility for your work life means

    A. planning your career path to keep your options open and your progress unobstructed.

    B. reacting emotionally to disappointments on the job.

    C. placing responsibility for obstacles on those who are creating them (bosses, coworkers, "the man").

    D. running with the immediate opportunities that face you, so you won't miss out on them.

11. Believing in Yourself: Change Your Inner Conversation

1. According to psychologist Albert Ellis, the following formula explains why people respond differently to the same event: A + B = C. In this formula, "A" stands for the Activating event, and "C" stands for the Consequence (how we feel about the activating event). What does "B" stand for?

    A. Behaviors

    B. Beliefs

    C. Brains

    D. Brawn

2. "I'm stupid" is a typical comment made by an Inner _____.

3. "He's stupid" is a typical comment made by an Inner _____.

4. Disputing irrational beliefs is best done by the

    A. Inner Critic.

    B. Inner Defender.

    C. Inner Guide.

    D. Inner Tube.

5. Being able to dispute irrational beliefs will help your self-esteem to grow.   TRUE   FALSE

12. Wise Choices in College: Reading

1. Reading is one of the most important ways of <u>C</u>ollecting knowledge; <u>C</u>ollecting knowledge is the first step in the CORE Learning System.   TRUE   FALSE

2. Active reading is characterized by intense mental engagement that leads to significant neural activity in the brain, assists deep and lasting learning, and leads to high grades.   TRUE   FALSE

3. When reading actively, the most significant information in the reading is in the supporting details.   TRUE   FALSE

4. Good readers don't read words; they read ideas, and ideas are found in chunks (groups of words).   TRUE   FALSE

5. Effective highlighting will result in 40 to 50 percent of a paragraph being marked for review.   TRUE   FALSE

Chapter 2: Essay Topics

1. Many people who commit crimes believe that they have been wronged by society and that this justifies their crimes. Write an essay to inform a group of prison inmates about the differences between a Creator and a Victim.

2. Some people have charged that North America has become a continent of Victims: Whenever North Americans don't like the way something is, the argument goes, they blame others instead of taking personal responsibility. Present an argument for a newspaper editorial supporting or contradicting this viewpoint.

3. Interview three or more instructors at your college, and find out their opinion on how well students accept personal responsibility for their education. Write an editorial for your college newspaper explaining what you discover.

4. Do most people use Victim language or Creator language? Take on the role of one who studies the way people use language. Go to a public place and listen to people talk. Write an article for a local magazine detailing what your research uncovers.

5. Recall a time when you received extraordinarily good or bad service from someone at a business where you were a customer. If the service was extraordinarily good, write a letter to the owner of the business explaining how an employee went "above and beyond" to accept personal responsibility for meeting your needs as a customer. If the service was extraordinarily bad, write a letter to the owner of the business explaining how an employee shirked personal responsibility and created a poor experience for you as a customer.

6. Psychologist Albert Ellis said that irrational beliefs (which he called "stinkin' thinkin'") cause many of our problems. In an essay for your classmates, report on some of your own irrational beliefs that have gotten you off course and lowered your self-esteem. Offer rational beliefs that you could take on to dispute your stinkin' thinkin'.

7. Using the student essays in *On Course* as a model, write an essay about how you used a strategy from Chapter 2 to overcome a problem in your life—academic, personal, or even at work. First explain the problem; then discuss the strategy you used and how; finally, identify what happened. Your instructor may submit your essay for possible publication in the next edition of *On Course*. Additional directions for writing and submitting these essays can be found at http://oncourseworkshop.com.

Answer Key to Chapter 2 Quiz Questions

7. Adopting a Creator Mindset

Answers: 1. A   2. B   3. D   4. D   5. TRUE

8. Mastering Creator Language

Answers: 1. B   2. A   3. FALSE (Creator)   4. C   5. A

9. Making Wise Decisions

Answers: 1. TRUE   2. FALSE (Your Inner Guide will best help you define your present situation.)   3. D
4. TRUE   5. TRUE

10. On Course at Work: Personal Responsibility at Work

Answers: 1. TRUE   2. TRUE   3. TRUE   4. D   5. A

11. Believing in Yourself: Change Your Inner Conversation

Answers: 1. B   2. Critic   3. Defender   4. C   5. TRUE

12. Wise Choices in College: Reading

Answers: 1. TRUE   2. TRUE   3. FALSE (main idea)   4. TRUE   5. FALSE

Discovering Self-Motivation

Concept

Choosing a meaningful purpose gives our lives a direction and creates inner motivation. Many students have not defined a personally meaningful purpose for being in college, let alone for being in a particular course. Unfocused, these students are more likely to drift **from** rather than **to** academic success. By offering them the opportunity to choose personally meaningful outcomes that they would like to achieve in college or in life, we assist students to create internal motivation and thus positively impact their persistence in the face of life's inevitable obstacles.

EMPOWERS STUDENTS TO . . .

1. Design a life plan that replaces external motivation with internal motivation.
2. Create a sense of "self" founded on their unique combination of personal roles, goals, and dreams.
3. Revise or upgrade their personal goals and dreams as a result of being exposed to the variety of aspirations held by other students.
4. Persist when they encounter obstacles that stand between them and their college education (or any other major goal).
5. Develop positive, affirming self-talk and powerful visualizations that will support them in pursuing their goals and dreams in the face of both internal and external obstacles.
6. Make and keep commitments to themselves.

Remember also to use the all-purpose exercises mentioned in the Introduction, actively engaging students in the exploration of JOURNAL ENTRIES, CASE STUDIES, ONE STUDENT'S STORY, ON COURSE AT WORK, QUOTATIONS, CARTOONS, FOCUS QUESTIONS, CHAPTER-OPENING CHARTS, and STUDY SKILLS. Remind students to use letters to label any in-class writing they do in their journals.

Case Study in Critical Thinking: Popson's Dilemma

Purpose

To develop critical thinking skills by exploring a real-life situation concerning self-motivation.

Supplies and Setup

"Popson's Dilemma" in *On Course*.

Directions

1. [Have students read "Popson's Dilemma." One way to be sure everyone has read the selection before taking the next step is to have one student read the first paragraph aloud, another student read the second, and so on until the reading is complete. Then have students put in their scores for the eight professors.] [5 minutes]
2. [Find out by a show of hands how many students have picked each professor as number one—the best advice for motivating Professor Popson's students. If two or more characters are chosen as number one, move on to Step 3. In the unlikely event that everyone chooses the same character as number one (or there is otherwise little diversity in opinion), ask how many students have picked each character as number eight—the worst advice for motivating Professor Popson's students. Often there is more diversity of opinion here.] [5 minutes]
3. [Create groups of like-minded students.] *Since you agree in your group about whose advice is best (or worst) for motivating Professor Popson's students, decide how you are going to persuade other groups to agree with you.* [5–10 minutes]
4. [Have a spokesperson from each group present the group's position; then lead a debate on the issue by moving the discussion from group to group, allowing students to explain their positions in more detail and rebut opposing views. Invite students to demonstrate a change in their opinions by getting up and going to the group with which they now agree.] [5–20 minutes]
5. [Quick-Write and/or Class Discussion] *What did you learn from this discussion about self-motivation? What motivates you? If, like the student in the case study, you begin to lose your motivation in college, what could you do to get it back? What's the life lesson here for you?* [e.g., "No one else can really motivate us; we're each responsible for creating our own motivation."] [5–10 minutes]

Approximate Time: 25–50 minutes

Instructor Notes

1. So as not to stifle discussion, I don't tell students what my scores are.
2. This class discussion is an excellent prewriting activity to be followed by students writing a persuasion essay supporting their opinion in the debate. Because students are now sharply aware of opposing views, they often write much more thorough and persuasive essays than would be the case without the debate.
3. An optional step for this activity is to ask students to do a Quick-Write and then a discussion about the Diving Deeper question: Is there an approach not mentioned by one of the eight professors that would be even more motivating to you?

Journal Entry 9 Creating Inner Motivation

EXERCISE 9-1: V × E = M

Purpose

To help students identify courses in which they have low motivation and provide them with an opportunity to find ways to increase their motivation.

Supplies and Setup

A copy of the "V × E = M" handout (p. 98). Students should have completed Journal Entry 9.

Directions

1. [Have students individually fill out the "V × E = M" handout.] [5 minutes]
2. [Have students get in pairs.] *Partner A, show your handout to Partner B and identify the course in which your motivation score is the lowest and explain why. Partner B, give suggestions to Partner A about how to raise his or her inner motivation. Apply what you know about the motivating power of the value and expectation of success.* [5–10 minutes]
3. *Now reverse roles. Partner B, show your handout to Partner A and identify the course in which your motivation score is the lowest and explain why. Partner A, give suggestions to Partner B about how to raise his or her inner motivation. Apply what you know about the motivating power of the value and expectation of success.* [5–10 minutes]
4. [Quick-Write and/or Class Discussion] *What was your experience of this activity? Who found that they were able to raise their motivation for a course? How? What did you learn or relearn from this discussion about self-motivation?* [e.g., "I can actually increase my motivation by thinking differently about the value I place on passing a course or learning the content of a course."] [5–10 minutes]

Approximate Time: 20–30 minutes

Instructor Notes

1. If time allows, have students also discuss the course for which they have their second-lowest score for motivation.
2. List on the board (and perhaps copy and hand out to students) all the ways they found to raise their value and expectancy for success in their courses.

V × E = M

In the "Course" column, list all of the courses you are taking this semester. In the "Value" column, give a score from 0–10 (10 high), indicating the value to you of each course (consider the value of both the outcomes and experiences of the course). In the "Expectation" column, give a score from 0–10 (10 high), indicating your expectation of being able to achieve your desired outcomes and experiences in each course with a reasonable effort. Multiply the two scores to determine your level of motivation for each course (0–100).

	COURSE	VALUE	×	EXPECTATION	=	MOTIVATION
1.						
2.						
3.						
4.						
5.						
6.						

EXERCISE 9-2: Roles and Dreams

Purpose

To assist students to identify dreams that they have in their various life roles. By showing specifically how college will contribute to these valued outcomes and experiences, we create the conditions for inner motivation to flourish.

Supplies and Setup

A copy of the "Roles and Dreams" handout (p. 100) for each student; students in pairs (Student A and Student B). Post the following three questions on the board or PowerPoint slide: *"What is one of your roles? What outcomes do you want in this role? What experience are you looking for?"*

Directions

1. *We each play many roles in life. A role is any function to which we regularly devote large chunks of time and energy. Write a list of your current roles, beginning with your role as "student." Continue your list with other roles that you play in your life. As you write them down, say them aloud as a reminder to others of their roles.*

2. *Student A, you'll ask student B the following three questions, pausing after each for B to answer: "What is one of your roles? What do you want in this role? What experience are you looking for?" After you have asked the three questions once and they have been answered, ask them again; B can consider the same role or a different one. If B can't think of a desired outcome or experience in a role, ask, "What do you REALLY want in this role? What do you REALLY want to experience in this role?"*

3. *Student B, you'll respond each time to A's question. You can repeat the same role as many times as you want, but try to do all of your roles at least once. Any questions? Ready. Begin.* [A demonstration (DEMO) here will help illustrate the process.] [5 minutes]

4. [After both partners have answered the questions aloud.] *Now fill in the boxes on your Roles and Dreams form. Identify your roles and what you really want—your dreams—in each role. What, for example, is your absolute biggest dream as a student? Is it a two-year associate's degree? A four-year bachelor's degree? A master's degree? A doctorate? Don't worry at this time about how you'll do it. What do you really want? Feel free to use words, pictures, symbols—whatever. It only has to make sense to you.* [5–10 minutes]

5. *Now we're going to do a walk-around. Take your Roles and Dreams form with you and meet someone. Introduce yourself; then tell one of your roles and a dream.* [DEMO by offering one of your own roles and dreams.] *After each of you has shared a role and dream, move on to another partner and do it again. No one owns a dream, so if you hear one you like, add it to your Roles and Dreams form. Make it your own!* [5–10 minutes, or as long as the energy in the room is high]

6. [Quick-Write and/or Class Discussion] *What's on your mind right now about your dreams? How will college contribute to the achievement of your life dreams? What's the life lesson here for you?* [e.g., "When I realize that college is an important step on the way to my dream, it's easy to stay self-motivated in my classes."] [5–10 minutes]

Approximate Time: 20–30 minutes

Instructor Notes

Giving a DEMO of what you want the students to do is essential in this (and in most) exercises. If you DEMO the process clearly, the students will move confidently and smoothly through it. Without a good DEMO, the activity often breaks down into confusion and requests for clarification.

Roles and Dreams

Role: _____

My dream:

Role: _____

My dream:

Role: _____

My dream:

Role: _____

My dream:

Role: _____

My dream:

Role: _____

My dream:

EXERCISE 9-3: Guess My Dream

Purpose

To offer students an opportunity to re-evaluate their dreams, make a public statement of their dreams, and hear the dreams of others.

Supplies and Setup

"Guess My Dream" handout (p. 102); pens; students in groups of four or five

Directions

1. *Finish the 10 sentence stems on the "Guess My Dream" handout.* [5–8 minutes]
2. *Decide who will go first in your group. Read sentences 1–9 to the group, but don't read sentence 10. After you read sentences 1–9, your group will have two minutes to guess your dream. After your group has guessed the dream or time runs out, read sentence 10. I'll let you know when it's time to move on to the next person.* [5 minutes per person]
3. [Quick-Write and/or Class Discussion] *What's on your mind right now about your dreams? What is the value of having dreams? Where do you suppose dreams come from? If you don't have a dream, how could you get one? What's the life lesson here for you?* [e.g.,"Some people have a difficult time taking ownership of a big dream."] [5–10 minutes]

Approximate Time: 20–40 minutes

Instructor Notes

1. Be sensitive to students who have yet to identify their dreams. Remind them that many successful people took years to find a dream that felt right to them. In the meantime, they set a goal to find a personally meaningful dream.
2. Remind everyone with a dream to stay open to an even more wonderful dream coming along.
3. Remind all students that one of the major values of having a personally meaningful dream is that it motivates us to do the difficult tasks that must be done to achieve success.

Guess My Dream

1. I really love to . . .

2. I'm very good at . . .

3. What I really want to have is . . .

4. What I really want to do is . . .

5. What I really want to be is . . .

6. Work that I would do even if I didn't get paid is . . .

7. After I'm gone, I want to be remembered for . . .

8. Someone I really admire for his or her achievements is . . .

9. The best compliment anyone can say to me is . . .

10. One of my biggest dreams is . . .

Journal Entry 🔟 Designing a Compelling Life Plan

EXERCISE 10-1: Looking Back

Purpose

To offer students an opportunity to consider the quality of their present life plan.

Supplies and Setup

Journals; students in pairs (Student A and Student B). Have students exchange journals.

Directions

1. *Partner A, imagine that it is many years from now and you are close to the end of your life. Partner B has come to visit you in the last few days of your life. Partner B will ask, "Have you had a rich and personally fulfilling life?" Partner A, answer "Yes" or "No" and then tell your partner why. Partner B, write your partner's reasons in his or her journal. Any questions? If not, begin with Partner B asking, "Have you had a rich and personally fulfilling life?"* [5 minutes]
2. *Now, Partner B will ask the same question. Only this time, Partner A, give the opposite answer. For example, if you said "Yes" before, now say "No, I have not had a rich and personally fulfilling life." Then go on to explain why. Once again, Partner B will record your reasons. Any questions? If not, begin. Partner B, ask your friend, "Have you had a rich and personally fulfilling life?"* [5 minutes]
3. [Reverse roles and repeat Steps 1 and 2.] [10 minutes]
4. *Exchange journals and read over the lists that your partner has recorded for you.*
5. [Quick-Write and/or Class Discussion] *What was your experience of doing this activity? What did you learn by doing this exercise? Are there any changes you want to make in your life plan? What's the life lesson here for you?* [e.g.,"Many people probably die without having done much more than talk about their dreams. I'm not going to let that happen to me."] [5–15 minutes]

Approximate Time: 25–40 minutes

Instructor Notes

If possible, it is more effective to have the "dying" partner lying down.

Source: Adapted from Jessica Dibb, Inspiration Seminars.

EXERCISE 10-2: Eulogy for Myself

Purpose

To offer students an opportunity to consider the quality of their present life plan.

Supplies and Setup

Paper and pens for each student

Directions

1. *Imagine that you have died. The person who knows you best in life undertakes the task of delivering the eulogy at your funeral. Write the eulogy this person would deliver. Write it neatly enough that someone else can read it. Do not put your name on it.* [10 minutes]
2. [Collect all the eulogies and redistribute them so that no one knows whose eulogy he or she has.]

3. *I'd like a volunteer to come up front and read the eulogy that you have.* [Have as many eulogies read as you have time for: 2–3 minutes each.]
4. [Quick-Write and/or Class Discussion] *How did you feel during this activity? What did you learn from writing and listening to the eulogies? Are there any changes you want to make now in your life plan? What's the life lesson here for you?* [e.g.,"I'm not going to live forever, so I better start taking steps to make my life something I'll be proud of."] [5–15 minutes]

Approximate Time: 20–45 minutes

Instructor Notes

1. After a eulogy is read, you can have students try to guess whose it is, explaining their choices. Then the true author of the eulogy can identify himself or herself, or not.
2. A time-saving alternative is to have students write one sentence they would like carved on their gravestones.
3. Another alternative is to have students imagine that they are at their retirement party and someone is making a speech about them.

Journal Entry **11** Committing to Your Goals and Dreams

EXERCISE 11-1: Draw Your Dreams

Purpose

To assist students to visualize their dreams, thus creating greater commitment to the dreams.

Supplies and Setup

Dozens of felt-tip pens of various colors; journal books (or blank sheets of paper); students in groups of four to six

Directions

1. [Pass around the felt-tip pens, and ask students to take some. Later, they can exchange with others if they want other colors.]
2. *Turn to the next clean page in your journal (or take out a blank sheet of paper). Using the colored markers, draw a picture or symbol of your greatest dream or dreams in life. You don't have to be a good artist; just use your imagination to create a picture of your dream.* [10 minutes]
3. *Each person in turn, show your drawing to your group and explain what your dream is. Be sure to (1) use present-tense verbs, (2) be specific and concrete in describing your drawing, and (3) present it with the energy and emotion that it deserves. If you finish describing your dream before I indicate it's time to move on, the other members of your group can ask you questions about your dream. Each person will have four minutes.* [15–25 minutes, depending on group size]
4. [Quick-Write and/or Class Discussion] *What was your experience of doing this activity? What's the life lesson here for you?* [e.g.,"When people talk about their dreams in the present tense, they often describe them as if they already exist."] [5–10 minutes]

Approximate Time: 25–40 minutes

Instructor Notes

1. Some Inner Critics will say, "But I can't draw. I'm no artist." Make it very clear that this is not an art contest. It is simply an opportunity to create a visual image of their dreams, something that they are all perfectly capable of doing.
2. An alternative to drawing is to have students create a collage.

3. Students will enjoy seeing your picture and hearing you explain it as well! Drawing your dream is powerful, and I urge you to get some of the power for yourself. I have pictures of my dreams framed and hanging in my bedroom for inspiration.

4. If you have a student with a particularly powerful dream, consider videotaping him or her explaining it, and use the tape to inspire future classes.

EXERCISE 11-2: I Have a Dream

Purpose

To offer students an illustration of the motivating power of commitment to a dream.

Supplies and Setup

Video of Dr. Martin Luther King's "I Have a Dream" speech. Most likely your college library has (or can get) a copy. [Many "I Have a Dream" videos on the Internet have been disabled; although as of this writing one is available on YouTube.]

Directions

1. *I'd like to introduce you to someone who had one of the most motivating dreams of the twentieth century.* [Explain the context for students who are unaware of the racial strife in 1968. Show all or part of "I Have a Dream." The last six or seven minutes are particularly stirring.] [6–15 minutes]

2. [Quick-Write and/or Class Discussion] *What's on your mind or in your heart after hearing Dr. King's dream? How committed do you suppose Dr. King was to his dream? How do you suppose he developed such a commitment to his dream? What did his dream motivate him to do? What difference do you suppose Martin Luther King's dream made in the quality of his life? If you have a dream, how committed are you to its fulfillment? How do you suppose you could strengthen your commitment? What difference would increasing your commitment to your dream make to your life? What's the life lesson here for you?* [e.g., "Dreams give you the courage to make difficult choices."] [10–20 minutes]

Approximate Time: 15–30 minutes

Instructor Notes

I have watched this speech numerous times, and it never fails to move me. In addition to the moral imperative of his message, I'm also strongly affected by the reality that Dr. King had such a commitment to his dream that he was motivated to present it to a quarter of a million people at the Lincoln Memorial and to many millions more on film. Dr. King's example causes me to ask myself, "What dream do I have about which I feel that much passion and commitment?"

Journal Entry 12 Believing in Yourself: Write a Personal Affirmation

EXERCISE 12-1: Revising Toxic Messages

Purpose

To demonstrate how affirmations can dispute the toxic messages of the Inner Critic.

Supplies and Setup

Journals; students in pairs (Student A and Student B).

Directions

1. *Draw a line down the middle of the next clean page in your journal.*
2. *What you are about to write will NOT be shared with anyone unless you choose to. On the left-hand side of the page, write any criticisms you can ever recall hearing from significant adults in your life. Skip a line after each one. For example, maybe your mother once told you, "You're the most selfish child I've ever known." Or your father told you, "You're the laziest child in the world." Or your teacher told you, "Your writing is poor." [Pause as they write.] What criticisms do you recall about your thinking ability? . . . Your emotions? . . . Your body? . . . Your schoolwork? . . . Your physical abilities? . . . The kind of person you are?* [5 minutes]
3. *What you are about to write WILL be shared with others. Now, write in the right-hand column a positive statement that reclaims the quality that you were criticized for. For example, if the criticism is "You're lazy," you'd counter with "I am a hard worker." If the criticism is "You're stupid," you'd counter with "I am intelligent."* [5 minutes]
4. *Partner A, read only your positive statements to Partner B. Partner B, listen carefully, and when your partner is done, tell your partner what you heard: "I heard you say that you are a hard worker and you are intelligent."* [2–4 minutes, based on the energy level of the room]
5. *Now reverse roles. Partner B, you read your positive statements, and, Partner A, you say what you heard.* [2–4 minutes]
6. *[Quick-Write and/or Class Discussion] How did it feel to say those positive statements? What did it feel like to listen to your partner's positive statements? How have the negative voices in your head hindered you in the past? How would your life be different if you heard the positive statements more? What's the life lesson here for you?* [e.g.,"If I refuse to allow negative thoughts to occupy my mind, I'll feel a lot better about myself, and I'll probably get a lot more done, too."] [5–15 minutes]

Approximate Time: 20–35 minutes

Instructor Notes

This activity makes a great setup for the affirmation writing process in Journal Entry 12.

EXERCISE 12-2: Affirmation Milling

Purpose

To take ownership of one's personal affirmation and hear other people's affirmations. This activity also builds a sense of community in the classroom.

Supplies and Setup

3×5 cards, two per student. Students need to have already completed Journal Entry 12, having written their personal affirmations.

Directions

1. *Open your journals to the page where you wrote your affirmations for Journal Entry 12. Make two copies of your affirmation on the 3×5 cards.*
2. *Now we're going to get up, walk around the room, and greet other people in the room with our name and our affirmations. You can take your cards if you want.*
3. *Here's what it will look like: You'll walk up to someone like this. [DEMO this by actually going up to a student.] Then you'll shake hands and say your name and affirmation like this: "Hi, my name is Skip, and I am a bold, happy, loving man." Your partner will respond, "Yes, you are!" And you reply, "I know!" [Encourage the student you're demonstrating with to say that to you.] Now your partner will say his or her name and affirmation, and you'll respond, "Yes, you are!" and your partner will reply, "I know!" [Encourage the student you're demonstrating with to say his or her affirmation, and you respond with a rousing "Yes, you are!" Ham it up and be lighthearted!]* [2 minutes]
4. *Okay, let's do it. And have fun! Keep meeting people with your affirmation until I call stop.* [2–4 minutes]
5. *[Quick-Write and/or Class Discussion] What was your experience of doing this activity? How do you feel right now? What's on your mind? Were you aware of any voices in your head while you were doing it? What were they saying? Whose voices were they? When would be great times to say your affirmation to yourself? What's the life lesson here for*

you? [e.g., "The more I say positive things about myself, the more I believe them, and when I believe them, I start acting like they are true."]

Approximate Time: 10–20 minutes

Instructor Notes

1. The messages students often hear in their heads while doing this activity are "I feel stupid doing this" or "Others will think I'm weird." This is the voice of the Inner Critic. Other messages might include "The teacher is stupid for making us do this" or "This activity is the dumbest thing I've ever experienced." This is the voice of the Inner Defender. Help students acknowledge these voices without judgment so they can begin to hear the more supportive voices of their Inner Guides in their affirmations.

2. Very rarely (in my experience), a student will not want to share his or her affirmation with classmates. (Some cultures, for example, frown on saying such positive things about oneself.) Remind students that they can always pass on doing an exercise.

3. I collect one card with the students' affirmations from each student. I print the affirmations on certificates or paper frames (available from office supply stores) and give them out at the next class. Students love to get this official-looking copy of their affirmation!

Taking Notes

TAKING NOTES EXERCISE 1: Academic Coaches (Option 2)

Purpose

To help students identify note-taking challenges in college classes and possible solutions to those problems.

Supplies and Setup

Whiteboard or easel pad for recording ideas from brainstorm. This activity is done over two class periods.

Directions

Note—this activity can be repeated with each study skill.

Day 1:

1. [Students in pairs] *With your partner, make a list of the challenges a student might face when trying to take complete and accurate notes during a college class. For example, one challenge is misunderstanding what the main idea of the class session is. Another challenge occurs when the professor talks very fast. List as many note-taking challenges as you can in five minutes. Begin!* [5 minutes]

2. [Conduct a class brainstorm of the challenges of taking complete and accurate notes during a college class. Encourage students to identify challenges that might occur during lectures, class discussions, class activities, and labs. Record the items on a whiteboard or easel pad.] [10 minutes]

3. *In a moment, I'm going to ask you each to vote for the four challenges that are most like your own. So look over the list and decide which four you will vote for.* [Pause while students decide. Then ask them to vote for four and tally the votes for each challenge. Identify the four challenges that received the most votes.] [5–10 minutes]

4. [Have each pair join another pair, creating groups of four students. Extra students make a group of five.] *You are now in your "home group." Decide who will become your home group's Academic Coach for each of the four note-taking challenges. This person will learn strategies for overcoming the challenge and coach the rest of you at our next class. Because teaching something is a great way to learn it, you might want to choose the note-taking challenge that gives you the most difficulty. If you have five in your group, two people double up on one of the challenges.* [5 minutes]

5. [Assign homework to read "Wise Choices in College: Taking Notes."] *As you read, look for the best strategies for overcoming the note-taking challenge so you can coach your home team on them in our next class. Obviously if you're absent or unprepared, your group is going to suffer. What questions do you have?* [5 minutes]

Day 2:

6. [Have students re-form their home groups so they will know where to go in Step 7.] *Before you do any coaching, you're going to leave your home group and meet with other coaches who chose the same note-taking challenge that you did. You'll have 15 minutes in your expert coaches' group to exchange ideas and come up with the very best strategies. Then, you'll return to your home group to coach others in the strategies that you have learned.* [Indicate corners of the room where each group of expert coaches is to work, and have students move to their group.] [20 minutes]

7. *Return to your home group. Go around the group, with each coach teaching just one strategy to the group. If there's time, keep going around the group, sharing only one strategy at a time.* [20 minutes]

8. [Class Discussion] *What were the best solutions you learned for our first note-taking challenge? The second note-taking challenge? The third? The fourth? How did it affect your learning to know that you were going to be coaching your group?* [10–20 minutes]

Approximate Time: **Class 1**: 20–35 minutes; **Class 2**: 50–60 minutes

TAKING NOTES EXERCISE 2: The Lecture

Purpose

To offer students an opportunity to assess their note-taking skills.

Supplies and Setup

You will need the ability to show a lecture, using either a DVD or the Internet. The advantage of using a pre-recorded lecture (as opposed to presenting one live) is that students can go back later and see where they missed key concepts, main ideas, and supporting details. Here are some of the many lectures that can be viewed on the Internet:

- http://www.YouTube.com: Search for **Psych 1—General Psychology—Lecture 2** (approximately 40 minutes). This is one of a series of lectures from University of California–Berkeley and is the most academic of the lectures listed here.
- http://www.YouTube.com: Search for **Randy Pausch Last Lecture** (the full version is approximately 75 minutes, but there are shorter versions available as well). This is the most inspirational of the lectures listed here (it also reinforces many of the concepts presented in *On Course*).
- http://www.Ted.com: Search for **Ken Robinson says schools kill creativity** (approximately 20 minutes).
- http://www.Ted.com: Search for **Robert Wright: How cooperation (eventually) trumps conflict** (approximately 20 minutes). This lecture is also a good one to show in Chapter 5: Interdependence.

Note: The directions assume that you will show the lecture during class. As an alternative, you can assign Step 1 for homework, which will save class time for having students assess and discuss their notes. Of course, to save time, you could also choose to show only part of the lecture.

Directions

1. *I am going to show a video of a lecture. As you listen, please take the very best notes you know how. Make every effort to record completely and accurately the key concepts, main ideas, and supporting details.* [If some students don't have note-taking materials, you may want to discuss the importance of bringing such materials to every class.] [Show the video.] [10–60 minutes, depending on the length of the lecture and how much you choose to show]

2. [Place students in pairs. I recommend putting the following directions on the board, a handout, or a PowerPoint slide, rather than giving them orally.] *Compare notes with your partner and . . .*
   A. *Identify at least two similarities.*
   B. *Identify at least two differences.*
   C. *Identify at least two strengths for each person's notes.*

    D. *Identify at least two areas for improvement for each person's notes.*

    E. *Identify your greatest challenges in taking good notes on this lecture.*

    F. *On a scale of 0–10 (with 10 high), rate the completeness and accuracy of your own notes.* [10–15 minutes]

3. [Journal Writing and/or Class Discussion] *What happened while you were taking notes? What difficulties did you encounter? If you were to sum up the speaker's lecture in one sentence, what would you say? What similarities did you notice between your notes and your partner's notes? What differences? What strengths did you find in your notes? What score did you give your own notes and why? What areas for improvement did you find in your own notes? Regarding note-taking, what will you do differently?* [10–25 minutes]

Approximate Time: 30–105 minutes (depending on whether you show the lecture video in class)

Instructor Notes

You can have students do this activity before and/or after they read about note-taking in the text. If the activity is done before and after students read about note-taking, they can assess changes (and hopefully improvements) in their note-taking skills.

TAKING NOTES EXERCISE 3: A Picture is Worth a Thousand Words

Purpose

Students typically struggle with taking notes from a graph, chart, or map. When an entire slide in a presentation consists of a graph, chart, or map, the students look at it in class, listen to the professor speak, but either don't know what to write down or don't write anything in their notebooks. This exercise will help students understand not only the importance of writing something down but what to write down.

Supplies and Setup

A premade PowerPoint presentation consisting of three or four slides. Use at least one graph, one map, and one chart (some suggestions follow). Before class, the instructor should study each one so that he or she can speak for a minute or two on each slide, essentially replicating a lecture.

Directions

1. Tell the students you will be discussing three or four slides in class that are important, and then proceed through the slides and your one- to two-minute lecture on each.
2. When finished, have students pair up and compare notes: What is the same? What is different?
3. Get back together in one group and discuss what types of multiple-choice questions could be asked on an exam where the answer would come from these slides.

Approximate Time: 25–45 minutes (depending on the length of discussion time)

Instructor Notes

It's important for students to understand the meaning of *purpose*. What is the professor's purpose in showing a graph, chart, or map as opposed to a slide with words? Next, students need to understand the parts of each. For example, does the graph, chart, or map have a title? Are there words on it? A legend? And, finally, what are the areas that the professor is focusing on during the discussion? Search the Internet to find representative images. Here are some examples:

- A map from Arbor Day detailing changes in hardiness zones (search at www.arborday.org)
- A chart from an Excel spreadsheet tutorial
- A graph from the Business Insider (search at www.businessinsider.com)

Source: Submitted by Melanie Marine, University of Wisconsin–Oshkosh, WI.

TAKING NOTES EXERCISE 4: Studying is a Process

Purpose

Students typically identify college as an extension of high school, instead of an extension of the work place. This activity will help them understand that studying in college is a multiple-step process that takes place over time.

Supplies and Setup

None

Directions

1. After discussing the note-taking section in class, assign students to submit one full class period's lecture notes to you. (Depending on how often you meet, a general-type class that has an exam in two to three weeks would be best.) Read over these notes and write feedback on them, then give them back to the students in the next class period.

2. That next class period, discuss the text section on organizing study materials section. For the next class period, have the students create a study guide from the *Wise Choices in College* section on Organizing Study Materials in the textbook.

3. The third class period, have the students show their study guides to their classmates, and explain two things: why did they choose that particular study guide and how creating the study guide has helped them retain information about that lecture. Then, assign students to create three or four test questions that could possibly come from that lecture, and have this due for the next class period (just the questions).

4. The fourth class period, discuss the text section on taking tests section. During class, have students take the test questions they developed in Step 3 and write each of them as a complete multiple-choice question, like their professor would have on the exam. At the end of class, make sure they turn in these questions.

5. At the beginning of the fifth class period, hand them their quizzes they developed in Step 4 back, and give them five minutes to take this "pop quiz." After the five minutes, allow them to grade their "quizzes." Then conduct a class discussion on this process. How did they do on the quiz? Why do they feel they got the score they did? What did they like? Not like? Did they discover anything about themselves? About studying? Etc.

Approximate Time: portions of four or five course periods (depending on the length of your course, as well as how long each class period is.)

Instructor Notes

1. If you have access to your students' schedules, you may find that a number of them have courses in common. You can divide them into groups based on courses they have in common and do this assignment, but add a "group study" component between weeks 2 and 3 and then again between weeks 3 and 4.

2. The most important part of this long assignment is the discussion at the end. Many of my students constantly say "I don't have any homework to do." They are still thinking in "high school mode," where class was held every day, they had worksheets to complete on a regular basis, and the teacher told them every single day what needed to be done. Especially if your campus has a high number of first-generation college students, "how to study" can become a serious problem. By taking one lecture step by step through the entire process, you are essentially making the students study. Letting them know that this is the process for every lecture in every class will show them what they need to accomplish to be a successful students!

Source: Submitted by Melanie Marine, University of Wisconsin–Oshkosh, WI.

TAKING NOTES EXERCISE 5: Paula Dean Is Coming to Dinner!

Purpose

To provide students with a fun way to practice their favored note-taking technique using a video.

Supplies and Setup

Any Paula Deen Food Network video, computer, projector

Directions

1. I have students get into teams and brainstorm a list of annoying and distracting qualities that instructors/lecturers have.
2. I then have students watch a short Paula Deen Food Network video and take notes using their preferred method. I tell students there will be a quiz at the end.
3. Students now look at their brainstormed lists and decide if Paula displays any of these qualities in the video clip. Note: She always does!
4. As a class, we look at each quality and talk about some possible methods that a student could use in order to overcome the annoying and/or distracting instructor lecturing quality.
5. I give a short, oral quiz on the video. I allow them to use their notes.
6. I then assign a reflective writing assignment. The students identify the top three annoying or distracting qualities are in their current instructors. Then they explain what techniques they are going to use to overcome these annoying or distracting qualities. They report back after two weeks to see if any improvements have been made.

Approximate Time: 55–75 minutes (plus homework)

Instructor Notes

1. Paula Deen is a well-known Food Network star. She is charismatic, but she also has a tendency to venture off topic, use Southern slang, and giggle—a lot. These are all distracting characteristics that a student may find in an instructor or even in a video that is being shown in class. The purpose of using Paula Deen is to re-create some of these "barriers" that students face when trying to actively listen and take down important information.

Source: Submitted by Katy Gofort, Tri-County Technical College, SC.

Embracing Change: Do One Different Thing This Week

You can wait until someone else (such as your instructor) motivates you—or you can be a Creator and do it for yourself. From the following list, pick ONE new belief or behavior that you will experiment with for one week. Check off each day that you do the action. See if this new choice increases the **value** you place on your academic efforts, increases your **expectations** that you will be successful in your academic efforts, or both. After seven days, assess your results. If your outcomes and experiences improve, you now have a tool you can use for the rest of your life.

From the following list, choose one belief or behavior you think will make the greatest positive impact on your self-motivation or self-esteem:

1. Think: "I choose all of the outcomes and experiences for my life."
2. Review and, if appropriate, revise my desired outcomes and desired experiences for this semester (recorded in Journal Entry 9).
3. Set a goal using the DAPPS rule.
4. Review my life plan (recorded in Journal Entry 10).
5. Focusing on an additional role in my life, write another page of my life plan.
6. Reread my visualization of achieving my goal or dream as a student (recorded in Journal Entry 11).
7. Write a visualization in which I am achieving a goal or dream in another life role.
8. Demonstrate self-motivation at my workplace.
9. Say my affirmation _____ times every day (recorded in Journal Entry 12).
10. Your choice: A different belief or behavior you learned in this chapter with which you would like to experiment.

Now, write the one you chose under "My Commitment" in the following chart. Then, track yourself for one week, putting a check in the appropriate box when you keep your commitment. After seven days, assess your results. If your outcomes and experiences improve, you now have a tool you can use to heighten your self-motivation for the rest of your life.

My Commitment						
Day 1	Day 2	Day 3	Day 4	Day 5	Day 6	Day 7

During my seven-day experiment, what happened?

As a result of what happened, what did I learn or relearn?

Chapter 3: Quiz Questions

(Please visit the Instructor Companion website for *On Course* at login.cengage.com or speak with your Cengage Learning sales representative to find electronic versions of the Quiz Questions.)

13. Creating Inner Motivation

1. In two major surveys, college and university educators identified lack of _____ as the number one barrier to student success.

2. According to American College Testing (ACT), in public four-year colleges in the United States, about _____ percent of students fail to return for their second year.

    A. 10

    B. 20

    C. 33

    D. 50

3. According to American College Testing (ACT), in public two-year colleges in the United States, about _____ percent of students fail to return for their second year.

    A. 10

    B. 20

    C. 33

    D. 50

4. In the formula $V \times E = $ Motivation, the letter E stands for _____.

    A. energy

    B. effort

    C. evidence

    D. expectation

5. According to recent U.S. Census Bureau data, how much more do Americans with a four-year college degree earn in a lifetime, on average, than people with a high school degree?

    A. $400,000

    B. $900,000

    C. $1,600,000

    D. $2,100,000

14. Designing a Compelling Life Plan

1. According to psychologist Brian Tracy, many people resist setting life goals because they don't know how.
   TRUE   FALSE

2. A "life role" is an activity to which we regularly devote large amounts of _____ and energy.

3. The DAPPS rule is an acronym, a memory device to assist us in remembering the five qualities of an effective
   _____.

4. The five letters in DAPPS stand for Dated, Achievable, Personal, Positive, and _____.
   [Capitalize the word.]

5. Which of the following is the most effective goal, according to the criteria of the DAPPS rule?

   A. Do well academically this semester.

   B. Work hard to get good grades.

   C. Achieve a grade point average of 3.5 or better this semester.

   D. Have more fun.

15. Committing to Your Goals and Dreams

1. A _____ is an unbending intention, a single-mindedness of purpose that promises to overcome all obstacles regardless of how you may feel at any particular moment.

2. When it comes to accomplishing goals and dreams, commitment creates _____.

3. Because of his commitment to return to Hawaii to visit his new girlfriend, the author earned money for the trip by selling magazine subscriptions door to door.   TRUE   FALSE

4. Cathy Turner used visualizations to help her win two Olympic gold medals in speed skating.   TRUE   FALSE

5. Which of the following is NOT a key to effective visualizing?

   A. relaxing

   B. using present-tense verbs

   C. being specific

   D. feeling your feelings

   E. Listening to your favorite music

16. *On Course* at Work: Self-Motivation at Work

1. Designing my career path has nothing to do with writing goals.   TRUE   FALSE

2. A motivating career goal need not have the DAPPS qualities.   TRUE   FALSE

3. To stay self-motivated, you'll want to match your career choice and college major with your parents' recommendations and desired income level.   TRUE   FALSE

4. Once you have begun your career, you

    A. will continue to find self-motivating strategies helpful.

    B. will no longer need to use your life plan (you've arrived).

    C. will never be asked to set goals or create work plans.

    D. all of the above.

    E. none of the above.

5. Some of the most motivated students we see in college are those who view college as

    A. an easy way to fill the time until they determine what they "really" want to do.

    B. the way to win the heart of someone they love.

    C. the next logical step on the path to their career goals.

    D. a way to win their parents' approval.

17. Believing in Yourself: Write a Personal Affirmation

1. As adults, we must depend on others to tell us what we should believe about ourselves.   TRUE   FALSE

2. A personal _____ is a statement about ourselves in which we claim our desired qualities as if we already have them in abundance.

3. If your affirmation seems like a lie, remind yourself that when you say your affirmation, you are prematurely telling the _____.

4. If you want to strengthen your affirmation, which of the following would you NOT do?

    A. Realize that you already possess the qualities you desire.

    B. Listen to your Inner Critic.

    C. Repeat your affirmation over and over as a reminder.

    D. Make choices consistent with your affirmation qualities.

5. If you want to further strengthen your affirmation, which of the following would you NOT do?

    A. Criticize other people before they criticize you.

    B. Be careful about the words you use to describe yourself.

    C. Say your affirmation when life tests you and then act consistently with your affirmation qualities.

    D. Record your affirmation and listen to it often.

18. *Wise Choices in College:* Taking Notes

1. In the pursuit of a four-year degree, students spend nearly 400 hours in a formal classroom.   TRUE   FALSE

2. The goal of taking notes is to get down "everything that the instructor says."   TRUE   FALSE

3. Victims allow wandering thoughts to sabotage their learning.   TRUE   FALSE

4. In a study by Kenneth Kiewra, it was found that lecture notes taken by first-year students contain, on average, only _____ of the critical ideas presented during a class.

    A. 5 percent

    B. 11 percent

    C. 75 percent

    D. half

    E. the first and last

5. When taking notes in the class of a speed-talker, what can you do to be a speed-note-taker?

    A. Condense: listen for a minute, note the key concept or main idea, then paraphrase in your own words.

    B. Leave blank spaces for missed material—you can talk with a classmate after class to fill in the blanks.

    C. Create your own personal shorthand—use a system of abbreviations.

    D. All of the above.

    E. None of the above.

Chapter 3: Essay Topics

1. Many students are unsuccessful in college because they don't see how college is going to help them create the life they want to live. Write an essay in which you define both what you want to accomplish in your life and how college is going to be an important steppingstone to that success.

2. Some critics suggest that today's college students have no sense of commitment to causes bigger than themselves. If this is an unfair criticism of you as a college student, write a letter to the editor of your local newspaper in which you define exactly what important cause(s) you feel committed to and why.

3. The ability to have a clear picture of the future you want to create is a great help in creating it. Write an essay in which you describe in detail what you would like to have, do, and be 20 years from now.

4. Personal affirmations are helpful for countering the negative self-talk of our Inner Critic. Write an essay in which you explore the messages you consistently get from your Inner Critic, where you think you got them from, and the kind of self-talk that you plan to engage in to minimize the negative effect your self-judgments will have on your success.

5. Some people find it extremely difficult to identify their personal goals and dreams. If this is true for you, write a formal letter to your teacher describing your lack of goals and dreams, speculate on why this is so, explain how you feel about it, and suggest what, if anything, you plan to do about this situation.

6. Using the student essays in *On Course* as a model, write an essay about how you used a strategy from Chapter 3 to overcome a problem in your life—academic, personal, or even at work. First, explain the problem; then, discuss the strategy you used and how you put it into action; finally, identify what happened. Your instructor may submit your essay for possible publication in the next edition of *On Course*. Additional directions for writing and submitting these essays can be found at http://oncourseworkshop.com.

Answer Key to Chapter 3 Quiz Questions

13. Creating Inner Motivation

Answers: 1. motivation   2. C   3. D   4. D   5. B

14. Designing a Compelling Life Plan

Answers: 1. TRUE   2. time   3. goal   4. Specific   5. C

15. Committing to Your Goals and Dreams

Answers: 1. commitment   2. method   3. FALSE (He sold an article to *Sports Illustrated* magazine.)   4. TRUE   5. E

16. *On Course* at Work: Self-Motivation at Work

Answers: 1. FALSE   2. FALSE   3. FALSE   4. A   5. C

17. Believing in Yourself: Write a Personal Affirmation

Answers: 1. FALSE   2. affirmation   3. truth   4. B   5. A

18. *Wise Choices in College:* Taking Notes

Answers: 1. TRUE   2. FALSE   3. TRUE   4. B   5. D

Mastering Self-Management

Concept

Most major life goals, such as earning a college degree, are achieved by taking purposeful actions consistently over time. Raised in a culture that relishes instant gratification, many students have not learned the rewards of taking persistent, small steps toward a distant personal goal. Without an effective action plan, many students fail to initiate the steps they are perfectly capable of taking to achieve their goals. By regularly offering them an opportunity to identify, record, and take their next-action steps, and by acknowledging them for taking these actions (regardless of the outcome), we help students develop effective self-management and reap the benefits of taking persistent, purposeful actions.

EMPOWERS STUDENTS TO . . .

1. Live life actively, rather than passively, understanding that the key to effectiveness is not time management but self-management.
2. Choose, prioritize, and schedule purposeful actions that will move them toward their goals and dreams.
3. Use effective self-management tools (e.g., monthly planners, next-actions lists, tracking forms, 32-day commitments) to get and stay on course.
4. Replace compliance with or defiance against outer rules with cooperation with inner rules that, over time, develop into supportive habits.
5. Develop self-discipline, including the abilities to focus and to persist in the face of obstacles.
6. Raise personal standards about the quality of the work they do.
7. Visualize themselves successfully doing purposeful actions.

Remember also to use the all-purpose exercises mentioned in the Introduction, actively engaging students in the exploration of JOURNAL ENTRIES, CASE STUDIES, ONE STUDENT'S STORY, ON COURSE AT WORK, QUOTATIONS, CARTOONS, FOCUS QUESTIONS, CHAPTER-OPENING CHARTS and STUDY SKILLS. Remind students to use letters to label any in-class writing they do in their journals.

Case Study in Critical Thinking: The Procrastinators

Purpose
To develop critical thinking skills by exploring a real-life situation concerning self-management.

Supplies and Setup
"The Procrastinators" in *On Course*

Directions

1. [Have students read "The Procrastinators." One way to be sure everyone has read the selection before taking the next step is to have one student read the first paragraph aloud, another student read the second, and so on until the reading is complete.] [5 minutes]

2. [Find out by a show of hands how many students have picked each character as having the more challenging self-management problem. In the unlikely event that everyone chooses the same character, attempt to sway some students by playing devil's advocate. Once you have reasonable diversity of opinion, move on to Step 3.] [5 minutes]

3. [Create two groups of like-minded students.] *Since you agree in your group about which student has the more challenging self-management problem, decide how you are going to persuade members of the other group to agree.* [5–10 minutes]

4. [Have a spokesperson from each group present the group's position; then lead a debate on the issue by moving the discussion back and forth, allowing students to explain their positions in more detail and rebut opposing views. Where possible, elicit students' personal experiences with self-management problems. Ask them to explain their self-management system—that is, how they get done what they need to do to achieve their goals and dreams. Invite students to demonstrate a change in their opinion by getting up and going to the other group.] [5–20 minutes]

5. [Create the role-play suggested in the second question of "The Procrastinators." One student role-plays Tracy or Ricardo; another student role-plays a mentor suggesting specific self-management strategies that Tracy or Ricardo could use to get on course in college.] [5–15 minutes]

6. [Quick-Write and/or Class Discussion] *What did you learn from this discussion about self-management? What changes will you make in your self-management system? What's the life lesson here for you?* [e.g., "Feeling overwhelmed can be the result of bad self-management decisions."] [5–10 minutes]

Approximate Time: 30–65 minutes

Instructor Notes

1. So as not to stifle discussion, I don't reveal which student I think has the more challenging self-management problem.

2. This class discussion is an excellent prewriting activity to be followed by students writing a persuasion essay that supports their opinion in the debate. Because students are now sharply aware of views opposing their own, they often write much more thorough and persuasive essays than would be the case without the debate.

3. An optional step for this activity is to ask students to do a Quick-Write and then a discussion about the Diving Deeper question: Which person's situation, Ricardo's or Tracy's, is more like yours? Explain the similarity and identify what you do to keep up with all of the things you need to do.

Journal Entry 13 Acting on Purpose

EXERCISE 13-1: Time Wasters

Purpose

To raise students' awareness about how they waste time in Quadrants III and IV and to offer students an opportunity to experience a week in which they consciously avoid one of their most common unpurposeful behaviors.

Supplies and Setup

Students in groups of five. One person in each group needs a pen and paper. Write the following on the whiteboard (or put on a PowerPoint slide): **I waste time by . . .**

Directions

1. *Decide who will be your group's recorder. That person needs a pen and paper. The person to the left of your recorder will go first. That person will complete the following sentence stem: "I waste time by. . . ." Going clockwise, the next person will complete the sentence again. Keep going around and around until I say stop. It's perfectly okay to repeat what someone else has said, but try not to repeat yourself. The recorder will make a list of all the different ways that people in your group waste time.* [5 minutes]

2. *Let's hear from the recorder in each group. What are the top three ways people in your group waste time?* [You may want to record the responses on the whiteboard or easel pad. Continue with all groups.] [5–10 minutes, depending on number of groups]

3. [Quick-Write and/or Class Discussion] *What did you learn from this exchange of ideas? What Quadrant III and IV actions are habits of yours? Which ones would most benefit you to eliminate? What's the life lesson here for you?* [e.g., "When I'm not working on a goal that is important to me, I waste a lot of time."] [5–15 minutes]

4. *I'd like to invite you to try an experiment this week, an experiment that could change the quality of your life. The experiment is to say "No" to one Quadrant III or Quadrant IV action that is a habit of yours. You can use the Embracing Change form in this chapter to track your results. Keeping this commitment will free up time for actions in Quadrants I and II. Remember, this is for just one week. After that you can decide if you want to stop completely. So, who'd be willing to make the commitment to yourself to give up one unpurposeful action for a week?* [You may wish to keep a record of the commitments and follow up on them in a subsequent class.] [5–10 minutes]

Approximate Time: 20–35 minutes

Instructor Notes

1. Make sure students are clear about the kinds of behaviors that occur in each of the four quadrants: Quadrant I (Important and Urgent), Quadrant II (Important and Not Urgent), Quadrant III (Unimportant and Urgent), Quadrant BB (Unimportant and Not Urgent).

2. Additionally, help students understand that what makes an action "Important" is whether or not it moves them toward a desired outcome or experience (not someone else's opinion).

EXERCISE 13-2: Who Wants This Prize?

Purpose

To demonstrate that wanting something is not enough; one also has to take purposeful actions.

Supplies and Setup

A prize of value to your students. (A sure bet is a dollar bill, but you can probably be more creative than that—perhaps a student planner or gift card.)

Directions

1. [Hold up the prize.] *I have a prize here.* [Describe it, making it very desirable.] *Who would like it?* [Keep asking the question until someone comes up and takes it from you or until a few minutes go by.] [3–4 minutes]

2. [Quick-Write and/or Class Discussion] *How many of you wanted the prize? Who got it? What did he or she do that no one else did? What is the life lesson here for you?* [e.g., "It's not enough to just want something; you have to take positive actions or you won't get it."] [5–10 minutes]

3. [In preparation for our later consideration of rules, valuable groundwork can be laid and an interesting discussion begun with the following questions.] *For all of you who didn't come forward to take the prize, what messages do you have in your heads that stopped you? Where did you get these rules? In what circumstances will these rules help you? Hinder you? What's the life lesson here for you?* [e.g., "Some of the things I believe are the very things that will keep me from taking the actions I need to take to succeed."] [5–10 minutes]

Approximate Time: 10–25 minutes

EXERCISE 13-3: Time-Saving Apps

Purpose

To identify and share applications for phones and computers that involve time management.

Supplies and Setup

Computers and/or cell phones [Instructors, please note: Make sure all students in your class use or have access to a computer, tablet, or smart phone before doing this activity.]

Directions

1. *Do you use your computer, cell phone, or other technology to help manage your time more efficiently? Let's look into applications that save us time and share these helpful resources with each other!*
2. *There are hundreds of FREE applications for phones and computers, and many of them involve time management. Select a free time management application and review it. (If you do an Internet search for "free time management applications," you will find thousands of hits.)*
   Review Format:
   1. What is the name of the application, and how might others find it?
   2. Describe what the application does to help a person save time.
   3. Rate this application on a scale of 1 (not helpful) to 10 (extremely helpful). Consider the following in your rating: How easy was this application to install and use? Does it do what it is supposed to do?
   4. Would you recommend this application to others? Why or why not?
3. Have students present their findings in class.

Approximate Time: 20 minutes to find and load the application; one week to test the application; 20–30 minutes for students to present their findings.

Instructor Notes

This assignment can be used as an online (e.g., Moodle Forum) assignment. Students may post their application reviews and respond to other student posts.

Source: Submitted by Laura Marlow, Sue Heath Olesiuk, Shelly Blackburn, and Barbara Brownsmith Campbell, Asheville-Buncombe Technical Community College, NC.

Journal Entry 14 Employing Self-Management Tools

EXERCISE 14-1: Rocks and Sugar

Purpose

To demonstrate the value of doing purposeful actions first.

Supplies and Setup

Two 1-quart glass jars, one empty and the other about three-fourths full of sugar; enough irregularly shaped rocks to nearly fill the empty glass jar

Directions

1. *We're going to imagine that this empty glass jar is a day in your life. The sugar represents unimportant actions: Quadrant III and IV actions. They are sweet at the moment, but they don't move us toward our goals and dreams. They provide instant gratification with no long-term benefit. What are some examples of these low-priority actions?* [e.g., talking for hours on the phone, watching TV, playing video games, surfing social networking sites, partying every night] *These rocks represent your important actions: Quadrant I and II actions. Important actions move*

us steadily toward our goals and dreams. Important actions build a strong foundation for success. What are some examples of important actions? [e.g., studying for a test, going to classes, applying for a job, exercising]

2. *Now I'm going to pour the sugar into this empty jar which—keep in mind—represents a day in your life. So on this day, you're choosing to do unimportant actions first. Now, I'm going to add the rocks, which represent your important actions. What do you notice?* [Very few of the rocks will fit in the jar.]

3. *Now, we'll do it a different way. First, I'll put all the rocks into the empty jar. This represents choosing to do your purposeful actions first. Now, I'm going to pour the sugar into the jar after the rocks. What do you notice this time?* [The sugar fills in between the rocks, and much, perhaps all, of the sugar will go into the jar.] [5 minutes for the whole demonstration]

4. [Quick-Write and/or Class Discussion] *What is the life lesson in the rocks and sugar demonstration for you?* [e.g., "When you do your important tasks first, you can accomplish more toward your goals and dreams."] [5–10 minutes]

Approximate Time: 10–15 minutes

Instructor Notes

1. The key to a successful demonstration is having rocks that are so irregular that they do not sit tight against one another in the jar, thus leaving room for the sugar to settle in between them.

2. Worth stressing: We can't manage time, but we can manage our own actions. The key is making wise choices. Doing important actions first is a wise choice.

3. A video with a similar message is titled "Keep Priorities Straight—A Jar of Life." You can search for this short video at www.youtube.com.

Source: Adapted from a demonstration by Stephen Covey.

EXERCISE 14-2: Time Savers

Purpose

To discover specific strategies for making the most of every 24 hours.

Supplies and Setup

Groups of four to five students. The group recorder needs a pen and paper.

Directions

1. *Almost everyone has developed strategies for saving time. In your group, have a discussion of your best ideas for saving time, and have one person record each suggestion. Here are a few examples:*

   - *I record my favorite television shows on my digital recorder and watch them later at night when I'm too tired to study. Also, I can fast-forward through the commercials, allowing me to watch an hour show in about 40 minutes. I figure this saves me at least two hours each week.*

   - *I carry a list of telephone calls that I have to make. Any time I have a few minutes, I pull out my list and make a call. I figure this saves me at least an hour each week.*

   - *On Sundays I cook large batches of food and freeze them in sizes just right for one meal. During the week, I pull out a frozen meal, heat it, and eat. I figure this saves me about three to four hours per week. This strategy saves me money as well as time because with meals already prepared, I'm much less inclined to go out to eat.*

   So, your job is to come up with a list of great ways to save time. Any questions? Okay, begin. [5–10 minutes]

2. *Now let's have the recorder report each group's best ideas.* [You may want to write them on the board or on an overhead transparency.] [5–10 minutes]

3. [Quick-Write and/or Class Discussion] *Which of these time savers will you try this week? What's the life lesson here for you?* [e.g., "I may not be able to add hours to a day, but I can take actions that will make it seem like I have more time."] [5–15 minutes]

Approximate Time: 20–30 minutes

Instructor Notes

Worth stressing: We can't manage time, but we can manage our own actions. The key is making wise choices.

Journal Entry 15 Developing Self-Discipline

EXERCISE 15-1: Focused Hands

Purpose

To demonstrate the importance of staying focused on the task at hand.

Supplies and Setup

Pairs of students (Student A and Student B) standing facing one another.

Directions

1. *Place your hands in front of you, palms facing and about one inch from your partner's but not touching. Partner A, your job is to move your hands up, down, back, forward, around—any way you want (but you can't move your feet). Partner B, your job is to follow your partner's hands, always keeping your palms about one inch from your partner's palms. Your hands should never touch.* [Demonstrate (DEMO) the process with a student.] *Any questions? Okay, go.* [2 minutes]
2. *What did you notice?* [3 minutes]
3. [Switch roles and repeat Steps 1 and 2.] [5 minutes]
4. [Quick-Write and/or Class Discussion] *What's the life lesson here for you?* [Almost always someone will write or express the idea of "focus." With that comment as a transition, lead the discussion to an in-depth consideration of "focus" with questions like these:] *What happened when you lost focus on your goal? What caused you to lose focus? How did you regain focus? When have you lost focus in your life? What happened? How strong is your focus right now on college? What could you do to strengthen your focus?* [5–15 minutes]

Approximate Time: 10–25 minutes

Source: Various presenters. The first time I saw this exercise, it was led by David Ellis.

EXERCISE 15-2: The Graduation Game

Purpose

To demonstrate that graduation and other life successes are usually the result of students taking small, purposeful actions persistently over time. This activity takes a bit more setup than most in this manual, but it's well worth it. Students will be talking about 3-foot tosses the rest of the semester.

Supplies and Setup

Ring toss set (use 1 post and 3–6 rings); tape on the floor marking 30 feet at 3-foot intervals; board or easel pad to keep score

Directions

1. *What's a big project you want to complete or goal you want to achieve?* [List some responses on the board.] *The question we're going to address is, "What's the best way for you to successfully complete all of the steps that need to be taken to complete this project or achieve this goal?"*
2. *First, though, we're going to play the Graduation Game. This game teaches an important lesson about HOW to complete a project or achieve an important goal, such as earning a college degree.*
3. *I need three volunteers to play.* [You can play with any number from 2–30, but the more players there are, the longer the game takes.]

4. *Every player has the same goal in this game—to graduate as quickly as possible.*

5. *In this game, you graduate when you earn 30 or more credits.*

6. *You earn credits by making a ringer. Each ringer earns credits equal to the distance thrown, and you can throw from any distance you choose. For example, a ringer from 6 feet earns 6 credits; a ringer from 24 feet earns 24 credits, and so on. You can throw from the same distance every time or you can change the distance every time—it's your choice.*

7. *Everyone playing will take turns tossing the rings until someone earns 30 or more credits and graduates. Before you toss each time, I'll write on the board the number representing the distance from which you're going to toss. After you toss, I'll circle the number if you get a ringer. The first person to total 30 or more credits graduates!* [When someone gets 30 or more credits and "graduates," allow everyone to complete the same number of tosses, then stop the game.]

8. [Quick-Write and/or Class Discussion] *So, what lesson does the ring-toss game teach us about successfully completing a large project, goal, or dream?* [e.g., "Life is a breeze in persistent 3-foot tosses . . . Life is hard by the yard but a cinch by the inch . . . You can eat a whale if you do it one bite at a time . . . You have to climb a mountain one step at a time."] *What would a 30-foot toss look like in college?* [e.g., "Not studying all semester, then cramming the night before an exam; taking 20 credits in one semester while working full-time."] *What would a 3-foot toss look like in college?* [e.g., "Coming to every class; handing in every assignment when due; asking questions when you have them."] [Some students will argue that 3-foot tosses are no challenge and that it's more exciting to take longer tosses. In the likely event that the person who graduated first took many 3-foot tosses, point that out. Remind them that they have every right to choose the excitement of a 30-foot toss, but it might be at the expense of achieving their goals or dreams. It's a strange choice to pick adrenalin over success, but, sadly, many people do it.] *Now let's apply this lesson to the rest of our lives: In life, what distance do you typically toss from? Are you a 30-foot tosser, a 15-foot tosser, a 3-foot tosser? Are you happy with the outcomes and experiences you've been creating this way? Are there any changes you plan to make in the way you pursue your goals and dreams? Let's look at the large projects we listed earlier. What are some 3-foot tosses for each of these projects?*

Approximate Time: 30–55 minutes, depending most on the length of discussion

Instructor Notes

1. In my experience, the person with the most 3-foot tosses almost always wins, but even if another person wins, you can make the point that sometimes someone wins the lottery, too. The fact remains that most of the time, 3-foot tosses lead to success, so it still comes down to a choice of which way we will pursue our goals and dreams. Do you want to trust your future success to one lucky 30-foot toss or a series of effective 3-foot tosses?

2. Another point to make is the value of knowing one's skill level. For some people a 9-foot toss might be as easy as a 3-foot toss for someone else. Also, there is value in stretching a bit beyond our skill level by taking a "reasonable risk" in the service of learning and growth.

3. This game creates a powerful metaphor to which you can return over and over. When someone is pondering an action to take toward his or her goal, you can say, "So what would a 3-foot toss look like in this situation?" or "That sounds like a 30-foot toss to me. Could you break that into smaller, 3-foot tosses?

4. Consider asking players to say their names and affirmations before tossing the ring. In the process, classmates learn one another's names and affirmations.

5. When one student has reached 30 credits, allow all other students one more toss. Some will need to take a desperation toss from 15–30 feet. Ask, *What is the equivalent desperation toss in a class when you have fallen way behind?* Answers: Staying up all night cramming for a test or even buying a paper from the Internet. Poor self-management can force a student to choose between failing and cheating.

6. Listen for negative self-talk and do some coaching. For example, a student may say, "I can't do this." You might reply, "If you keep saying 'I can't do this,' do you think that helps or hinders you in your efforts to make a ringer? What comment would be more helpful?"

Source: This is a variation on a demonstration I first saw done by Ron and Mary Hulnick at the University of Santa Monica.

Journal Entry 16 Believing in Yourself: Develop Self-Confidence

EXERCISE 16-1: Victories

Purpose

To offer students an opportunity to acknowledge their successes, thus building self-confidence.

Supplies and Setup

Chime, students sitting in pairs (Student A and Student B), pen and 25 3 × 5 index cards for each student

Directions

1. *Everyone has accomplished goals, and each goal—whether large or small—is a personal victory. Victims focus on what they have not accomplished in life; Creators acknowledge their victories in life. What are some victories you have experienced in the last year?* [Elicit some examples of victories, large and small—for example, graduation from high school, turned in English paper on time.] [1 minute]
2. *Working alone for now, create your own personal victory deck by writing one victory on each card.* [10 minutes]
3. *When I say go, start telling your partners about some of your victories in life. Alternate back and forth, sharing as many victories as you can as fast as you can. If you think of another of your victories, write it quickly on a blank card. After a minute or so, I'll ring the chime and call for either A's or B's to "FLY." All A's or B's will leap up, find an empty seat, sit down with a new partner, and immediately start exchanging victories. Again, go back and forth, telling each other about victories you have created in your life. Then I'll ring the chime and shout for A's or B's to "FLY" again, and one of you will dash off to a new partner to do it all over again.* [DEMO the process, telling your victories quickly to model a sense of urgency.] [3–5 minutes]
4. *So, any questions? Get ready, and start telling your victories NOW!* [6–10 minutes, depending on how many partner changes you want]
5. [Quick-Write and/or Class Discussion] *What was your experience? What was it like to hear your partner telling you about victories? What was it like to speak of your own victories? Did your Inner Critic try to block you from telling your victories? How? How do you feel right now? What would it do for your self-confidence if you acknowledged your victories more often? What's the life lesson here for you?* [e.g., "I've got more victories than I thought I did, and saying them out loud makes me feel proud of what I've accomplished."] *What could you do with your "victory deck" beyond this class?* [e.g., "Keep adding victories to it every day. Read the cards every day."] [10–20 minutes]

Approximate Time: 30–40 minutes

Instructor Notes

1. Some Inner Critics will accuse the students of "bragging." I acknowledge to students that they might not want to go around telling everyone about their victories, but they surely would get value from acknowledging them to close friends and to themselves.
2. You can use the same process to have students acknowledge their talents, skills, and personal strengths.

EXERCISE 16-2: Visualizing My Success

Purpose

To practice visualizing successfully doing a purposeful action.

Supplies and Setup

Groups of five to six students standing in a circle [Equipment for optional step: video camera and TV/DVD for playback]

Directions

1. *Think of one of your most challenging goals. Now think of a **purpose**ful action that you need to take to achieve this goal. Even better is to think of a **purpose**ful action that you've been avoiding for some reason. [After 1–2 minutes, ask:] Has everyone thought of a **purpose**ful action you could take? [Give more time or coaching, as needed.]*

2. *Each of you will act out your **purpose**ful action, and your group will try to guess what it is that you're doing. Each person will have 2 minutes. [You might want to DEMO acting out one of your own purposeful actions, such as sitting down to grade a set of exams or painting your living room.] [10 minutes]*

3. *[Optional: Make a video recording of one or more students from each group acting out their visualizations. You can then show the scenes to the whole class for discussion. With the students' permission, you can also use these recordings as a DEMO for a future class.]*

4. *[Quick-Write and/or Class Discussion] What did you learn about visualizing from this exercise? What's the life lesson here for you? [e.g., "Visualizing myself doing something scary makes it seem less intimidating."] [5–10 minutes]*

Approximate Time: 15–25 minutes

Instructor Notes

Here's an alternative that requires time outside of class. Put students in pairs. Give each student the assignment to choose and actually carry out a purposeful action that will move him or her toward an important goal, especially one he or she has been postponing. With a video camera, partners record each other doing the action (such as going to see a teacher for a conference or studying for a math test). This approach, of course, requires arranging for the students to have access to a video camera, or it may be that enough students in your class have smart phones that can record video. With this approach, you can show the recordings in class, then discuss the power of actually seeing the purposeful action being done. You could later post videos on a class website or YouTube.

EXERCISE 16-3: Talents

Purpose

To offer students an opportunity to acknowledge their talents and skills.

Supplies and Setup

Entire class standing in a large circle

Directions

1. *Creators raise their self-esteem by acknowledging their talents and skills, at least to themselves. They're good at certain things and, without being conceited, they know it. So be a Creator and think of a talent or a skill that you have. You don't need to be an expert, just think of something that you're fairly good at. [2 minutes]*

2. *When you're ready, you'll walk into the middle of the circle and tell us one thing that you're good at. Anyone else with that same talent will also step into the circle. We'll applaud to acknowledge you all for your talents and skills. Then return to the outside circle, and someone else will step into the circle and tell us one of his or her talents. You can go as many times as you want; just be aware of those who haven't had a chance to go. Notice if your Inner Critic or Inner Defender tries to block you from telling us or acknowledging your talents. [2 minutes for directions]*

3. *So, I'll start. "I'm good at . . ."* [Tell something you're good at, then invite others with the same talent or skill to step into the circle with you, and urge those in the outside circle to give resounding applause. Encourage an enthusiastic response to set the pattern for students who follow you. Then take your place in the circle and wait for others to do what you've modeled.] [5–15 minutes, depending on the size of the group and energy generated by the exercise]

4. *[Quick-Write and/or Class Discussion] What was your experience? What was it like to tell about your talents? What was it like to acknowledge that you have talents that someone else named? What was it like to be applauded for your talents? To applaud others? Did your Inner Critic or Inner Defender try to block you from telling or acknowledging your talents? What was the chatter in your head? How did you respond? How do you feel right now? What would it do for*

your self-confidence if you acknowledged your talents often? What's the life lesson here for you? [e.g., "It's a lot easier to acknowledge other people for their talents than it is to acknowledge myself for my own talents."]

Approximate Time: 20–30 minutes

Instructor Notes

By this time in the semester, most students will be comfortable coming into the circle. If you have a few shy students, you might (near the end of the allotted time) say, "Some of you haven't chosen to go yet, and that's okay. But this is a great opportunity for you to experiment with a bold new behavior. What do you say? We'll give you extra applause. C'mon, you can do it!" The key here is to be encouraging without singling anyone out. Almost always a few shy students will say, "Oh, all right . . .," and you've helped them choose an empowering new behavior.

Organizing Study Materials

ORGANIZING EXERCISE 1: CONCEPT MAPS

Purpose

To provide students with practice in organizing key concepts, main and secondary ideas, and major and minor supporting details with the use of a concept map.

Supplies and Setup

Sticky notes in five colors (about 25 of each color for each group of three or four students); two easel pad pages and markers for each group of students; tape to hang easel pad pages on the wall. Assign students to read Creating a Self-Management System and "Wise Choices in College: Organizing Study Materials" (both in *On Course*, Chapter 4) before coming to class. Encourage them to mark and annotate the reading assignment as they learned to do in the "Wise Choices in College: Reading" section in Chapter 2.

Directions

1. [Review with students the idea of levels of significance of information: key concepts, main and secondary ideas, major and minor supporting details. These ideas were first introduced in Chapter 2, "Wise Choices in College: Reading."] [5 minutes]
2. [With students in groups, provide each group with sticky notes in five colors (about 25 of each color). Designate a color for each of the five levels of significance. For example:

    Green = Key Concept

    Yellow = Main Idea

    Blue = Secondary Idea

    Orange = Major Supporting Detail

    Pink = Minor Supporting Detail] [5 minutes]
3. *Read through Creating a Self-Management System and create a sticky note for each key concept, main idea, secondary idea, major supporting detail, and minor supporting detail. Write the information on the appropriate-color sticky note and post it on one easel pad page.* **During this part of the activity, no one may talk.** [10 minutes]
4. [Review how to create a concept map.] [5 minutes]
5. *Move sticky notes around on your easel pad page until they form a helpful concept map. Then use your markers to draw the concept map on your other easel pad page.* **You may talk during this part of the activity.** *When you are finished, tape your group's concept map on the wall.* [10 minutes]
6. [Gallery Walk: Invite students to walk around, viewing the concept maps of other groups. Ask students to draw a star with a colored marker on the best concept map created by a group other than their own.] [5 minutes]

7. [Class Discussion] [Identify the concept map that has the most stars.] *What do you like about this concept map? What would you add or change to improve it? What did you learn/relearn? How will you use concept maps to organize study materials? Are there courses for which concept maps might be ideal? Less than ideal?* [Time permitting, you could repeat the discussion about the concept map that has the second most stars.] [10–20 minutes]

Approximate Time: 50–60 minutes

ORGANIZING EXERCISE 2: CORNELL STUDY SHEETS

Purpose

To provide students with practice in creating effective Cornell study sheets.

Supplies and Setup

One 9 × 12 envelope for each group; 3 blue index cards for each student; 3 green index cards for each student; 2 white index cards for each student; one "Cornell Study Sheet" handout (p. 131) for each student. In a previous class, assign students to read Believing in Yourself: Develop Self-Confidence and write Journal Entry 16.

Directions

1. [Place students in groups of four; if you have extra students, create one to three groups of five. Give each group one large envelope. Distribute to each student: 3 blue index cards, 3 green index cards, 2 white index cards, and 1 Cornell Study Sheet handout.] [5 minutes]

2. *The first step of creating a Cornell study sheet is to copy your polished notes into Section A. Usually, these notes will be either an outline or a concept map. You can see that Section A of your Cornell Study Sheet handout has been completed with an informal outline. The second step of creating a Cornell study sheet is writing questions in Section B about the information found in Section A. Take your three blue index cards and write one question on each about the information found in Section A; then place the cards in your group's envelope. This is an individual activity, so there should be no talking at this time.* [5 minutes]

3. *The third step of creating a Cornell study sheet is writing key concepts, terms, or names in Section B alongside their definitions or explanations in Section A. Take your three green index cards and write one key concept, term, or name from Section A on each card; then place the cards in your group's envelope.* [5 minutes]

4. *The fourth step of creating a Cornell study sheet is writing in Section C a summary of the information in Section A. Take one white index card and write a summary of the information in Section A. The second white card is available in case you want to copy over what you wrote on your first card. When you have completed writing your summary, place the white index card in your group's envelope.* [5–10 minutes]

5. *Exchange envelopes with another team. Then exchange again with another team. Empty the contents of the envelope and group the cards by color. Starting with the blue cards, read and discuss each question with your group members. Then each person, individually, choose the questions you think would be most helpful to study this material and write them in Section B on your Cornell Study Sheet handout.* [5–10 minutes]

6. *Now go through the green cards with your group. Again, read and discuss each key term with your group members. Then each person, individually, choose the key terms you think would be most helpful to study this material and write them in Section B on your Cornell Study Sheet handout.* [5 minutes]

7. *Now go through the white cards. Read and discuss each summary. Then each person, individually, choose the summary you think would be most helpful to study this material and write it in Section B on your Cornell Study Sheet handout. Feel free to revise the summary if you think you can improve upon it.* [10 minutes]

8. [Journal Writing and/or Class Discussion] *What did you learn/relearn about using Cornell study sheets to organize your study materials? What is a plus (positive) about Cornell study sheets? What is a minus (negative) about Cornell study sheets? What do you find most interesting about Cornell study sheets?* [10 minutes]

Approximate Time: 50–60 minutes

Instructor Notes

1. Obviously, any color index cards will work fine as long as you have three different colors.
2. The purpose of exchanging envelopes twice in Step 5 is to make it highly unlikely that students know whose cards they are working with.
3. You can reduce the time of this activity by reducing the number of students in each group.

Cornell Study Sheet

"Develop Self-Confidence"

Importance of self-confidence: We are unlikely to accomplish more than we believe we can.
- Example: Student wasn't sure she was "cut out for college."

Three ways to develop greater self-confidence

1. Create a success identity

   How: Stack one small victory on another
   - Example: Nathan McCall—After spending time in prison, he built self-confidence by graduating from college, getting a job with newspaper, becoming bureau chief, and publishing best seller. Each victory raised his self-confidence.

2. Celebrate your successes and talents

   How: Acknowledge small and large victories
   —Victory cards: write at least one success/day on an index card and read through the deck every day.
   —Celebrate and reward yourself for successes, even small ones: dinner out, movie, etc.
   - Example: 8-yr-old girl writes praise on her school work

3. Visualize purposeful actions done well

   How: Create mental picture using all five senses
   —Experiment by psychologist Charles Garfield: Visualizing helped a group of nervous speakers improve more than two other groups that didn't visualize.

Result: These actions increase self-confidence and lead to a core belief that says, "I CAN."

ORGANIZING EXERCISE 3: COMPARE AND CONTRAST CHARTS

Purpose

Students typically struggle with test questions that use phrases similar to "all of the following are true EXCEPT" and "which of the follow is NOT true." Using a compare and contrast chart to help differentiate between similar information can help students see what they might be tested on.

Supplies and Setup

Copies of the "Compare and Contrast Chart Notes" and the "Compare and Contrast Chart" (pp. 133–135), enough small wipe boards to give one to each group of two to three students (or students can write the charts on the board in the classroom, or they can write on pieces of paper and use a doc cam to show the other students)

Directions

1. Prior to class, assign for homework *Wise Choices in College: Organizing Study Materials* in Chapter 4.
2. Place students into pairs or groups of three. Give each group the sheet with the notes on it. Have the students fill out the blank Compare and Contrast Chart using the notes on the handout.
3. When all students are finished, have one student from each group show the rest of the class the Compare and Contrast Chart that his or her group created. The student must explain to the class HOW each row is either similar or different.

Approximate Time: 25–45 minutes (depending on the length of discussion time)

Instructor Notes

1. It's important to point out that empty boxes are okay; that is something that would be remembered on a test (for example "Which of the following Indigenous groups did NOT have a writing system?").
2. Additionally, upon completion of the Compare and Contrast Chart, either the instructor or students could give examples of possible test questions—for example, "All of the following are true about the Mayans EXCEPT. . . ."
3. Ideally, if all your students are enrolled in a paired class, asking the instructor of that class to give you notes to go through and then choosing different sections of similar material would be most meaningful. Additionally, you could divide students into groups based on courses they are enrolled in together, have them bring their notebooks from that class, and then have them create the Compare and Contrast Chart for a future exam.

Source: Submitted by Melanie Marine, University of Wisconsin–Oshkosh, WI.

Compare and Contrast Chart Notes

	Use the following notes to develop your chart:
The Maya	Developed in Guatemalan highlands
	Spread to Honduras, Belize, and Yucatan
	Architecture: pyramids—Chichen Itza
	Advanced in math, astronomy, calendar
	Writing system (glyphs)
	Collapse: 1. military conflict (most probable) 2. Natural disaster 3. Soil exhaustion 4. Epidemic disease
The Aztec	1325 AD establishment of Tenochtitlan on an island in Lake Texcoco
	Adopted Toltec culture
	Subjects had to pay tribute to rulers
	Very militaristic; importance of human sacrifices
	Conquered in 1519 by Cortes: superior weapons, alliances with subjugated tribes, legend predicted return of fair-skinned god assisted by a native woman
The Inca	Large empire stretching from Ecuador to Chile
	Focused on the city of Cuzco
	Taxes were paid through labor (mita)
	Extensive road network with bridges
	Imperial relay runners (Chasqui)
	Sophisticated architecture: mortarless masonry
	Advance agriculture: terracing
	No writing or calendar
	Kept records with strings and knots = Quipus
	Conquered in 1532

Compare and Contrast Chart

Category	Maya	Aztec	Inca
Where developed?			
Agriculture?			
Architecture?			
Tribute/taxes?			
Advanced in/distinguishing characteristic?			
Writing system?			
Focused on what city?			
Collapsed/Conquered?			
Toltecs?			

Example: Completed Compare and Contrast Chart

Category	Mayas	Aztecs	Incas
Where developed?	Developed in Guatemalan highlands in 3000 BC Spread to Honduras, Yucatan TolPeninsula	Tenochtitlan developed on an island in Lake Texcoco in 1325 AD	Large empire stretching from Ecuador to Chile
Agriculture?	Based on subsistence agriculture		Advanced agriculture = terracing
Architecture?	Architecture = pyramids		Architecture = mortarless masonry
Tribute/taxes?		Subjects had to pay tribute to rulers = taxes	Taxes were paid through labor (mita);
Advanced in/distinguishing characteristic?	Advanced in math, astronomy, and calendars		no calendar
Writing system?	Writing was called glyphs		No writing; kept records with Quipus using Imperial relay runners (Chasqui)
Focused on what city?	Focused on city of Chichen Itza in the Yucatan		Focused on city of Cuzco
Collapsed/Conquered?	Collapsed because: Military conflict Natural disaster Soil exhaustion Epidemic diseases	Conquest of the Aztec Empire: 1519: Cortes Alliances with subjugated tribes Legend predicted return of a fair-skinned god assisted by a native woman	Conquered in 1532
Toltecs	Much of Mayan area conquered by Toltecs	Aztecs adopted the Toltec culture	

Embracing Change: Do One Different Thing This Week

Creators take important actions daily, both urgent (Quadrant I) and not urgent (Quadrant II). From the following list, pick ONE new belief or behavior you think will improve your self-management. Then experiment with it for a week to see if this new choice helps you create more positive outcomes and experiences.

1. Think: "I am taking all of the actions necessary to achieve my goals and dreams."
2. Pause, look at what I am doing, and decide what quadrant I am in at that moment.
3. Use a monthly calendar.
4. Use a next-actions list.
5. Use a tracking form.
6. Make and keep a 32-day commitment.
7. Demonstrate effective self-management skills at my workplace.
8. Celebrate a success, big or small.
9. Visualize myself taking a purposeful action.
10. Your choice: A different belief or behavior you learned in this chapter with which you would like to experiment.

   Now, write the one you chose under "My Commitment" in the following chart. Then, track yourself for one week, putting a check in the appropriate box when you keep your commitment. After seven days, assess your results. If your outcomes and experiences improve, you now have a tool you can use to improve your self-management for the rest of your life. As author and philosopher Henry David Thoreau noted, "Things do not change, we change."

My Commitment						
Day 1	Day 2	Day 3	Day 4	Day 5	Day 6	Day 7

During my seven-day experiment, what happened?

As a result of what happened, what did I learn or relearn?

Chapter 4: Quiz Questions

(Please visit the Instructor Companion website for *On Course* at login.cengage.com or contact your local Cengage Learning sales representative to find electronic versions of the Quiz Questions.)

19. Acting on Purpose

For questions 1–4, choose two of the following to fill in the blanks:

IMPORTANT, UNIMPORTANT, URGENT, NOT URGENT [Capitalize all answers.]

1. Quadrant I actions are IMPORTANT and ___.

2. Quadrant II actions are IMPORTANT and ___.

3. Quadrant III actions are UNIMPORTANT and ___.

4. Quadrant IV actions are UNIMPORTANT and ___.

5. Creators spend as much time as possible in Quadrant

   A. I.

   B. II.

   C. III.

   D. IV.

20. Mastering Effective Self-Management

1. It is possible to manage time.   TRUE   FALSE

2. A self-management tool that provides an overview of upcoming commitments, appointments, and assignments by dates is a

   A. next-actions list.

   B. tracking form.

   C. calendar.

3. A self-management tool that records, by life roles, all important tasks to do that day or as soon as possible afterward is a

   A. next-actions list.

   B. tracking form.

   C. calendar.

4. A self-management tool that records and tracks, for two weeks, all of the outer and inner actions that need to be done repeatedly to reach a particular goal is called a

   A. next-actions list.

   B. tracking form.

   C. calendar.

5. Researchers at the University of Georgia found that students' self-management skills and attitudes are even better predictors of their grades in college than their Scholastic Aptitude Test (SAT) scores.   TRUE   FALSE

21. Developing Self-Discipline

1. Self-discipline is commitment made visible through purposeful actions.   TRUE   FALSE

2. Self-discipline has three essential ingredients: commitment, focus, and creativity.   TRUE   FALSE.

3. According to *On Course*, for many college and university students the time to beware of losing focus is at midterm.   TRUE   FALSE

4. A self-management tool for tracking the daily completion of one action long enough to create or eliminate a habit is called a

   A. 32-day commitment.

   B. next-actions list.

   C. tracking form.

   D. calendar.

5. People are either born with self-discipline or they're not.   TRUE   FALSE

22. *On Course* at Work: Self-Management at Work

1. The self-management skills you learn in college will make success in the workplace more likely.   TRUE   FALSE

2. These Quadrant II actions will look great on your resume: volunteer work, internships, and club memberships related to your future career.   TRUE   FALSE

3. Success in the workplace means having the self-discipline to spend the majority of your time in Quadrant III.   TRUE   FALSE

4. When beginning a job search, which of the following self-management tools will serve you well?

   A. tracking form for directing your outer and inner action steps toward your employment goals

   B. next-actions list for keeping track of essential one-time actions such as returning calls or sending thank-you notes after an interview

   C. monthly calendars for avoiding the embarrassment of arriving late or having to cancel an interview because of a scheduling conflict

   D. all of the above

   E. none of the above

5. Imagine that you have a big project at work that is due tomorrow. It's after dinner and you're about ready to write the final draft of the report when your brother-in-law calls. His wife is out of town, and he asks you to watch their kids (ages three, four, and seven) while he goes to his high school reunion that night. If you agree to watch his children instead of finishing your project, which of Quadrants I–IV will you be in?

   A. I

   B. II

   C. III

   D. IV

23. Believing in Yourself: Develop Self-Confidence

1. Self-esteem is strengthened by increased self-confidence.   TRUE   FALSE

2. Self-confidence is the core belief that I _____. [Capitalize all letters.]

3. By creating one small success after another, eventually you create a success identity, which is one way to build your self-confidence.   TRUE   FALSE

4. Which of the three following groups, studied by psychologist Charles Garfield, improved the most in speechmaking abilities?

   A. **Group 1** read and studied how to give public speeches, but delivered no actual speeches.

   B. **Group 2** read about speechmaking and also gave two talks each week to small audiences of classmates and friends.

   C. **Group 3** read about effective speaking and gave one talk each week to small groups. This group also watched videotapes of effective speakers and, twice a day, mentally rehearsed giving effective speeches of their own.

5. Genuine self-confidence results from a history of trying to be successful.   TRUE   FALSE

24. *Wise Choices in College*: Organizing Study Materials

1. Quality processing leads to a deep understanding of what we are learning.   TRUE   FALSE

2. After **C**ollecting information (for example, through reading and taking notes) from course materials, we begin to develop a deep understanding of what we are learning by immediately **R**ehearsing the knowledge we have **C**ollected.   TRUE   FALSE

3. The goal of **O**rganizing our **C**ollected information is the creation of many different kinds of effective study materials.   TRUE   FALSE

4. Creators hold the core belief that their ability to learn can be improved.   TRUE   FALSE

5. Good learners condense the information they have **C**ollected (from reading assignments and taking notes) into the key concepts, main ideas, and supporting details of the course.   TRUE   FALSE

Chapter 4: Essay Topics

1. Students new to college are often overwhelmed by their newfound freedom to make almost unlimited choices. As a result of bad choices, some first-year students do much less well than they are capable of doing. Write an essay in which you warn these students about the bad choices they will probably be tempted to make and recommend the most important actions they should take to resist those temptations and be successful in college.

2. Choosing to do a 32-day commitment offers you an intense learning experience. Write an essay for your classmates in which you discuss your experience with a 32-day commitment, including the life lessons you learned from the experience. Consider, among other things, how your thoughts, feelings, and actions changed over the course of the 32 days. It is not necessary that you had a successful 32-day commitment to write this essay. In fact, there will be much to learn from a 32-day commitment that you had trouble keeping.

3. Many people find that they don't get as much accomplished in their lives as they want. Yet they resist undertaking any sort of self-management system, saying they aren't comfortable using tools like a monthly calendar, next-action list, 32-day commitment, or a tracking form. Write an essay for people who have difficulty using a written self-management plan, suggesting how they might accomplish more in their lives with self-management strategies that are consistent with their personalities. As much as possible, use your own experience to support your opinions.

4. There are numerous electronic and paper self-management tools on the market today (e.g., iPod, iPad, BlackBerry, FranklinCovey Planner, Day Runner, Day Timer, etc.). Write a consumer report essay in which you discuss the strengths and weaknesses of one of these tools. You can report on a tool that you own and use, or you can go to an office supply or electronics store and familiarize yourself with one of the tools there. Award the product 1 to 5 (high) stars for its value, and then explain your reasons for the score.

5. One of the ways that people build confidence is by taking positive risks. Write an essay in which you fully describe the biggest risk(s) you have taken in your life, what you learned from your experience(s), and how your overall confidence has been affected.

6. People's confidence in their ability to succeed at something has a great deal to do with the level of their eventual success. Write an essay for fellow college students in which you explain how confident you feel about succeeding in college. Fully explore what you believe are the causes of your present level of academic confidence, and propose what you will do to raise your confidence higher.

7. Using the student essays in *On Course* as a model, write an essay about how you used a strategy from Chapter 4 to overcome a problem in your life—academic, personal, or even at work. First explain the problem; then discuss the strategy you used and how; finally, identify what happened. Your instructor may submit your essay for possible publication in the next edition of *On Course*. Additional directions for writing and submitting these essays can be found at http://oncourseworkshop.com.

Answer Key to Chapter 4 Quiz Questions

19. Acting on Purpose

Answers: 1. URGENT   2. NOT URGENT   3. URGENT   4. NOT URGENT   5. B

20. Mastering Effective Self-Management

Answers: 1. FALSE (We can only manage ourselves and our own actions.)   2. C   3. A   4. B   5. TRUE

21. Developing Self-Discipline

Answers: 1. TRUE   2. FALSE (persistence, not creativity)   3. TRUE   4. A   5. FALSE

22. *On Course* at Work: Self-Management at Work

Answers: 1. TRUE   2. TRUE   3. FALSE   4. D   5. C

23. Believing in Yourself: Develop Self-Confidence

Answers: 1. TRUE   2. CAN   3. TRUE   4. C.   5. FALSE (a history of success, not *trying to be successful*)

24. *Wise Choices in College*: Organizing Study Materials

Answers: 1. TRUE   2. FALSE (The Collected information needs to be Organized before it is Rehearsed.)
3. TRUE   4. TRUE   5. TRUE

Chapter 5

Developing Interdependence

Concept

The world provides valuable resources for those who choose interdependence over independence, dependence, or codependence. Many students, however, do not utilize the abundant human resources available to assist them to achieve their goals more easily and enjoyably. Worse, many students are entangled in a web of toxic relationships. Without positive assistance, many students find the achievement of personal, academic, and professional goals to be difficult, even impossible. By offering students the skills to build and nurture mutually supportive relationships, we empower them to benefit from resources that might otherwise go untapped, to experience the uplift of giving and receiving assistance, and to achieve goals that otherwise might be difficult or even impossible. Additionally, in a world that is becoming increasingly diverse, students' academic and life success is affected by their cultural intelligence, which Brooks Peterson, author of *Cultural Intelligence: A Guide to Working with People from Other Cultures*, defines as

Knowledge about cultures (facts and cultural traits)

+ Awareness (of yourself and others)

+ Specific skills (behaviors)

EMPOWERS STUDENTS TO . . .

1. Develop interdependence, reinforcing mutual cooperation rather than competition.
2. Identify valuable resources that can assist them in reaching their goals.
3. Request assistance in achieving their goals.
4. Create a network of support for college and beyond.
5. Develop personal bonds of friendship and appreciation that can support them to persist in a course or in college.
6. Communicate more effectively both as speakers and listeners.
7. Develop cultural intelligence and respect for differences.
8. Reduce anxiety and reluctance about trusting others, increasing a sense of safety and willingness to interact positively with the people in their lives.

Remember also to use the all-purpose exercises mentioned in the Introduction, actively engaging students in the exploration of JOURNAL ENTRIES, CASE STUDIES, ONE STUDENT'S STORY, ON COURSE AT WORK, QUOTATIONS, CARTOONS, FOCUS QUESTIONS, CHAPTER-OPENING CHARTS, and STUDY SKILLS. Remind students to use letters to label any in-class writing they do in their journals.

Case Study In Critical Thinking: Professor Rogers's Trial

Purpose

To develop critical thinking skills by exploring a real-life situation concerning interdependence and the ability to work well with others.

Supplies and Setup

"Professor Rogers' Trial" in *On Course*.

Directions

1. [Have students read "Professor Rogers's Trial." One way to be sure everyone has read the selection before taking the next step is to have one student read the first paragraph aloud, another student read the second, and so on until the reading is complete. Then have students put in their scores for the four characters.] [5 minutes]
2. [Find out by a show of hands how many students have picked each character as number one—having the greatest responsibility for the team's grade of D. If two or more characters are chosen as number one, move on to Step 3. In the unlikely event that everyone chooses the same character as number one (or there is otherwise little diversity in opinion), ask how many students have picked each character as number four—having the least responsibility for the team's grade of D.] [5 minutes]
3. [Create groups of like-minded students.] *Choose a spokesperson for your group. Then provide your spokesperson with evidence from the story that will persuade others to agree with your group.* [5–10 minutes]
4. [Have a spokesperson from each group present the group's position; then lead a debate by moving the discussion from group to group, allowing students to explain their positions in more detail and rebut opposing views. Invite students to demonstrate a change in their opinions by getting up and going to the group with which they now agree.] [5–20 minutes]
5. [Quick-Write and/or Class Discussion] *What is the life lesson here about interdependence and working collaboratively?* [e.g., "Groups sometimes have members who are not contributors. Other group members can employ a Creator mindset and still make the most of the group experience."] [5–10 minutes]

Approximate Time: 25–50 minutes

Instructor Notes

1. So as not to stifle discussion, I don't tell students what my scores are.
2. This class discussion is an excellent prewriting activity to be followed by students writing a persuasion essay supporting their opinions in the debate. Because students are now sharply aware of views opposed to their own, they often write much more thorough and persuasive essays than would be the case without the debate.
3. An optional step for this activity is to ask students to do a Quick-Write and then a discussion about the Diving Deeper question: Imagine that you have been assigned to a group project in one of your college courses and that the student whom you scored as most responsible for the group's grade of D (Anthony, Silvia, or Donald) is in your group. What positive actions could you take to help your group be a success despite this person? One by one, make a list of positive options for dealing with difficult group members like Anthony (a bossy dictator), Silvia (an emotional time bomb), and Donald (a disengaged loafer).
4. One aspect that helps the effectiveness of this activity is the creation of a vocabulary that allows students to address group problems effectively. Students will say to each other, "You're starting to act bossy like Anthony" or "Don't be a Donald—help us out here." This shorthand helps some groups solve problems that might otherwise sabotage their collaborative efforts.

Journal Entry **17** Creating a Support System

EXERCISE 17-1: The Chair Lift

Purpose

To demonstrate that some goals are difficult, or even impossible, to achieve alone, but they are relatively easy to accomplish with help.

Supplies and Setup

Two volunteers (ideally Volunteer A is larger than Volunteer B); one chair. Have Volunteer A (the larger person) sit in the chair and Volunteer B stand behind the chair.

Directions

1. *Everyone in the room will have a goal during this activity.* [To the class] *Your goal is to listen to the goal I give to B and decide how you would attempt to accomplish the goal.* [To A] *You've got the easiest goal of all. Your goal is to stay seated in the chair. You may not stand up. Can you handle that?* [To B] *Your goal is to cause the chair with A sitting in it to be 12 inches in the air as soon as possible. That is, every part of the chair and A, including feet, must be at least 12 inches in the air. Ready? Go.* [It's important that you say "cause the chair," not "lift the chair."] [2 minutes]

2. [Listen for B's self-talk. B's Inner Critic will very likely say things like, "I can't do that" or "I'm not strong enough." Whatever B says, for now simply repeat the directions.] *Remember, your goal is to cause the chair with A sitting in it to be 12 inches in the air as soon as possible. That is, every part of the chair and A, including feet, must be at least 12 inches in the air. Ready? Go.* [3–5 minutes]

3. [Now, encourage B, saying that the goal *can* be accomplished with the right approach. If B doesn't achieve the goal after a couple of minutes, ask B if the class can offer suggestions. Eventually, someone will suggest that B needs help. If B asks, "Can I ask for help?" simply repeat the directions, stressing "**cause** the chair." Notice that you have never told B to lift the chair. Eventually, you will have volunteers come to help B lift the chair with A in it. **IMPORTANT:** Be sure there are at least four strong people lifting, and ask each one if his or her back is okay. Tell them to lift with their legs, not their backs. The point here is to guard against injury. I have done this activity many times, and no one has ever gotten hurt—but I am always very careful!] [2–5 minutes]

4. [Quick-Write and/or Class Discussion] [To B] *What beliefs originally kept you from achieving your goal?* [e.g., "I had to lift the chair by myself."] *So, what's the life lesson for you of the chair-lift exercise?* [e.g., "A goal that I couldn't accomplish alone became easy with help."] *Can you identify other goals you have that are difficult because you're trying to accomplish them alone? Whom could you ask for help? Will you? When is it best to be independent, and when is it best to be interdependent?* [These same questions can also be asked of the rest of the students.] [5–10 minutes]

Approximate Time: 10–25 minutes

Instructor Notes

If you noticed some self-talk, which is clearly B's Inner Critic or Inner Defender, you might want to spend a few minutes discussing how those voices interfered with his or her success and how to work with that inner voice.

EXERCISE 17-2: The Scavenger Hunt

Purpose

To assist students to learn about your college's resources for student success and to demonstrate that some goals are impossible to achieve alone but are relatively easy to achieve with help.

Supplies and Setup

"The Scavenger Hunt" handout (page 147).

Directions

[IMPORTANT: Read Steps 1–5 of the directions exactly as given.]

1. *The way* **you all** *can win the Scavenger Hunt is by accumulating the maximum number of points available.*
2. *The way* **you each** *accumulate points is to fill in the correct answer in any of the three columns.*
3. *If* **you** *are a winner, you will win a prize.*
4. *Let's synchronize our watches. It's now ___. You must be back in this room by ___ to be a winner.* [Allow about 20 minutes for the Scavenger Hunt.]
5. *The Scavenger Hunt will not start until everyone is ready. Are you ready?* [This is the time when students could form teams so they could all be winners; chances are, however, they will dash out of the door, operating independently and competitively.] *If ready, let the Scavenger Hunt begin.* [Steps 1–5: 3–5 minutes]
6. [Upon students' return, go over the resources they have discovered.] [10–15 minutes]
7. *Now let's see who won the Scavenger Hunt. Remember, I said, "The way* **you all** *can win the Scavenger Hunt is by accumulating the maximum number of points available." What is the maximum number of points available?* [72 points—there are 72 boxes to be filled in on the Scavenger Hunt form.] *Did anyone accumulate the maximum number of points available? What is the only way you could win this game?* [The only way to win the game is by working cooperatively with others. Discuss the students' assumption that they were in competition with one another and that only one person could be a winner when, in fact, the directions allow everyone to be a winner. In what other areas of their lives do they compete, even when cooperation would be more beneficial?] [10 minutes]
8. [Quick-Write and/or Class Discussion] *What is the life lesson for you of the Scavenger Hunt?* [e.g., "For some tasks, many people can accomplish with ease what one person cannot accomplish alone. One of the challenges in life is choosing when it is better to be independent and when it is better to be interdependent."] [5–10 minutes]

Approximate Time: 30–50 minutes

Scavenger Hunt

YOUR DESIRE OR PROBLEM	NAME OF COLLEGE OFFICE OR RESOURCE	LOCATION	PERSON TO SEE
1. Need money for tuition and books			
2. Can't decide what major to choose			
3. Want to drop a course			
4. Need help with writing skills			
5. Want to participate in clubs and activities			
6. Need to withdraw from a course			
7. Have a problem with a college bill			
8. Feel physically ill			
9. Need information about transferring to another college			
10. Need to exchange textbooks			
11. Have a personal problem			
12. Need a computer to type an essay			
13. Want career information			
14. Want to write for the school newspaper			
15. Need tutoring in reading			
16. Want services for disabled students			
17. Want to serve in student government			
18. Need books for a research paper			
19. Want to transfer credits to another college			
20. Need a part-time job			
21. Need a parking permit			
22. Want to play intramural sports			
23. Need tutoring in math			
24. Have complaint about a teacher			

EXERCISE 17-3: The Interdependence Game

Purpose
To demonstrate the power of interdependence to solve problems.

Supplies and Setup
One volunteer up front; one recorder with pen and paper. You may wish to post the three sentence stems (Step 1 below) on the board or on a PowerPoint slide.

Directions

1. [To the student volunteer] *We're going to play the Interdependence Game. This is a game in which you can get immediate help on a problem you have. You could leave here today with one of your problems solved. Here's how the game works. All you need to do is read and complete these three sentence stems:* **My goal is . . . My problem is . . . The help I'd like is . . . .** *What specific help do you need to solve your problem? Do you need information? Advice? Assistance?* [Demonstrate (DEMO) the Interdependence Game process with a problem of your own, or you could tell a story of how the Interdependence Game helped someone in a previous class. For example, Vicki's **goal** was to move to Florida at the end of the semester; her **problem** was that she had to paint her apartment before she could get her deposit back; the **help** she wanted was for classmates to come to a painting party and help her paint the inside of her house. Three people showed up that day and helped her paint her apartment. One of the people helping that day was a man Vicki had never met; he had come along with his friend. Vicki and the man started dating, and Vicki decided not to move to Florida. So Vicki not only got a painted apartment, she got a new relationship as well. The life lesson: You never know what you'll get when you start asking for help.] [5 minutes]
2. [To the class] *After A explains the situation, if you have information, advice, or assistance to offer, raise your hand and A will call on you. You have 30 seconds to respond, and our recorder will write down your ideas. If your idea will take longer, give a brief explanation, and invite the volunteer to meet you after class for the full version. We'll try to get 10 ideas in 5 minutes.* [Do as many additional volunteers as time allows, about 5–6 minutes each.]
3. [Quick-Write and/or Class Discussion] *What is the life lesson for you of the Interdependence Game?* [e.g., "To get the help you need, sometimes all you need to do is ask for it."] [5–10 minutes]

Approximate Time: About 10–35 minutes

Instructor Notes
A key to the success of the Interdependence Game is to keep it moving. Don't let any suggestion for help last more than 30 seconds before you say, "What a great idea . . . how about meeting after class to finish explaining your idea. Now, quick, let's get another great idea." For the same reason, the person with the problem should not respond to those who are giving suggestions.

EXERCISE 17-4: Study-Team Bingo

Purpose
To help students find possible study-team members.

Supplies and Setup
"Study-Team Bingo" handout (page 150)

Directions

1. *In the empty boxes on the top row of your Study-Team Bingo sheet, put the names of the courses you are taking this semester, including this one. If you don't have enough courses to fill in all four columns, put our course at the top of more than one column. If you have more than four courses, write your four most challenging courses.* [2 minutes]

2. *Now we're going to play Study-Team Bingo. Your goal is first to find someone in our class who is taking one of your courses written at the top of any column. Next, go down that column and see if the person has any of the qualities described in the boxes by asking questions such as "Are you a part-time student? Have you attended another college? Do you exercise regularly?"* [1 minute]

3. *If the person answers "Yes," write the person's full name (first **and** last) in the box. You may use the same person in more than one box in a column if the description applies. Move on to another person, then another. The person who has the most boxes filled in when time is called is the winner.* [10 minutes]

4. [Ring a chime or call "Stop."] *Count the number of boxes you've filled in.* [Optional: Have the winner(s) come up front and read the name and information in each of the filled-in boxes, inviting the named person to stand. This assists everyone to learn who's in the class and what some of their skills and experiences are.]

5. [Quick-Write and/or Class Discussion] *What's the life lesson here for you?* [e.g.,"Many people around me have the skills and talents to help me achieve my goals."] *How could you apply this lesson to be more successful in college and in life? Are you willing to do that? How?* [5–15 minutes]

6. *I hope you'll think about creating a study team with the people who are in your classes. Remember, there are four steps to creating a helpful study team: (1) Choose the team yourself. (2) Agree on team goals. (3) Agree on meeting times, dates, and place. (4) Create team rules (e.g., to each meeting bring 10 questions on 3 × 5 cards with answers and sources on back).*

Approximate Time: 15–30 minutes

Instructor Notes

The movie *Stand and Deliver*—available from most DVD rental services—dramatizes the value of belonging to a supportive study group and choosing a wise and caring mentor. You might want to show parts of the movie in class to generate additional Quick-Writes and class discussions.

Study-Team Bingo

is part-time student	is part-time student	is part-time student	is part-time student
is full-time student	is full-time student	is full-time student	is full-time student
loves going to college	loves going to college	loves going to college	loves going to college
types 30 wpm or more	types 30 wpm or more	types 30 wpm or more	types 30 wpm or more
has child under 10	has child under 10	has child under 10	has child under 10
has scholarship aid	has scholarship aid	has scholarship aid	has scholarship aid
uses Microsoft Word	uses Microsoft Word	uses Microsoft Word	uses Microsoft Word
drives to school	drives to school	drives to school	drives to school
will get 4-year degree	will get 4-year degree	will get 4-year degree	will get 4-year degree
lives in your zip code	lives in your zip code	lives in your zip code	lives in your zip code
works full-time	works full-time	works full-time	works full-time
has work-study job	has work-study job	has work-study job	has work-study job
belongs to a study group	belongs to a study group	belongs to a study group	belongs to a study group
has same career goal as you	has same career goal as you	has same career goal as you	has same career goal as you
is good at math	is good at math	is good at math	is good at math
out of school 10+ years	out of school 10+ years	out of school 10+ years	out of school 10+ years
attended other college	attended other college	attended other college	attended other college
exercises regularly	exercises regularly	exercises regularly	exercises regularly
is grandparent	is grandparent	is grandparent	is grandparent
has 20+ college credits	has 20+ college credits	has 20+ college credits	has 20+ college credits

EXERCISE 17-5: Your Relationship Bank Account

Purpose

To demonstrate how we make deposits and withdrawals from the relationship bank accounts we have with family, friends, and associates in our support network.

Supplies and Setup

Pen and paper

Directions

1. *I want you to think about one of your best friends. Create a picture of this person in your mind. Now, on a sheet of paper write the number 100. This represents the present balance that your friend has in a relationship bank account with you.*

2. *I'll now ask you to imagine that your friend did the actions that I'm about to read to you. After you hear each one, make an appropriate deposit or withdrawal from your friendship account. For example, if your friend does something that strengthens your relationship, you might add 10 or 20 points to his or her account. If your friend does something that weakens your relationship, you might subtract points from the account.*

   A. *You and your friend agree to meet for lunch at noon. Your friend shows up an hour late and offers no explanation.* [After reading each situation, remind students to make a deposit or a withdrawal—that is, add or subtract from the starting balance of 100.]

   B. *You mention to your friend that you're having difficulty understanding one of your college courses. Your friend says, "I passed that course last semester. I'll be glad to give you some help." Your friend comes to your house the next day and tutors you for two hours.*

   C. *Your friend introduces you to a new group of people, telling them that you are the best friend he or she has in the world.*

   D. *On Friday, you and your friend agree to meet at the library at 4:00 on Monday for a study session. On the way to the library on Monday, you see your friend talking and laughing with a group of people. Your friend never shows up at the library as promised. Later your friend apologizes, "I'm really sorry I didn't meet you. I tried to get there, but I was in a conference with my history teacher, and he just kept talking. There was nothing I could do."*

   E. *You're moving to a new place to live, and you've decided to move the furniture yourself. You mention to your friend that you've asked about 10 people to come over on Saturday morning to help you move. Your friend doesn't offer to assist and doesn't show up on Saturday.*

   F. *A person you barely know tells you that some people were criticizing you, and your friend stood up for you.*
   [5 minutes]

3. [Quick-Write and/or Class Discussion] *What is the present balance in your friendship account with this person? What behavior caused you to make the biggest withdrawal from your friend's account? Why? What rule of yours did your friend keep or break? What behavior caused you to make the biggest deposit? Why? What rule of yours did your friend keep or break? If you were a college professor, what behaviors would make a large deposit in your relationship account with a student? What behaviors would make a large withdrawal in your relationship account with a student? What is the life lesson here for you?* [e.g., "Behaviors that greatly bother one person in a relationship may not bother another person much at all." Or "I never realized how my choices might affect how my professors think and feel about me."]
   [10–25 minutes]

Approximate Time: 15–30 minutes

Instructor Notes

Points worth stressing: We deposit points when a friend lives by our rules, and we withdraw points when a friend defies our rules. You can use this exercise to preview the discussion of beliefs and rules in Chapter 6.

EXERCISE 17-6: Tootsie Roll Pops

Purpose

To help students increase respect for differences and gain a deeper understanding of universal similarities.

Supplies and Setup

Tootsie Roll Pops—one per student; two columns on the board, labeled "On the Outside" and "On the Inside"; one Tootsie Roll Pop cracked open (for students who have never seen one)

Directions

1. [Hold up both a Tootsie Roll Pop and a cracked one.] *A Tootsie Roll Pop is a candy-coated sucker on the outside with chewy chocolate on the inside. On a piece of paper, write words or phrases that describe both the outside* [e.g., hard, different-colored wrappers, different flavors, requires 600 to 800 licks to get to the center] *and on the inside* [e.g., soft, chewy, supported by a lollipop stick]. [3 minutes]
2. *Call out some of the words and phrases written as I record them on the board.*
3. [Quick Write and/or Class Discussion] *How are Tootsie Roll Pops like people—on the outside and on the inside? How can you compare the different flavors of Tootsie Roll Pops with outer differences among people? If you choose Tootsie Roll Pops by the wrapper color, do you also select friends by appearance (clothes, hairstyle)? Why do Tootsie Roll Pops and people have a hard exterior? Just as you look forward to reaching the Tootsie Roll Pop's sweet center, what reward do you get from making the effort to get to know new people? Think about a time you judged someone from the outside, then later found that the person was different on the inside. Just as the Tootsie Roll Pop gets "held up" by the lollipop stick, who are some people in your life you use for support? Do you try different flavors of Tootsie Roll Pops? Do you always choose the same types of friends, or do you sometimes move outside of your comfort zone to get to know new people? What's the life lesson here for you?* [e.g., "I want to find the 'soft center' of several of my classmates who seem unfriendly." Or "I wish to melt my 'hard shell' so that other students can see I really am sweet on the inside." Or "I usually hang out with people who are similar to me on the outside, and now I want to find people who are like me on the inside."] [10 minutes]
4. *Enjoy eating your Tootsie Roll Pop—a sweet ending our life lesson!*

Approximate Time: 20 minutes

Instructor Notes

1. A summary of the main concepts may include the following. *Everyone has something valuable inside that we may not see at first. The "soft center" of people represents what we all have in common: feelings, hopes, dreams, fears, and insecurities. To feel safe and protected, people often use a hard outside to hide their soft core. However, a tough outer shell may prevent others from getting to know what is truly special about us. Making the effort to get to know what makes someone special on the inside helps us learn, grow, and practice tolerance.*
2. For students with special dietary needs: Tootsie Roll Pops are gluten-free, peanut-free, nut-product-free, and Kosher-certified.

Source: Submitted by Cris Davis and LuAnn Wood, Century College, MN; adapted from Lois Rothberg, retired from Pikesville Middle School, Pikesville, Maryland, *www.tolerance.org.*

EXERCISE 17-7: Team Juggling

Purpose

To experience an activity that illustrates the empowerment possible when people in a group work interdependently versus trying to do the activity independently.

Supplies and Setup

Five tennis balls; groups stand in a circle facing in.

RULES: [Post on board or PowerPoint]

1. Always call your partner's name before you toss to him or her.
2. Always have eye contact before you toss.
3. Always toss underhanded.
4. If you drop the ball, don't leave the circle to retrieve it—just keep going.

Directions

1. [Group stands in a circle, facing the center, with hands raised in the air. Starting with the facilitator (usually the instructor), each person chooses a "toss to" partner on the other side of the circle and asks the person his or her name. As someone is chosen as a "toss to" a partner, that person drops his or her hands until each player has a partner to "toss to." The final person tosses back to the facilitator.
2. **WARM UP**: As a warm-up, the facilitator begins the game by starting with one ball. Each person catches and tosses the ball following the rules (call partner's name, eye contact, and toss underhanded), establishing a pattern. One person calls the name of and tosses the ball to his or her "toss to" partner on the other side of the circle. That person then tosses the ball to his or her "toss to" partner, and so on until everyone has tossed and caught the ball once. The last catcher tosses the ball back to the facilitator who began the first throw and the group runs through the sequence once again for practice. Now the real juggling can begin.
3. **THE GAME**: With one ball on its way around the circle, the facilitator adds another, so that there are now two balls in the air following the catch-and-toss pattern. The facilitator then adds another ball until all five balls are in play. After the balls are in play for a few minutes, players should be watching carefully for midair collisions, trying to toss the ball so that the intended receiver can catch it. The facilitator may stop the game (by collecting all five balls as they are tossed to him or her) to process what's happening (see processing questions) and remind players that they should keep in mind that this is an interdependent venture. The objective is to keep as many balls in the air as possible. If one drops, pick it up quickly if possible or, if not, let it go to keep the pattern going.

Approximate Time: 20 minutes

Instructor Notes

Once processing of the following questions has been completed, the facilitator once again tosses the ball to his or her partner and begins the patterns until all five balls are once again in play. The facilitator stops the action to process every so often. It's fun to ask the group a few questions as you "pause" the game, such as:

1. What's working?
2. What's not working?
3. Is there anything you'd like to change to make it work better?
4. Is there anything you'd like to say to your partner that would help you to be a better team player?
5. If something isn't working, what can you do to fix it? (e.g., Slow down or speed up your throw to make the multi-tasking more manageable.)
6. Does the group want more of a challenge? (e.g., Add more balls, speed up the process, eliminate calling of names to see if the group members can keep the focus and pattern going.)
7. What are some results we notice when as a team, we creatively change the rules?

Additional Process Questions

1. What was that like for you? What are your reactions to this game?
2. What are some "team" aspects of this game?
   [e.g., "If everyone doesn't do their part = the objective isn't met."]
   [e.g., "If everyone does their small part well—paying attention and following the rules—we work together to create something amazing that we couldn't create alone."]
3. What worked? Give examples.
4. What didn't work? Give examples and share—how did you problem solve this?
5. Was it challenging to enlist the support of teammates to make the process work more smoothly? Why or why not?
6. How does this game relate to our lives and working dependently, independently, or interdependently?

7. What have you learned about your role as a team player?
8. What could we learn from this game to apply to our own experiences (at home, at work with coworkers, at work with customers, with fellow students and instructors)?
9. What have you learned about interdependence?
10. What's the life lesson?

Source: Submitted by Sherry Lichte-Baird, Rio Salado College, AZ

Journal Entry 18 Strengthening Relationships with Active Listening

EXERCISE 18-1: Circle of Reflection

Purpose

To practice listening actively. To explore thoughts and feelings about asking for assistance.

Supplies and Setup

Students sitting in trios (Students A, B, and C)

Directions

1. *We're going to practice listening actively. Here's how it works: Person A speaks a thought to B about the topic of asking for help. This "thought" can be an opinion, a story, or anything having to do with asking for help. B reflects A's thoughts and feelings. A confirms or corrects. (If A corrects, B now reflects the correction.) When B has accurately reflected A's thought, B speaks a thought to C about asking for help. C reflects B's thoughts and feelings. B confirms or corrects. When C has accurately reflected B's thought, C speaks a thought to A about asking for help. And the process of reflecting keeps going around the circle.* [You may want to provide these directions on a handout or post them on a PowerPoint slide. A sample DEMO follows. Emphasize not changing speakers until the speaker confirms that the listener has gotten the thought and feeling—the complete message—correct.]

2. *Whoever isn't the speaker or the listener is the observer. The observer's job is to identify any talking that doesn't follow the reflecting format. Keep going around your circle until I call stop.* [8–10 minutes]

3. [Quick-Write and/or Class Discussion] *What was your experience when you were the active listener? What was your experience when you were being actively listened to? What did you notice when you were the observer? What did you learn about active listening? What did you learn about asking for help? What is the life lesson here for you?* [e.g., "Some people listen without really hearing."] [10–20 minutes]

Approximate Time: 20–30 minutes

Instructor Notes

1. Here's a sample DEMO as a model for the interactions in this activity:

   A to B: I really don't like asking for help. [States thought]

   B to A: What I heard is that you don't like to ask for help. [Reflection]

   A to B: That's right. [Confirms accuracy of B's reflection]

   B to C: Well, I don't mind asking for help. In fact, my brother would probably tell you that I ask for help all the time. Maybe I ask for too much help. [States thought]

   C to B: What I heard is that you don't mind asking for help. [Reflection]

   B to C: Right, but also, sometimes I think I ask for too much help. [Corrects C's reflection]

   C to B: Okay, now I've got it. You don't mind asking for help, but you're wondering if you ask for too much help. [Reflection]

B to C: That's it. [Confirms C's reflection]

C to A: Actually, I've never thought much about asking for help.

[The process returns to A for a reflection, and it keeps going around the circle until time is called.]

2. If you want to illustrate how poorly people listen to one another, show a recording of a few minutes from one of the conflict-oriented TV talk shows, such as the *Jerry Springer Show*.

EXERCISE 18-2: The Sounds of Silence

Purpose

To demonstrate the value of silence and careful observation while actively listening.

Supplies and Setup

Chime; students sitting in pairs facing one another, each with journal and a pen

Directions

1. *The first part of this activity is to be done without talking. Please don't say a word until I tell you it's okay to talk again. Sit with your partner in total silence and observe each other. Don't say a word until I ring the chime* [or call "Stop"]. [2 minutes]

2. [Quick-Write] *In your journal, write an answer to this question: What did you observe about your partner during the silence? Be complete. Later, you'll be sharing with your partner what you wrote.* [Many people will report not observing much, feeling rather uncomfortable, and wondering how much longer the silence would last. In other words, they were more aware of themselves than their partner.] [4 minutes]

3. *Now sit with your partner again, and this time, see what you can learn about him or her just by observing him or her in silence. Use your powers of observation and intuition. Don't say a word until I ring the chime* [or call "Stop"]. [2 minutes]

4. [Quick Write] *In your journal, write an answer to this question: What did you observe about your partner this time? Be complete.* [Many people will report more meaningful observations about their partners this time.] [3 minutes]

5. *Alternate reading your first entry to one another. Then read your second entry to one another. Then take a few minutes to have a conversation about what you observed and learned about each other.* [7 minutes]

6. [Quick-Write and/or Class Discussion] *What was the experience like for you? How might silence contribute to a more complete communication? What can you look for in another person that tells you something about that person or what he or she is experiencing at the moment? What is the life lesson here for you?* [e.g., "You can look at a person without really seeing him or her."] [5–15 minutes]

Approximate Time: 25–40 minutes

Journal Entry 19 Respecting Cultural Differences

EXERCISE 19-1: What's in a Name?

Purpose

To enable students to get to know their classmates—including their cultures—and begin to create a comfortable learning community where students feel safe to risk new behaviors and adopt new beliefs and attitudes.

Supplies and Setup

Pens and journals. If without their journals, students can write on notebook paper and later copy or type this writing into their journals.

Directions

1. *Write your full name on the top of a blank page in your journal. Now, write the story of your name. Where did it come from? How do you feel about it? How do you think your name has influenced who you are? Does your name reflect the culture with which you most identify; if so, how? Add anything else that comes to mind about your name as you write.* [Teacher DEMOs by telling the story of his or her name.] [5–8 minutes]

2. [Move students into groups of four.] *The person in your group who will have the next birthday goes first. That person reads the story of his or her name to the group. Then go clockwise around your group until each person has read. When everyone has finished reading, have a discussion about any patterns that you notice about the names in your group. For example, perhaps you'll find that many of you in your group were named for a relative or that most of you prefer a different name. Later, one of you will report on what your group discovered about your names, so be sure to take notes about your group members' names. You have 10 minutes. What questions do you have?* [Respond to questions, if any.] *Please begin.* [10 minutes]

3. *Let's hear from someone in each group. What did you learn about the names of the people in your group? Any patterns? Any discoveries about the cultures of your group members? Any surprises? Any unusual stories?* [5–15 minutes]

Approximate Time: 20–30 minutes

Instructor Notes

This activity is also a great first-day ice-breaker, generating lively discussions. Most people enjoy talking about their names. Some people discover thoughts and feelings about their names that they didn't realize they had.

Source: This activity is a variation of an exercise I learned from Barbara Jaffe of El Camino College, CA

EXERCISE 19-2: Examining Stereotypes

Purpose

To help students become aware of the hurtful nature of stereotypes as well as ways to combat stereotypes.

Supplies and Setup

3×5 index cards (five for each student)

Directions

1. *Each of us has an identity that is composed of the many aspects that make us who we are. It is the unique combination of these aspects that makes us similar to some people as well as different from every other person. On each of the five index cards, write an important part of your identity. No one else will know which cards are yours. Here are some examples of aspects of identity. If you hear one that is important to your identity, write it on a card: woman, college student, Democrat, middle class, Asian, man, Republican, middle-aged, learning disabled, athlete, immigrant, black, southerner, Muslim, tall, white, Jewish, large, Native American, teenager, gay, Latino/a, surfer, jazz musician, Goth, "A" student, elderly, working class. What are some other aspects of identity?* [Ask students to brainstorm aloud.] [5–7 minutes]

2. *According to the* On Course *text, "A stereotype is a generalization about a group of people based on limited or even faulty evidence. Once we accept a generalization as true, we have a tendency to apply it to all individuals we encounter from that group. . . . Stereotypes about any group disrespect individuals from that group, denying them their uniqueness." On the back of each of your five index cards, write a stereotype you have heard about people who have the aspect as part of their identity. These stereotypes could be seemingly negative, such as "Women are weak." Or these stereotypes could be seemingly positive, such as "Asians are good at math." If you honestly can't think of a stereotype for an aspect of your identity, leave the back of the card blank. Remember, don't put your name on any of the cards."* [5–8 minutes]

3. [Collect only the cards that have both an aspect of identity on one side and a stereotype on the other. Shuffle the cards and pass them all out to students. Each student will likely have two or three cards.] [2 minutes]

4. [To a volunteer:] *Please read the identity on one of your cards.* [To the class:] *See if you can predict what stereotype is written on the back of the card.* [Ask the volunteer to read the stereotype.] *How do you suppose a person would feel to be stereotyped in that manner?* [Repeat as often as time allows, providing about three minutes for each card.] [3–30 minutes]

5. [Optional if time allows] [Collect the cards that have an aspect of identity on one side but no stereotype written on the other. Shuffle the cards and pass them all out to students. Ask volunteers to read an aspect from a card and ask the class to offer stereotypes they have heard about people with this aspect.] *How do you suppose a person would feel to be stereotyped in that manner?* [Repeat as often as time allows, providing about three minutes for each card.] [3–15 minutes]

6. *What ideas do you have for eliminating stereotypes in your own thinking?* [Example: "Don't assume someone either fits a stereotype or can speak for a whole culture."] [5–10 minutes]

Approximate Time: 25–70 minutes

Source: Adapted from an activity posted on the Teaching Tolerance website, www.tolerance.org.

EXERCISE 19-3: The Ladder of Prejudice

Purpose
To help students learn the range of harmful behaviors caused by prejudice and how to combat them.

Supplies and Setup
Post-It Notes (all the same color, five for each student). Post the following Ladder of Prejudice on the board or an easel pad (make the ladder large so that a number of Post-It Notes can be placed on the ladder during the activity):

The Ladder of Prejudice

The Fifth Rung: Extermination

The Fourth Rung: Physical Attack

The Third Rung: Discrimination

The Second Rung: Avoidance

The First Rung: Spoken Abuse

The ladder should be positioned so that students can place Post-It Notes on it unseen (like the privacy of a voting booth). For example, if the Ladder of Prejudice is on an easel pad, turn the pad to face away from the class. If the Ladder of Prejudice is on the board, move a screen in front of the board (or lower a screen from a ceiling mount if available). In either case, have students come up one at a time and place their Post-Its without anyone seeing where they place them.

Directions
1. *What is your understanding of the meaning of "prejudice"? Write a definition of "prejudice."* [3 minutes]
2. *Here's one definition: "Prejudice is pre-judgment, that is, a judgment or opinion (usually negative) that is formed without the benefit of knowledge or an examination of the facts." In other words, even though we don't have good reasons for it, we believe something is true, so we make choices as if it is true.* [2 minutes]
3. *Psychologist Gordon Allport, in his book* The Nature of Prejudice, *describes the hurtful choices that are the result of prejudice. He called this the "Ladder of Prejudice."* [Show the "Ladder of Prejudice."] *Let's start with the first rung: "Spoken Abuse." What's an example of a behavior on this rung?* [e.g., calling people insulting names] *The second rung is "Avoidance." What's an example of this rung?* [e.g., not going to places where people are different from you] *The third rung is "Discrimination." What's an example?* [e.g., not hiring someone for a job because of her age, race, or sexual orientation.] *The fourth rung is "Physical Attack." What's an example?* [e.g., pushing and shoving someone because he or she is different.] *And the fifth rung of Allport's Ladder of Prejudice is "Extermination." What's an example?* [e.g., U.S. government/Native Americans; Nazis/Jews] [5 minutes]
4. *Working by yourself, write on a Post-It Note something that happened here at school, in your community, or in the world that could be posted somewhere on the ladder. Don't put your name on the notes; they will remain anonymous.*

When you have completed a Post-It Note, please come up one at a time and stick it on the appropriate rung of the Ladder of Prejudice. Only one person may come up at a time so that everyone has complete privacy. You are welcome to add more than one Post-It if you wish. [10 minutes]

5. [Reveal the Ladder of Prejudice with the Post-It Notes attached. Have a volunteer read Post-Its on each rung, starting with Rung 1. Pause after each to ask, *What did you hear that you expected? What did you hear that you didn't expect? What can we do to make sure these things don't happen in our class? On our campus?* [Consider sharing this quotation from anthropologist Margaret Mead: "Never doubt that a small group of thoughtful, committed citizens can change the world; indeed, it is the only thing that ever has."] [20–30 minutes]

Approximate Time: 40–50 minutes

Instructor Notes

Stress that prejudice is a judgment made by the Inner Defender.

Source: This is a variation of an activity by Stefanie Fox of Kingsway Middle School posted at www.tolerance.org/activity/ladder-prejudice.

EXERCISE 19-4: Microaggressions

Purpose

To identify microaggressions and understand what messages they send to members of minority groups.

Supplies and Setup

"**Microaggressions**" handout (**page 160**), whiteboard with markers. Place students in groups of four to six. (This is a great activity for success teams, if you use them.)

Directions

1. *One of the ways we can work toward better intercultural communication is to be aware of when we use commonplace (intentional or unintentional) microaggressions in our interactions with others. Microaggressions are brief slights and insults that send demeaning messages to members of minority groups. This activity will help us identify and understand what these messages subtly say to others, especially to groups that are racially, ethnically, or otherwise different from the majority culture. Taking personal responsibility for using correct terminology and avoiding microaggressions is an important step in building trust and respect between and among various cultures.* [If possible show the brief video mentioned in the Instructor Notes section. It provides a good explanation and examples of microaggressions.] [5 minutes]

2. [Give out the Microaggressions handout.] *In your group, read through the rows together. In each row there is a blank cell. Discuss and fill in what you think the missing theme, action, or message is. When you are done filling out the sheet, write your responses on the board or poster paper that corresponds to the blank space in each row of your handout.* [15 minutes]

3. [Large-Group Discussion: First, talk through the examples the students offered, as well as adding any statements from the possible answers provided below the handout. Then discuss the following questions:] *Why are microaggressions hurtful? Are there any other examples of microaggressions you would be willing to share from your own personal and cultural background? What should someone do if he or she experiences a microaggression? What will you do with this information?* [15 minutes]

Approximate Time: 35 minutes (40 minutes if adding the video mentioned in the Instructor Notes)

Instructor Notes

1. Depending on the reading level of your students, you may need to explicitly explain some of the vocabulary used. As with any discussion on race and any "ism," it is important to have built a classroom of trust and respect. Reviewing your classroom civility rules prior to this activity helps set a Creator tone for this activity. We stress "listen deeply, avoid assumptions, and turn to wonder" to set the stage for this activity.

2. You may wish to introduce microaggressions by showing a four-minute video on YouTube by Derald Wing Sue, professor of psychology and education at Teacher's College, Columbia University. Sue explains what a microaggression is (with examples), how it manifests itself, how it impacts people, and what can be done to address it.

3. Possible answers for blanks in each row:
   1. You are not American. You are a foreigner.
   2. You are a credit to your race. You are so articulate. Asking an Asian person for help with a math or science problem.
   3. Statements that indicate that a white person does not want to acknowledge race.
   4. I am immune to races because I have friends of color. Your racial oppression is not different than my gender oppression. I can't be a racist. I'm like you.
   5. Assimilate to the dominate culture. Leave your cultural baggage outside.
   6. People of color are given extra unfair benefits because of their race. People of color are lazy and/or incompetent and need to work harder.

Source: Submitted by LuAnn Wood and Cris Davis, Century College, MN, based on and adapted from work by Tracey Wyman, Century College, MN.

Microaggressions

Microaggressions are commonplace verbal or behavioral indignities, whether intentional or unintentional, that communicate hostile, derogatory, or negative slights and insults to people because of their membership in a cultural sub-group.

THEME	MICROAGGRESSION	MESSAGE
1. Alien in Own Land When Asian Americans and Latino Americans are assumed to be foreign-born	"Where are you from?" "Where were you born?" "You speak good English." A person asking an Asian American to teach him or her words in his or her native language.	
2. Ascription of Intelligence Assigning intelligence to a person of color on the basis of their race		People of color are generally not as intelligent as whites. It is unusual for someone of your race to be intelligent. All Asians are intelligent and good in math/science.
3. Color Blindness	"When I look at you, I don't see color." "America is a melting pot." "There is only one race, the human race."	Denying a person of color's racial/ethnic experiences. Assimilate/acculturate to the dominant culture. Denying the individual as a racial/cultural being.
4. Denial of Individual Racism A statement made when whites deny their racial biases	"I'm not a racist. I have several black friends." "As a woman, I know what you go through as a racial minority."	
5. Pathologizing Cultural Values/ Communication Styles The notion that the values and communication styles of the dominant/white culture are ideal	Asking a black person: "Why do you have to be so loud/animated? Just calm down." To an Asian or Latino person: "Why are you so quiet? We want to know what you think. Be more verbal. Speak up more." Dismissing an individual who brings up race/culture in a work/school setting.	
6. Myth of Meritocracy Statements asserting that race does not play a role in life successes	"I believe the most qualified person should get the job." "Everyone can succeed in this society, if they work hard enough."	

Note: We are all going to make mistakes. Be genuine, honest, apologize, and learn from the mistake. Recognize and accept that your worldview is only one of many ways to understand and experience the world.

Journal Entry 20 Believing in Yourself: Be Assertive

EXERCISE 20-1: The Party

Purpose

To better understand placating, blaming, and leveling as communication styles.

Supplies and Setup

Chime (or another way to get the students' attention). Students should have read/written Journal Entry 20.

Directions

1. According to family therapist Virginia Satir, the two most common patterns of ineffective communication are **placating** and **blaming**. Both perpetuate low self-esteem. *In a few moments, we're going to have a party of placaters, blamers, and levelers. Let's examine how placaters, blamers, and levelers typically communicate.* [DEMO each of these three communication styles: **Placate**: "Even though I'm extremely busy, I'll be glad to drop everything I need to do in order to do what you want me to do." **Blame**: "You never make time for me; you are a terrible friend." **Level**: "I miss the times we used to spend together. Would you be willing to meet for coffee on Thursday or Friday?" Explain that these are the voices of the Inner Critic (placating), Inner Defender (blaming), and Inner Guide (leveling).]

2. *During our party, everyone born in January, February, March, or April will communicate as a placater. Those born in May, June July, or August, your style of communication will be blaming. If you were born in September, October, November, or December, your style of communication will be leveling. When you talk to people at this party, communicate in your assigned style.* [5–8 minutes]

3. *You can talk about anything you want to: sports, college, what you did this weekend, whatever you might talk about at a party. Okay, let the party begin!* [3–5 minutes]

4. [Ring the chime or call "Stop!"] *Stop where you are, close your eyes, and become aware of your breathing, thoughts, feelings, and body sensations.* [Pause] *How do you feel about yourself?* [Pause] *How do you feel about the people you have been talking to?* [Pause] *Now we're going to start the party again. But you're going to change communication styles. If you were placating, now use blaming. If you were blaming, now use leveling. If you were leveling, now use placating. Okay, let the party resume!* [5 minutes]

5. [Ring the chime or call "Stop!"] *Stop where you are, close your eyes, and again become aware of your breathing, thoughts, feelings, and body sensations.* [Pause] *How do you feel about yourself now?* [Pause] *How do you feel about the people you have been talking to?* [Pause] *In a moment, we're going to start the party again. But you're going to change communication styles one last time. If you were placating, now use blaming. If you were blaming, now use leveling. If you were leveling, now use placating. Okay, let the party resume!* [5 minutes]

6. [Ring the chime or call "Stop!"] *Stop where you are, close your eyes, and one more time become aware of your breathing, thoughts, feelings, and body sensations.* [Pause] *How do you feel about yourself now?* [Pause] *How do you feel about the people you have been talking to?* [Pause] *Okay, return to your seats.* [5 minutes]

7. [Quick-Write and/or Class Discussion] *What was your experience at this party? How did you feel about yourself as you spoke as a placater? As a blamer? As a leveler? How did you feel about other people as they used these three styles to communicate with you? Did you have a sense that any of these communication styles is the one you use most often? What is the life lesson here for you?* [e.g., "Speaking as a placater and blamer is exhausting."] [10–20 minutes]

Approximate Time: 30–50 minutes

EXERCISE 20-2: Make a Request—Now!

Purpose

To assist students to be more assertive about making requests, especially at college.

Supplies and Setup

Pen and paper

Directions

1. *Write down a problem that you are having here at college. Perhaps you're having a problem with a particular course, or with a particular assignment, or with finding a book you need, for example. Okay, let's hear some of the problems you have.* [Having some students share their problems will assist others to think of one of their own. Make sure everyone has thought of a problem before moving on to Step 2.] [5 minutes]

2. *Now make a list of requests you could make to assist you to solve this problem. For example, if your problem is that you're confused in your math course, you could request an appointment with your math teacher or a tutor to get help.* [5 minutes]

3. *Okay, let's hear your problem and the requests for help that you could make.* [As students read their lists of possible requests, listen for one in each list that the student could do immediately. Without telling them why, instruct each to put a star next to one request—the one you picked because the request could be made immediately.] [10 minutes]

4. [Each student should now have a request starred that he or she could make immediately.] *Get with a partner. You have five minutes to practice your request.* [5 minutes]

5. *Okay, now I want you to leave the class and go and make the request that has a star next to it. I want you back here in 15 minutes to report on your experience, no matter what it is.* [15 minutes]

6. [Quick-Write and/or Class Discussion] *What was your experience? Were you aware of your Inner Critic or Inner Defender talking to you as you went to make your request? How did you feel as you went to make the request? How did you feel after making the request (if you were able to)? What is the life lesson here for you?* [e.g.,"Making a request that is important to me is a great way to take care of myself."] [15 minutes]

Approximate Time: 50 minutes

Instructor Notes

Some students may not have been able (either because of inner or outer barriers) to make their requests. Be sure to remind them that they don't have to judge themselves for not succeeding this time. You may even want to suggest that they create a plan to try it again and report their results in the next class period. This activity is another of life's learning opportunities, not a reason to beat themselves up.

Rehearsing and Memorizing Study Materials

REHEARSING AND MEMORIZING STUDY MATERIALS EXERCISE 1: Quiz Me

Purpose

To offer students the experience of creating flashcards and rehearsing the answers to possible test questions.

Supplies and Setup

In a previous class, assign students to read Chapter 5 in *On Course*. Index cards, eight for each student; "Directions for Playing Quiz Me" handout (p. 164), one for each student. This activity is distributed over three class periods. Optional: Prizes for the winners.

Directions

Class 1:

1. [Discussion] *We're now going to look at a study strategy that will help you create deep and lasting learning . . . and help you earn better test scores. First, what kinds of questions can an instructor ask you on a test?* [List answers on the board: true/false, multiple choice, matching, fill in the blank (completion), short answer (paragraph), essay, problems, etc. Ask for a definition of each kind of question, perhaps putting an example of each on the board.] [5–10 minutes]

2. [Give out eight index cards to each student and the Directions for Playing Quiz Me handout. Have volunteers read aloud the Day 1 part of the directions. Review the directions and make sure that everyone understands.] *Your ticket to play the game in our next class is two identical sets of four flashcards. No cards, no play! If you know of anyone who's not here, tell them what they need to do before our next class. See you then!* [If you plan to give a prize, you could announce what the prize is as an extrinsic motivator for students to come prepared with their flashcards. Remind them again:] *No cards, no play. No play, no prize!* [5 minutes]

Class 2:

3. [As students arrive, collect one set of four cards from each student. Make sure that all cards have a question on one side and—on the other side—an answer, the page number where the answer is found in *On Course*, and the student's name. Now conduct the Quiz Me Game. Have volunteers read aloud the Day 2 part of the Quiz Me directions.] *What questions do you have?* [Respond as appropriate.] *Ready, begin.* [25 minutes]

4. [Determine who has the most cards and award a prize, if you wish. If there is a tie, you can either provide all winners with a prize or have a quiz-off, where each gets to ask the other player(s) to "Quiz me" until there is a winner.] [5 minutes]

5. [Journal Writing and/or Class Discussion] *What happened during the game? For what kind of courses would flashcards be a good way to rehearse information? What did you learn or relearn during the game? How will you use what you learned?* [5–10 minutes]

Class 3:

6. [After Class 2, go through the flashcards you collected, choose the best question from each student, and create a quiz using these questions.]

7. [At the start of Class 3, administer the unannounced quiz. You may want to put a short time limit, such as 30 seconds for each question. Thus a 20-question quiz would have a 10-minute time limit. After the test, have students exchange and grade quizzes as you elicit a correct answer for each question. Have students receive their quizzes back.] [15–20 minutes]

8. [Journal Writing and/or Class Discussion] *What did you say to yourself during the quiz? How did you feel during the quiz? What was your experience when you saw your own question on the quiz? What would it be like if you could predict all of the questions that an instructor asked on a test?* [If there are students who didn't participate in the previous days' activities—either because of absence or because of not having flashcards—ask them how they did on the quiz. Ask them if they think they would have done better if they had created flashcards and participated in the Quiz Me Game.] *How will this affect how you prepare for your next test?* [10–20 minutes]

Approximate Time: **Class 1:** 10–15 minutes; **Class 2:** 35–40 minutes; **Class 3:** 25–40 minutes

Instructor Notes

1. Optional: Instead of resolving "fouls" during the game, collect the offending cards and, after the game, have a class discussion about them. The issues will be (1) What is the correct answer? and/or (2) Is this a question that a fair instructor would ask?

2. If you encounter a lot of "fouls" being called, you may want to institute the "frivolous foul" rule. If you judge a foul claim to be frivolous, that player's opponent may take two cards from the player who called the frivolous foul.

Directions for Playing "Quiz Me"

Day 1: Preparation: In our next class, we are going to play a learning game called "Quiz Me." Your homework is to create two identical sets of four flashcards using information in Chapter 5 of *On Course*. Each set of four flashcards must contain one each of the following questions:

- true/false
- multiple choice
- matching
- fill in the blank (completion)

The four questions should be questions that you believe an instructor might actually ask on a test that is **challenging but fair**. In other words, they should be questions about key concepts, main or secondary ideas, or major or minor supporting details. No ridiculous questions that a fair instructor would never ask are allowed, such as "What is the third word on page 143?"

Unfair questions will be penalized. Here's how to create your flashcards. On one side of an index card, write a question. On the other side, write (1) the answer, (2) the page number where the information is found in the book, and (3) your name.

Be sure you create two identical sets of these four cards. To play, you must bring all eight cards to our next class.

Day 2: How to play Quiz Me: Everyone starts with four flashcards. The winner of "Quiz Me" is the person who has the most flashcards at the end of the game. Here's how you collect additional flashcards:

1. During the game, everyone will be walking around. You'll walk up to someone and say, "Quiz me." Your partner shows you the question on a flashcard, and you answer the question. If you answer correctly, you get the card. If you answer the question incorrectly, you do not get the card.
2. Your partner then says either, "Quiz me" or "Quiz me not." If your partner says "Quiz me," you show a question card, and your partner gives an answer. If the answer is correct, you lose your card. If the answer is incorrect, you keep your card. If your partner says, "Quiz me not," you each find another partner.
3. If you run out of cards, sit down.
4. As long as you still have flashcards, keep playing Quiz Me until the time is up.

The game will last a maximum of 20 minutes, and the person with the most flashcards at the end is the winner. Of course, if one person gets all of the cards before 20 minutes is up, that person is the winner.

FOULS: There are three conditions under which you may call a **foul** and ask for a ruling by the referee (the instructor). You can call a foul if you think . . .
(1) the answer on the flashcard is wrong and your answer is correct.
(2) your answer is an acceptable variation of the answer on the flashcard.
(3) the question is ridiculous, one that a fair instructor would never ask.

To call a foul: raise your hand, and the referee will come and arbitrate the dispute.

Result: If you call a foul and the ruling is in your favor, you get the flashcard. If you call a foul and the ruling goes against you, you must give two flashcards to your partner. (If you have only one or two card left, hand your card(s) over to your partner and exit the game.)

REHEARSING AND MEMORIZING STUDY MATERIALS EXERCISE 2: The Memory Box

Purpose

To have students learn and apply effective rehearsing and memorizing strategies.

Supplies and Setup

One box with 50 different small objects, some common and some not so common (examples: paperclip, piece of paper, book, comb, plastic bottle, birthday card, packet of sugar, pen, scissors, pencil sharpener, cell phone, 3 × 5 card, calendar page, flower, can of hair spray, etc.); have an additional 25 items available as well; table at front of room; students with paper and pens. Optional: prizes for members of the winning team. This activity is done over two class periods.

Directions

Day 1:

1. [Students in teams of five or six.] *We're going to play a game called the Memory Box. I'm going to take 50 objects from this box one at a time and place them on the table. Then, I am quickly going to put the items back in the box. Afterward, I will ask you each to make a list of as many of the 50 objects as you can remember.* [If someone asks if they can take notes, the answer is no.] [Remove an item from the box, display it for about five seconds, and then place it on the table where students can still see it. When 50 items are on the table, sweep them quickly back into the box where students can no longer see them.] [10 minutes]

2. *Now that the objects are back in a box, please make a list of as many of them as you can remember. You have five minutes, and you must work alone.* [5 minutes]

3. [Help students assess how many items they got right. Take the items out one at a time and have students check those they listed correctly. Each student then adds up the number he or she recalled correctly. Obviously, a perfect score would be 50.] [10 minutes]

4. [Have students create groups of four to six students. It is helpful, though not essential, for the groups to be the same size.] *On a sheet of paper, make a list of each person on your team and the number of items each person remembered correctly.* [To help students assess their lists accurately, take the items out one at a time as students check them off on their lists. Collect the team lists, showing the number of items that each person remembered. Bring these lists back to the next class.] [10 minutes]

5. *In our next class we are going to play the Memory Box game again with a few variations. I will again take 50 objects out of the box one at a time and place them on a table for viewing. They may be the same objects as last time, or they may be new objects. Next time, however,* **you will each be allowed to take notes as I remove the items from the box.** *After all items are back in the box, you will have 10 minutes working alone to organize, rehearse, and memorize your notes. After 10 minutes, I'll collect your notes, and you'll make a list of as many items as you can remember. Afterward, we'll see which team improved the most.* [Optional: *You now have the rest of the class period to make a plan for how you play next time.*] *You will find many helpful strategies in the "Rehearsing and Memorizing Study Materials" section in* On Course. *Of course your team is welcome to get together outside of class to continue mastering these skills, if you wish.* [5–15 minutes]

Day 2:

6. [Replace 25 of the items in the box with new items. Students should not be sitting with their teams.] *As in our last class, I'm going to take 50 objects from this box one at a time and place them on the table. Then, I am going to put them back in the box. This time you may take notes as I display the items.* [Remember that 25 of these items should be ones that the students have not seen previously. Remove an item from the box, display it for about five seconds, and then place it on the table where students can still see it. When 50 items are on the table, sweep them quickly back into the box where students can no longer see them.] [10 minutes]

7. *You now have 10 minutes to study your notes before the test. You must work alone.* [Afterward, collect all notes.] [10 minutes]

8. *Now, please make a list of as many objects as you can remember. You have five minutes and you must work alone.* [5 minutes]

9. [Help students assess how many items they got right. Take the items out one at a time and have students check those they listed correctly. Each student then adds up the number he or she recalled correctly. Once again, a perfect score would be 50.] [10 minutes]

10. [Have students reconvene their teams. Return to each team the score sheets you collected in the previous class.] *Now figure out how many more items your team remembered today than last time. To get the average improvement of each team member, divide your total improvement by the number of people on your team.* [On the board, record the results—average improvement—of each team.] [5 minutes]

11. [Discussion. Congratulate the team that improved the most. Ask the winning team (and later all teams) to discuss the following questions:] *What did you do differently the second time? How much did it help to take notes this time? Did you do anything to organize the notes you took? What strategies did you use to remember the items in your notes? Did you find it easier to remember items that you saw in both rounds of the game? Why or why not? What does this tell you about memory? What changes will you make in the way you study for tests?* [10–20 minutes]

Approximate Time: Class 1: 35–50 minutes; **Class 2:** 40–60 minutes

Embracing Change: Do One Different Thing This Week

Creators build mutually supportive relationships, giving and receiving help. Experiment with being more interdependent by picking ONE new belief or behavior from the following list and trying it for one week.

1. Think: "I am giving and receiving help."
2. Ask an instructor for help.
3. Seek help from a college resource.
4. Find and work with a study partner.
5. Create and meet with a study group.
6. Have a meaningful conversation with someone very different from myself.
7. Take a specific action to show respect to someone different from myself.
8. Use an "I" statement in assertively expressing something that upsets me.
9. Make a request for help with a problem.
10. Offer help to someone with a problem.
11. Say "no" to something someone requests of me.
12. Your choice: A different belief or behavior you learned in this chapter with which you would like to experiment.

Now, write the one you chose under "My Commitment" in the following chart. Then, track yourself for one week, putting a check in the appropriate box when you keep your commitment. After seven days, assess your results. If your outcomes and experiences improve, you now have a tool you can use for the rest of your life. As Russian author Leo Tolstoy said, "Everyone thinks of changing the world, but no one thinks of changing himself."

My Commitment						
Day 1	Day 2	Day 3	Day 4	Day 5	Day 6	Day 7

During my seven-day experiment, what happened?

As a result of what happened, what did I learn or relearn?

Chapter 5: Quiz Questions

(Please visit the Instructor Companion website for *On Course* at login.cengage.com or contact your local Cengage Learning sales representative to find electronic versions of the Quiz Questions.)

25. Creating a Support System

1. Individualistic cultures, such as mainstream North American culture, have an "I/me" orientation, and independence is highly regarded.   TRUE   FALSE

2. Collectivistic cultures, such as Latino, Asian, and Native American cultures, have a "we/us" orientation and independence is highly regarded.   TRUE   FALSE

3. Most college and university instructors hold office hours when students can visit them to ask questions about the course.   TRUE   FALSE

4. Certain steps must be taken to create an effective study group. Which of the following suggestions is NOT given in *On Course*?

    A. Choose only Creators.

    B. Choose group goals.

    C. Choose a group name.

    D. Choose group rules.

5. If you were having academic problems in a math class, which college resource would likely offer the most effective help?

    A. Student Activities Office

    B. Career Center

    C. Tutoring Lab

    D. Financial Aid Office

26. Strengthening Relationships with Active Listening

1. Good listeners clear their minds and listen for the entire message, including words, tone of voice, gestures, and facial expressions.   TRUE   FALSE

2. Suppose that you are listening to someone and you ask, "Could you say more about that?" You are using an active listening strategy called "reflection."   TRUE   FALSE

3. You are actively listening when you're actively waiting for the first opportunity to offer your own opinion on what the other person is saying.   TRUE   FALSE

4. Active listening is a way to demonstrate the high esteem with which you value the other person.   TRUE   FALSE

5. Listening effectively means that you accept 50 percent of the responsibility for receiving the same message that the speaker is sending, uncontaminated by your own thoughts or feelings.   TRUE   FALSE

27. Respecting Cultural Differences

1. According to the Pew Research Center, by 2050 whites will make up less than half of the population of the United States.   TRUE   FALSE

2. While there are many different verbal languages on Earth, nonverbal languages (such as the meaning of gestures) are pretty much the same for all people.   TRUE   FALSE

3. Ethnocentrism is the belief that

    A. all people are created equal.

    B. the way *we* do things is superior to the way *they* do things.

    C. prejudice is inherited, just like skin color.

    D. other people are usually right.

4. Jean Moule, an African American professor at Oregon State University, described the following experiences: "A man saw my face as I walked into the store and unconsciously checked his wallet. On the street, a woman catches my eye a half a block away and moves her purse from the handle of her baby's stroller to her side as she arranges the baby's blanket. In the airport, a man signals to his wife to move her purse so it is not over the back of her chair, adjacent to the one I am moving toward." These experiences are examples of _____.

5. If you witness or are the target of discrimination, bigotry, or hate crimes, which of the following is NOT a recommended choice in *On Course*?

    A. Ignore the incident.

    B. Report the offense to campus officials.

    C. Follow up to see that something is done.

    D. Request help from a group that has experience dealing with such injustices.

28. *On Course* at Work: Interdependence at Work

1. One advantage of choosing good attendance and completed assignments is that instructors will be more willing to help with job references or letters of recommendation.   TRUE   FALSE

2. A good choice for collaboration during your job search is to get to know individuals who are working in your field of interest.   TRUE   FALSE

3. A mentor is someone further along in his or her career development who is willing to assist newer employees.   TRUE   FALSE

4. In what ways will mutually supportive relationships assist you during a job search?

    A. They may be a source for good letters of recommendation or references.

    B. They may be a source of job openings that are unpublished or "invisible."

    C. They may assist you in staying on course when the job search is frustrating.

    D. All of the above.

    E. None of the above.

5. Once you are on the job (and let's imagine that it's your dream job), you can be sure that

   A. your work with collaboration has ended.

   B. your bosses will value those workers who "fly solo" and work independently.

   C. your ability to develop strong support networks at work may make you a "star."

   D. your coworkers will not be interested in your active listening skills or interdependent values.

29. Believing in Yourself: Be Assertive

1. Victims who _____ are placing themselves below others. They protect themselves from the sting of criticism and rejection by saying whatever they think will gain approval.

   A. blame

   B. level

   C. placate

2. Victims who _____ are placing themselves above others. They protect themselves from wounds of disappointment and failure by making others responsible for their problems.

   A. blame

   B. level

   C. placate

3. Creators who _____ (a term used by family therapist Virginia Satir) are telling the truth as they see it.

   A. blame

   B. level

   C. placate

4. Which of the following problems could you probably get help with at your college if you made a request to the proper person?

   A. academic problems

   B. money problems

   C. health problems

   D. problems deciding on a career

   E. all of the above

5. The DAPPS rule, which we use to remember the qualities of an effective goal, can also be used to remember the qualities of an effective request. The letters in DAPPS stand for Dated, Achievable, Personal, Positive, and _____.

30. *Wise Choices in College:* Rehearsing and Memorizing Study Materials

1. Reciting and reviewing study materials is to <u>R</u>ehearsing as creating a variety of study materials is to <u>O</u>rganizing.   TRUE   FALSE

2. One way to strengthen neural networks is to use many different kinds of <u>R</u>ehearsal strategies and distribute these efforts over time.   TRUE   FALSE

3. The key to developing the self-confidence that you can learn virtually anything is choosing effective study strategies and spending sufficient time on task.   TRUE   FALSE

4. There are generally two types of <u>R</u>ehearsal strategies: rote and collaborative.   TRUE   FALSE

5. The best way to distribute your study time is to do it all within the 24 hours before a test.   TRUE   FALSE

Chapter 5: Essay Topics

1. Many college students are very proud of being INDEPENDENT. Write an essay in which you persuade them that they would actually be better off if they were INTERDEPENDENT.

2. The deep culture of some students promotes independence (individualism), whereas the deep culture of other students promotes interdependence (collectivism). Write an opinion piece for your college newspaper in which you explore the advantages and disadvantages of each belief. Conclude by explaining when it would be beneficial for college students to choose to be independent and when it would be beneficial to choose to be interdependent.

3. Successful students often create study groups. Write a formal letter to three to five fellow students in one of your present classes persuading them to join you in forming a study group. Be sure to explain what a study group is, why one is important, and how you see the group working for mutual success.

4. Very few people are truly active listeners. Do a personal research project to answer the question: What behaviors typically interfere with listening well? You should be able to gather a great deal of information simply by observing people while they are engaged in a conversation. Feel free to gather information in any way that seems appropriate to answer your question. Write an essay revealing your discoveries.

5. Describe a time when you experienced a culture different from your own. Explain the differences in surface and/or deep cultures. Relate any challenges you had while interacting with others in this culture, how you dealt with the challenges, and what you learned.

6. There are times in most people's lives when they said "Yes" because they were not assertive enough to say "No." Write an essay about a time when you said "Yes" when "No" would have been a wiser choice. Explain the situation, including your thoughts that led to saying "Yes." Describe the consequences of your "Yes" in terms of the price you later paid. End your essay by explaining what you have learned about the power of saying "No" and how you expect this discovery to affect your life in the future.

7. Using the student essays in *On Course* as a model, write an essay about how you used a strategy from Chapter 5 to overcome a problem in your life—academic, personal, or even at work. First explain the problem; then discuss the strategy you used and how; finally, identify what happened. Your instructor may submit your essay for possible publication in the next edition of *On Course*. Additional directions for writing and submitting these essays can be found at http://oncourseworkshop.com.

Answer Key to Chapter 5 Quiz Questions

25. Creating a Support System

Answers: 1. TRUE   2. FALSE (Interdependence is highly regarded, not independence.)   3. TRUE   4. C (though a group name couldn't hurt)   5. C

26. Strengthening Relationships with Active Listening

Answers: 1. TRUE   FALSE (expansion)   2. FALSE   3. TRUE   4. FALSE (100 percent responsibility)

27. Respecting Cultural Differences

Answers: 1. TRUE (actually 47 percent)   2. FALSE   3. B   4. microaggressions   5. A

28. *On Course* at Work: Interdependence at Work

Answers: 1. TRUE   2. TRUE   3. TRUE   4. D   5. C

29. Believing in Yourself: Be Assertive

Answers: 1. C   2. A   3. B   4. E (You may want to confirm that all of these services are, in fact, available at your college.)   5. Specific

30. *Wise Choices in College*: Rehearsing and Memorizing Study Materials

Answers: 1. TRUE   2. TRUE   3. TRUE   4. FALSE (elaborative, not collaborative)   5. FALSE

Gaining Self-Awareness

Chapter
6

Concept

When discussing self-awareness, the thought that usually pops most quickly to mind is awareness of one's strengths and weaknesses, inclinations and disinclinations. However, there is another realm of self-awareness that may play an even bigger role than these characteristics in determining one's outcomes and experiences. Many people, despite their conscious intentions, make choices that sabotage their success. As a result of their self-defeating habit patterns (including behaviors, thoughts, emotions) and unconscious limiting beliefs, students with great potential can thwart the achievement of their most cherished goals and dreams. As a result, these students are their own greatest obstacle. By assisting students to become aware of their unconscious self-defeating habit patterns and limiting beliefs, we empower them to rewrite outdated life scripts and change their lives for the better.

EMPOWERS STUDENTS TO . . .

1. Recognize when they are off course from their goals and dreams.
2. Identify their self-defeating habit patterns of thought, behavior, and emotion.
3. Identify their unconscious limiting beliefs about themselves, other people, and the world.
4. Revise their outdated scripts, thereby becoming the author of their future.
5. Consciously take charge of the outcomes of their lives.

Remember also to use the all-purpose exercises mentioned in the Introduction, actively engaging students in the exploration of JOURNAL ENTRIES, CASE STUDIES, ONE STUDENT'S STORY, ON COURSE AT WORK, QUOTATIONS, CARTOONS, FOCUS QUESTIONS, CHAPTER-OPENING CHARTS, and STUDY SKILLS. Remind students to use letters to label any in-class writing they do in their journals.

Case Study in Critical Thinking: Strange Choices

Purpose

To develop critical thinking skills by exploring a real-life situation concerning self-awareness and the power of scripts to affect our choices.

Supplies and Setup

"Strange Choices" in *On Course.*

Directions

1. [Have students read "Strange Choices." One way to be sure everyone has read the selection before taking the next step is to have one student read the first paragraph aloud, another student read the second, and so on until the reading is complete. Then have students put in their scores for the six professors' students.] [5 minutes]

2. [Find out by a show of hands how many students have picked each professor's student as number 1—demonstrating the strangest choices (or, as we will see later, the most self-sabotaging script). If two or more characters are chosen as number 1, move on to step 3. In the unlikely event that everyone chooses the same character as number 1 (or there is otherwise little diversity in opinion), ask how many students have picked each character as number 6—demonstrating the least self-sabotaging script. Sometimes there is more diversity of opinion here.] [5 minutes]

3. [Create groups of like-minded students.] *Since you agree in your group about which student demonstrated the strangest choice, decide how you are going to persuade other groups to agree with you.* [5–10 minutes]

4. [Have a spokesperson from each group present the group's position; then lead a debate on the issue by moving the discussion from group to group, allowing students to explain their positions in more detail and rebut opposing views. Invite students to demonstrate a change in their opinions by getting up and going to the group with which they now agree. If spokespersons don't offer reasons for the student's "strange choice," encourage them to speculate on the causes. See if you can guide them to discover that unconscious beliefs are sometimes the cause of strange choices and that, as long as people are unaware of these beliefs they will make "strange" and perhaps self-sabotaging choices.] [5–20 minutes]

5. [Quick-Write and/or Class Discussion] *What did you learn from this discussion about strange choices? What's the life lesson here for you?* [e.g., "People sometimes make choices that seem strange to others because the choices sabotage the very goals the people say they want, like getting a college degree" Or "Sometimes we make bad choices and we don't even know why."] [5–10 minutes]

Approximate Time: 25–50 minutes

Instructor Notes

1. So as not to stifle discussion, I don't tell students what my scores are.

2. This class discussion is an excellent prewriting activity to be followed by students writing a persuasion essay supporting their opinions in the debate. Because students are now sharply aware of opposing views to their own, they often write much more thorough and persuasive essays than would be the case without the debate.

3. An optional step for this activity is to ask students to do a Quick-Write and then a discussion about the Diving Deeper question: Recall a course you once took in which you made a choice that your instructor might describe as "strange." Explain why you made that choice. Dive deep, exploring what *really* caused your choice.

Journal Entry 21 Recognizing When You Are Off Course

EXERCISE 21-1: On Course—Off Course

Purpose

To become conscious of whether one is on course or off course in the pursuit of one's goals and dreams.

Supplies and Setup

Students in pairs (Student A and Student B). Display the following listening skills on a PowerPoint slide or write them on the board:

- *Listen to understand*
- *Clear your mind and remain silent*
- *Ask the person to expand or clarify*
- *Reflect the other person's thoughts and feelings*

Directions

1. *Make a list of all of your life roles. Refer to Journal Entry 10 to remind yourself of the life roles you've chosen.* [3 minutes]

2. *On a scale of 0–10, rate how on course you are toward your goals and dreams in each of your life roles. A score of 0 means that you are totally off course in this role. A score of 10 means that you are totally on course in this role. Scores in*

between indicate various degrees of being on course or off course. Listen to the information available to you from your Inner Guide and score yourself now. [3 minutes]

3. *Partner A, tell Partner B each of your life roles and the scores you have given them. Explain each score. You have five minutes.* [Display the four listening skills.] *B, use your best active listening skills:*
   - *Listen to understand*
   - *Clear your mind and remain silent*
   - *Ask the person to expand or clarify*
   - *Reflect the other person's thoughts and feelings* [5 minutes]

4. *Now switch roles. Partner B, you explain your scores to Partner A, who will use his or her best listening skills. You have five minutes.* [5 minutes]

5. [Quick-Write and/or Class Discussion] *What did you discover? In what roles are you on course? In what roles are you off course? What self-sabotaging habits may have gotten you off course? What could you do about these habits? What is the life lesson here for you?* [e.g., "If I don't pay close attention, I can get far off course, and my Inner Defender won't even let me admit it."] [5–15 minutes]

Approximate Time: 20–30 minutes

EXERCISE 21-2: The Air Traffic Controller

Purpose

To demonstrate the value of responding as a Creator when receiving feedback about being off course.

Supplies and Setup

Have a volunteer stand on the opposite side of the room from you.

Directions

1. [To the volunteer] *Let's imagine for this demonstration that I'm an airplane pilot, and I am trying to fly to your airport in a terrible storm. You're the air traffic controller, and it's your job to guide me safely to your airport. If I'm headed toward you, say, "On course, on course, on course . . ." If I'm not headed toward you, say, "Off course, off course, off course . . ." Now I'm going to close my eyes because there's a storm in my life, and I can't see very well.* [Head toward the volunteer and make sure he continually says, "On course, on course . . ." Now head away from the volunteer and make sure he says, "Off course, off course . . ." Once you have him or her trained as an air traffic controller, you can go into your DEMO of what people often do when they receive feedback that they're off course.]

2. *Notice that I'm now getting feedback saying I'm off course. How do people often act when they're told they're off course?* [Elicit and dramatize various responses: anger, blame, tears, complaints, self-criticism, excuses, or just sitting down and giving up.] *Are any of these responses helping me get back on course?* [Naturally, the answer is NO.]

3. *Life constantly gives us feedback when we are off course. What kind of feedback might we get that we're off course in college?* [An F on a test.] *On a job?* [Demoted or fired.] *Concerning our health?* [We get sick or have a heart attack.] *In a relationship?* [Someone we love decides to leave us.] *Many people, when they get feedback that they're off course, resist the feedback. Does it help us get back on course to get angry, cry, blame, complain, make excuses, or quit? Whose voices are these, anyway?* [It's the Victim reacting from his or her Inner Defender and Inner Critic.]

4. *What would be a more effective way to respond to feedback that tells us we're off course?* [As a Creator listening to his or her Inner Guide.] *Would someone like to demonstrate how a Creator, listening to his her Inner Guide, would respond to the feedback from the air traffic controller?* [Have someone take your place. Have the person close his or her eyes and role-play the pilot of a plane moving on course and off course as it makes its way toward its destination. Ideally the student will simply take the off-course feedback and use it to change direction to get back on course.]

5. [Quick-Write and/or Class Discussion] *What's the life lesson here for you?* [e.g., "Even feedback that is uncomfortable to hear can be helpful in getting me back on course."] *How do you most often respond to feedback that you're off course? Are there any changes you wish to make?* [5–10 minutes]

Approximate Time: 10–20 minutes

EXERCISE 21-3: Can We Be Trained to Lose and Then Learn to Win?

Purpose

To help students learn that failures teach us about ourselves and prepare us for our successes in life.

Supplies and Setup

Journals; and computer/projector/Internet access; reflective questions on the white board, handout or PowerPoint slide (see Instructor Notes for questions).

Directions

1. [Introduce the activity to the students.] *We have all failed at something. Some people say that failures teach us more than successes do. Failures can actually prepare us for our successes. In this activity, you will view a clip from the movie* Seabiscuit *and reflect on times in your life when you felt like a failure and/or victim. You will then explore the positives that actually came from the experience and what you learned.*
2. *After the clip, you will answer some reflective questions. Be prepared to share your answers with the class.*
3. [After students view the video and respond in writing to the Reflective Questions, lead a discussion of their answers.]

Approximate Time: 25–55 minutes (depending on the length of discussion)

Instructor Notes

1. Search for Seabiscuit (1/10) Movie CLIP - The History of Seabiscuit (2003) HD on youTube for the clip associated with this activity.
2. This discussion can tie into self-awareness, self-esteem, choices students make, and so forth. It also opens up a good discussion about Victims and Creators. Students can continue to blame someone else who may very well have trained them to lose, but they will be the ones to suffer. There are many different directions you can go with this discussion.

Reflective Questions

1. In the clip, the narrator talks about how when Seabiscuit would not perform like the horses labeled as champions, he was instead trained to lose. When he began racing again, Seabiscuit did what he had been trained to do. He lost. Write about a time when you experienced failure at something because you were "trained to lose."
2. As we now know, Seabiscuit went on to become a champion. Were you able to get back on track after failing? How? If not, why do you think that is? What would you do differently now?

Source: Submitted by Katy Goforth, from Tri-County Technical College, SC

EXERCISE 21-4: What Color Are Your "Lenses"?

Purpose

To help students understand that the way we "view" the world has a huge impact on the choices we make at forks in the road.

Supplies and Setup

Several pairs of "fashion" glasses painted with different colored lenses. *Pebeo's Vitrea 160* transparent paints are available at Michael's and Hobby Lobby.

Directions

1. I bring to class with me several pairs of "fashion" glasses, their lenses painted with different transparent colors.
2. I ask for several student volunteers to participate in the activity. Each student is given a different pair of glasses to wear.

3. Once the students are wearing the glasses, I show them different items, starting with a plain white sheet of paper, and ask them to describe the color. The color they describe SHOULD correspond to the color of the lenses in their glasses.

4. After all of the students have given their responses, we discuss how our beliefs are like the "lenses" through which we see the world and how those "lenses" can color everything we see. If we see the world through the colored lens of an Inner Victim or Inner Defender, things will look much different than if we view them through the clear lens of the Inner Guide, thereby coloring the choices we make.

Approximate Time: 50 minutes. This activity can easily be completed during a regular 50-minute class period, although the discussion can be extended for as long as necessary.

Instructor Notes

1. I find that students understand the concepts of mindsets better when we have done this literal, physical exercise of seeing the world through different colors.

2. I sometimes give the students a journal assignment to write about the different "lenses" through which they see the world.

Source: Submitted by Lory Conrad, University of Arkansas—Fort Smith, AR

Journal Entry 22 Identifying Your Scripts

EXERCISE 22-1: What's Your Pattern?

Purpose

To dramatize and raise students' awareness about self-defeating patterns.

Supplies and Setup

Students in groups of three; "Character Cards" (page 181) cut into eight slips of paper, each with one situation on it. Use the skit subjects suggested or create your own.

Directions

1. [Have someone from each group pick a Character Card containing the cast and situation for the skit.] *Each group has five minutes to assign each person in the group to one of the roles in the skit. Your skit will be _____ minutes long.* [See Instructor Note 1 about length of skits.] *The character listed first on the Character Card will always say the first line of the skit, and the other two characters will simply play off that character's lead.*

2. *Whatever your role is, your character is to demonstrate a self-defeating pattern. You can choose one from the list of Self-Defeating Habit Patterns in the text immediately before Journal Entry 22, or you can simply role-play a self-defeating pattern you're familiar with. Before each skit, character 1 will read the Character Card to the audience so we know what role each person is playing. After each skit, we'll try to guess what each character's self-defeating pattern is.* [Check with each group to confirm that they are, indeed, choosing self-defeating patterns to dramatize.] [5–8 minutes]

3. [Get the actors in each skit to the front of the room, and turn them loose to role-play. Remind them to read their Character Cards aloud to the audience. Time the skits, and stop them if they exceed your allotted time. After each skit, have the audience guess what self-defeating patterns each person was dramatizing.]

4. [Quick-Write and/or Class Discussion] *What did you learn about self-defeating habit patterns? Did you recognize yourself in any of the skits? Did you discover any habit patterns of thought, behavior, or emotions that you want to change? What's the life lesson here for you?* [e.g., "It's easier to see someone else's self-defeating habit patterns than it is to see my own."] [10–25 minutes]

Approximate Time: 10–60 minutes, depending on how many groups and the length of each skit

Instructor Notes

1. Determine the length of each skit by the amount of time you have available for the presentation and discussion of all skits. If you have 30 minutes available for all skits and six groups, then allot five minutes per group. That would allow about three minutes for acting out the skit and two minutes for guessing the self-defeating pattern. With any luck, the point about the self-defeating patterns will be made before you need to stop the skit.

2. To create Character Cards for class, simply duplicate page 181 and cut it into eighths. If you need more than 8 Character Cards, make two copies of the page and create 16 cards. It is interesting to have two groups do the same skit to see the differences.

3. You could give out Character Cards in one class period and do the skits in class at the next meeting. You could also carry some skits over to another day if your students get really involved.

4. Once students are familiar with this activity, you could have each team create its own Character Cards.

Character Cards

1. **STUDENT A:** Has just gotten word that he or she has been turned down for a scholarship.

2. **DIRECTOR OF FINANCIAL AID:** This is the person who turned down Student A's application for a scholarship.

3. **STUDENT B:** The boyfriend or girlfriend of Student A. Just got a huge scholarship from the same director of financial aid.

---

1. **FRIEND 1:** Promised two other friends to buy them lottery tickets for Christmas. Asked them to each pick a number, bought the tickets, and held on to them. The ticket bought for Friend 2 wins $1,000,000. Friend 1's spouse threatens a divorce if Friend 1 gives the winning ticket to Friend 2.

2. **FRIEND 2**

3. **FRIEND 3**

---

1. **THE BOSS:** Owns a huge business, is looking for a vice president, and has narrowed the field to Applicants A and B. The boss has invited both applicants in at the same time for a final interview.

2. **APPLICANT A**

3. **APPLICANT B**

---

1. **STUDENT 1:** Organized these three students into a study group for a very difficult course. Always comes to the group prepared.

2. **STUDENT 2:** Sometimes comes to the group prepared.

3. **STUDENT 3:** Never comes to the group prepared and often misses the meetings.

---

1. **MOTHER:** Has discovered that her teenager has not been attending high school for the last three weeks. She has no idea where her teenager has been going every day.

2. **FATHER:** Dropped out of high school when he was a teenager.

3. **TEENAGER**

---

1. **SPOUSE 1:** Wants to return to college. Has been out of school for 10 years. Presently earns more money than Spouse 2 but dislikes the job.

2. **SPOUSE 2:** Worried about their family having enough money if Spouse 1 goes to college.

3. **PARENT OF SPOUSE 2:** Visiting from another state.

---

1. **DRIVER 1:** Was backing out of a parking space in a mall parking lot and was struck in the rear door by Driver 2 who was also backing out of a parking space. Driver 1's car has a huge dent. Driver 2's car is unhurt.

2. **DRIVER 2:** Thinks that Driver 1 is at fault for backing out so fast.

3. **POLICE OFFICER**

---

1. **STUDENT:** Has failed the professor's class; believes that the professor graded unfairly after the student disagreed with the professor in front of the class; has appealed the grade to the department chairperson.

2. **PROFESSOR**

3. **DEPARTMENT CHAIRPERSON**

EXERCISE 22-2: The Puzzle

Purpose

To discover self-defeating patterns and their underlying limiting beliefs.

Supplies and Setup

Have one jigsaw puzzle of about 35 pieces for each 10 to 12 students. Thus for a group of 35 students, have three puzzles available.

Directions

1. [Have students count off so that you form groups of 10–12 students. Thus, if you have 35 students, have them count off by three's. Place the puzzles, one for each group, where they can be picked up by students—perhaps on the front desk. Do not hand them to any particular student.] *Your goal is to assemble these puzzles. Please begin.* [If anyone asks a question, simply repeat the directions. Record what students are doing/saying as they work on the puzzles. Also note if there are any emotions that surface during the puzzle assembly (e.g., one student getting upset with another).] [5–10 minutes]

2. [When all puzzles are assembled, introduce the next part as follows.] *What's the value of heightened awareness?* [e.g., "Awareness allows us to see when we are off course and what options we have for getting back on course. Without awareness we will just keep heading off course without even realizing it. Awareness allows us to change so that we can achieve our goals and dreams."] *So our goal here is to see if we can each become aware of one or more patterns in our lives, especially those habits that may keep us from achieving the outcomes and experiences we desire. If we can become more aware of what we are doing that isn't working, then we have the option of making different choices that get us more of the outcomes and experiences we want.* [5 minutes]

3. *Some psychologists believe that the microcosm of our lives (the little things) sometimes reveal the macrocosm of our lives (the big things). For example, the way you go through the grocery store may reveal how you live your life. Do you go up and down every aisle or go right to what you need? Do you buy whatever brand you want or only the ones on sale? Do you chat in the check-out line or are you all business about finishing your shopping? For today, you're going to see what you can learn about how you live your life by examining how you did the puzzle. It's important to realize that none of this exploration is about "right" and "wrong." It's merely about becoming aware of how we live our lives. No one did the puzzle* right *and no one did the puzzle* wrong. *You just did the puzzle and we're going to examine what that looks like for each of us.* [Without naming names, give examples of what you saw, heard, and recorded as the puzzles were being assembled.] [5 minutes]

4. *Now we're going to begin a little experiment in self-awareness. Title a page in your journal: "How I did the puzzle is how I do my life." Then write as much as you can to prove that this statement is true. Don't worry about whether it really IS true; for now, just pretend it is, and make your case by giving examples wherever possible. Consider questions such as "What were you thinking, feeling, and doing while your group was working on the puzzle? Where else in your life do you think, feel, or do that?" You'll have about eight minutes to write; then you'll share what you wrote with someone else. By the way, everybody "did the puzzle." Whatever you did from the time I put the puzzles out until the puzzles were put together (even if you were out of the room) is "how you did the puzzle." And, once more, please understand that this is not about whether you did this activity "right" or "wrong." This is only about seeing how aware you are about what you were thinking, saying, doing, and feeling during the puzzle . . . and then seeing if you can find examples of how you have done the same thing at other times in your life. So go ahead and make a case for the idea, "How I did the puzzle is how I do my life."* [10 minutes]

5. *Now meet with a partner, and read and discuss what you wrote. See if either of you found any truth to the idea that "How I did the puzzle is how I do my life."* [10 minutes]

6. [Class Discussion] *So, did anyone find truth in the statement that "How I did the puzzle is how I do my life"? Do these habit patterns support or limit you in achieving your desired outcomes and experiences? Are there any changes you'd like to make in your beliefs, behaviors, thoughts, or feelings? What is the life lesson here for you?* [e.g., "Self-aware people make choices with minimal contamination from their past experiences."] [10–20 minutes]

Approximate Time: 45–65 minutes

Instructor Notes

1. This puzzle exercise is a very powerful means for generating discussion and insight about habit patterns and their underlying beliefs. Given time, many people will make extraordinary discoveries about their scripts.
2. Keep the puzzle groups large enough—10 to 12 people—so that it is difficult for everyone to work on the puzzle at the same time. This arrangement creates some stress and tends to cause habitual scripts to emerge. Among other discoveries, participants may notice their patterns of participating/withdrawing and of competing/cooperating.

Journal Entry 23 Rewriting Your Outdated Scripts

EXERCISE 23-1: What I Did Instead

Purpose

To raise students' awareness about limiting core beliefs that may cause them to make unwise choices and how they can revise these beliefs.

Supplies and Setup

Each student needs a pen and a piece of paper.

Directions

1. *Think of a time when you missed or were late to a class for a poor reason. On a piece of paper, write what you did instead of attending or getting to class on time. Don't put your name on the paper. For example, you might write, "Instead of going to math class, I stayed home to watch television." Or, "Instead of arriving on time to my English class, I stopped in the cafeteria, got into a conversation with a friend, and talked too long." [3 minutes]*
2. [Collect the papers and redistribute them so no one knows whose paper he or she has.] [2 minutes]
3. *Look at what the person chose to do instead of attending class or being on time. Write a list of possible **limiting core beliefs** that may have led to this choice. In other words, why do you think the student REALLY was late or absent? For example, if the student chose, instead of going to English class on time, to continue a conversation with a friend in the cafeteria, you might suggest the following possible core beliefs:*

   "I'm not smart enough to pass this class."

   "Going to college is a waste of time."

   "Teachers don't care whether I do well in college."

   "When I'm tired, I'm not motivated to go to class."

   "It doesn't matter if I'm late."

   "I can't be rude and just walk away from a conversation."
4. *Now get a partner. Partner A, read the core beliefs on your list to your partner. After reading each belief, Partner A tell Partner B whether this core belief is actually one of your own. Partner B, ask questions to help A explore each core belief and take ownership if appropriate. Discuss what would be a more empowering core belief to adopt. When I ring the chime, reverse roles. [10–15 minutes]*
5. [Quick-Write and/or Class Discussion] *What did you learn about your limiting core beliefs from this activity? Did you discover a limiting core belief that you will actively seek to rewrite? What's the life lesson here for you?* [e.g., "Core beliefs that I'm not even aware of can cause me to make unwise choices. I need to become more aware of my core beliefs."] [5–15 minutes]

Approximate Time: 25–35 minutes

Instructor Notes

When students are speculating in Step 3 about the other person's limiting core beliefs, they may be projecting their own scripts onto another. So it is likely that at least some, if not all, of the core beliefs on their lists are actually their own.

EXERCISE 23-2: Author, Author

Purpose

To practice changing a limiting script into an empowering script.

Supplies and Setup

Ten index cards for each student

Directions

1. *By now you're probably aware of some of your limiting beliefs. As you know, if you revise your limiting beliefs, you'll change your patterns of thought, behavior, and emotion.*
2. *Write five of your limiting beliefs, one each on five index cards. No one will ever see these cards, so be honest with yourself. Write limiting beliefs you have about life, about people, and especially about yourself. For example, one of the students mentioned in* On Course *believed, "I am the half-brain in the family, so I'll never be able to go to college." If you can't think of five limiting beliefs, then make some up so that you have five cards, each with a limiting belief. Please note, however, that you'll get much more value from this activity if you use your own limiting beliefs.* [5–8 minutes]
3. *Next, translate each of your limiting beliefs into empowering beliefs. Write each empowering belief on a separate index card. For example, the student in* On Course *might have revised her limiting belief to read, "I am smart and doing great in college."* [5–10 minutes]
4. *Now, rip up and throw your limiting beliefs into the trash can. Who would like to read one [or more] of their empowering beliefs to the class?* [5 minutes]
5. *[Quick-Write and/or Class Discussion]* When are times that it might be particularly important to remind yourself of these empowering beliefs? How can you remember to think these beliefs even at the most difficult times? So, what's the life lesson here for you? [e.g., "It isn't easy, but I can change my core beliefs."] *[10–20 minutes]*

Approximate Time: 20–40 minutes

Instructor Notes

Suggest that students carry their empowering belief cards with them or post them at home where they will see them often.

EXERCISE 23-3: Making Academic Course Corrections

Purpose

To help students become aware of and revise self-defeating behaviors, beliefs, and attitudes that get them off course in challenging college courses.

Supplies and Setup

"Making Academic Course Corrections" handout (page 186); students in pairs [Student A and Student B]

Directions

1. *Decide which of your present college courses is the most challenging for you. Then complete each of the 13 sentences on the handout as it relates to this challenging course. For example, if your most challenging course this semester is Math 110, you'd write "So far in Math 110 . . . (1) I've been absent four times." You will be sharing your answers with a partner. Obviously, to get value from this exercise, you must be honest.* [10 minutes]
2. *Partner A, read your completed sentences to Partner B. Afterward, Partner B, tell your partner any behaviors, beliefs, or attitudes you heard that might sabotage his or her success. Where possible, suggest more empowering behaviors, beliefs, or attitudes that your partner could choose.* [10 minutes]

3. *Switch roles, and repeat the same process.* [10 minutes]
4. [Quick-Write and/or Class Discussion] *Are there any changes you intend to make in your behaviors, beliefs, or attitudes? Why? What is the life lesson here for you?* [e.g., "If I don't notice when I am off course and make a course correction, then I become my own worst enemy."] [5–10 minutes]

Approximate Time: 25–30 minutes

Making Academic Course Corrections

Fill in the blank below with the name of a current college course that is the most challenging for you. Then complete the following sentences, letting your Inner Guide tell the truth.

So far in _____ . . .
     [course name]

1. I've been absent _____ times.

2. I've been late _____ times.

3. I've studied for this course an average of _____ hours per week.

4. I've completed _____ percent of the assignments.

5. I've done my work at _____ percent of my best effort.

6. I've participated actively in _____ percent of the classes I've attended.

7. I've attended _____ study group meetings.

8. I've attended _____ conferences with my instructor.

9. I've gotten tutoring for this subject _____ times this semester.

10. If I keep doing what I've been doing, the grade I'll probably get in this course is _____.

11. The advantages of my doing well in this course are . . .

12. The disadvantages of my doing poorly in this course are . . .

13. Changes I will make to improve my results in this course are . . .

EXERCISE 23-4: The Party Game

Purpose

To get students interacting with one another; to orient students to the importance of preferred people-environments in thinking about future careers; to help students find potential study buddies and/or study groups.

Supplies and Setup

Six pieces of paper with the letters R I A S E C on each piece, overhead transparency or handout of "The Party" (page 188).

Directions

1. [Announce to the class that you are all going to go to a "party." This should elicit cheers. Around the room, you have placed or taped pieces of paper with one of these letters on it: R I A S E C.]
2. [On a screen or white board, put up the diagram of "The Party Game." (You can copy the one on the next page.) Ask the students to read the six descriptors, and then go to the "lettered" area of the room where they would most like to "party" with people who share the same interests.]
3. [Once they are at a letter, ask the students to introduce themselves to their fellow partygoers. Ask them to talk about what they are attracted to: social or artistic ability, athletic or math and science ability, and so on. If there are any students standing alone by a letter, go over and have the same conversation with them. Once it appears that a good chat has occurred, give the next set of directions:] *Everyone in the corner you have chosen leaves for another party across town, except you. Find another corner and repeat the intros and chat.*
4. [Once they are it appears that this has occurred, repeat the instructions one last time.]
5. [After the third round, ask students to return to their seats and write down all three letters of the hexagon "corners" in the order that they visited. Guide the conversation about what they observed—did they encounter the same student(s) in all three groups? Could one of them be a potential study buddy or study team member?]
6. [Then, if you wish, you can take this conversation further and talk about possible careers or majors, using a variety of websites that discuss Holland codes. My favorite is the University of Missouri website, which has (with permission) titled this the "Career Interests" game: http://career.missouri.edu/students/majors-careers/skills-interests/career-interest-game/.]

Approximate Time: 25–30 minutes

Instructor Notes

1. I really play this up in the introduction of the activity as a fun party. I also suggest to students that they really do know the type of environment with which they are comfortable, and to trust their instincts.
2. Dick Bolles, author of *What Color Is Your Parachute?*, has written about the importance of environmental factors as a part of career planning. Learning about the environment in which we would most like to work, including the kind of people we are surrounded by, is a fun activity for the next class meeting after the activity.
3. The late Dr. John L. Holland believed that there are six primary people/environments. They are referenced in your *On Course* textbook in the "Self-Awareness at Work" section. Dr. Holland also created the *Self-Directed Search* assessment, also referenced in the text.

Source: Submitted by Lea Beth Lewis, California State Fullerton, CA. Adapted from *What Color Is Your Parachute?* by Richard Nelson Bolles

Realistic:
People who have athletic or mechanical ability, prefer to work with objects, machines, tools, or animals, or prefer to be outdoors.

Investigative:
People who like to observe, learn, investigate, analyze, evaluate, or solve problems.

Conventional:
People who like to work with data, have clerical or numerical ability, and who carry things out in detail or follow through on others' instructions.

Artistic:
People who have artistic, innovating, or intuitive abilities, and like to work in unstructured situations, using their imagination or creativity.

Enterprising:
People who like to work with people— influencing, persuading or performing, or leading or managing for organizational goals or for economic gain.

Social:
People who like to work with people— to inform, enlighten, help, train, develop, or cure them, or who are skilled with words.

Imagine walking into a room in which a party is taking place. At this party, people with the same or similar interests have (for some reason) all gathered in the same corner of the room.

1. Which corner of the room would you instinctively be drawn to as the group of people you would most enjoy being with for the longest time? (Leave aside any question of shyness, or whether you would have to talk to them.) Write the letter of that corner here: ☐

2. After 15 minutes, everyone in the corner you have chosen leaves for another party across town, except you. Of the groups that still remain now, which corner or group would you be drawn to the most, as the people you would most enjoy being with for the longest time? Write the letter of that corner here: ☐

3. After 15 minutes, everyone in the corner you have chosen leaves for another party across town, except you. Of the groups that still remain now, which corner or group would you be drawn to the most, as the people you would most enjoy being with for the longest time? Write the letter of that corner here: ☐

The three letters you just chose, in the three steps, are called your "Holland Code."

Journal Entry 24 Believing in Yourself: Write Your Own Rules

EXERCISE 24-1: Changing Habits

Purpose

To see that rules followed over time become habits; to identify and modify self-defeating habits and rules.

Supplies and Setup

Students sitting in pairs (Student A and Student B). Write the following three sentence stems on the board or display on a PowerPoint slide):
1. One habit I have that supports my success is . . .
2. One habit I have that hinders my success is . . .
3. One habit I would benefit from having is . . .

Directions

1. *Partner A will read and complete the three sentences until I call "Stop." For example, you might say . . .*
   1. *One habit I have that supports my success is . . . I always get places on time.*
   2. *One habit I have that hinders my success is . . . smoking cigarettes.*
   3. *One habit I would benefit from having is . . . exercising more.*

   Remember that habits include behaviors, thoughts, feelings, and beliefs. Keep going until I call stop.
2. *Partner B, tell Partner A what you heard him or her say. For example, "I heard you say that your smoking is a habit that hinders your success. And I heard you say that you always get places on time." [3–5 minutes]*
3. *[Reverse roles and repeat steps 1 and 2.] [3–5 minutes]*
4. *[Quick-Write and/or Class Discussion] What are some of the habits you mentioned that support your success? That hinder your success? Are there any habits that you would like to get rid of? Are there any new habits that you would like to adopt? How could you do that? [e.g., doing a 32-day commitment] How are habits like rules? What is the life lesson here for you? [e.g., "I need to make a habit of not letting habits run my life."] [10–15 minutes]*

Approximate Time: 15–30 minutes

Instructor Notes

An important point to bring out in the discussion is that the rules we adopt—whether consciously or unconsciously—eventually turn into habits. It isn't easy to adopt a new habit or eliminate an old habit, but, with the exercise of intention and self-discipline, we can choose to do that. You may wish to conclude this activity by inviting students to make a 32-day commitment (Journal Entry 15) to create a new empowering habit or extinguish an old self-sabotaging one.

EXERCISE 24-2: Role Model Rules

Purpose

To identify a role model who demonstrates excellence in the way he or she lives and to determine the habits or rules this person uses to create success.

Supplies and Setup

Students in groups of three with pens and journals or paper.

Directions

1. *Write the name of a person who, in your opinion, has created success. This role model can be anyone, whether you know the person or not.* [1–2 minutes]

2. *Under your role model's name, list all of the reasons why you chose this person. In other words, what has this person accomplished, and what does this person do consistently that impresses you?* [5 minutes]

3. *Given what your role model has accomplished and what this person does consistently, what are most likely his or her habits or rules for life? Make a list. For example, your role model's rules might include: "Do all tasks with excellence. Perform good deeds for others. Be cheerful."*

4. *Now, each person in your group reads aloud what you wrote, both why you chose your role model and what his or her rules may be. Choose one person to start and go clockwise until everyone has had a chance to read.* [10 minutes]

5. *[Quick-Write and/or Class Discussion] What did you learn about creating greater success in your life? Is there a rule you identified or heard that you would* not *want to adopt? Is there one new success rule you would benefit from adopting today? What's the life lesson here for you?* [e.g., "People don't get to be successful by accident; they operate by personal rules that act as an inner compass, and this compass keeps them on course."] [5–15 minutes]

Approximate Time: 25–40 minutes

Taking Tests

TAKING TESTS EXERCISE 1: THE TEST-SMART GAME

Purpose

To have students practice creating a test-smart plan.

Supplies and Setup

"Creating a Test-Smart Plan" handout (p. 190), one copy for each student. You may prefer to project each question (table) one at a time on a PowerPoint slide so students can't work ahead. Optional: prizes for members of the winning team.

Directions

1. [Place students in groups of three to five. You may want to ask students to name their team. Otherwise give each team a number and place the team name/number on the whiteboard.] [5 minutes]

2. [Discussion] *What does it mean to be "test-smart"?* [Lead discussion to the concept that being test-smart means knowing how to earn the maximum number of points possible on any test. As such, one of the most important elements of creating a test-smart plan is strategically allocating the available time to earn the most points possible. The best approach is to spend more time on high-point and easy questions and less time on low-point and difficult questions.] [5 minutes]

3. [Distribute the handout.] *On your handout, look at the example history test.* [Explain how the numbers in *each* column were derived. Confirm that students understand how to determine the following:
   A. Points available for each section of the test,
   B. Percent of total possible points for each section of the test, and
   C. The number of minutes that should then be allocated for each section of the test.] [5 minutes]

4. *We're now going to play the Test-Smart Game. Starting with Test 1: Mathematics, fill in the test-smart answers as a team. When you think you have all the answers correct for Test 1, place your paper face down and shout "Done." The round will be over when all teams have placed their answer sheets face down and shouted "Done." I'll keep track of the order of finishers. Starting with the first team done, we'll check the answers. If all of the answers for the test are correct, the first team done will earn points. If any answer is incorrect, we'll move on to the answers of the second team to call*

"Done." We'll keep going until we get to a team with all correct answers or until all teams are eliminated. If a team gets all correct answers, points will be awarded as follows:

First team to call Done: 10 points

Second team to call Done: 8 points

Third team to call Done: 6 points

Fourth team to call Done: 4 points

Fifth team to call Done: 2 points

Sixth team (and beyond) to call Done: 1 point

Questions? Start with Test 1: Mathematics Test. Begin! [15 minutes for first round]

5. [Keep track of the order in which teams turn over their answer sheets. When all teams have turned their answer sheets face down, check and discuss answers starting with the first team to turn its answer sheet face down. Discuss why answers are correct or incorrect. Track points earned for each team and offer kudos—or prizes—to the winning team.]

6. [Repeat steps 4 and 5 for Tests 2–4. If you wish, give a prize for the winning team.] [10–30 minutes, depending on number of additional rounds]

7. [Discussion] *What's the lesson here for being test-smart?* [5 minutes]

Approximate Time: 45–65 minutes

Creating a Test-Smart Plan

Test: History (example) Total Time: 60 minutes; possible points: 100	Points available for this section	Percent of total possible points	Minutes for this section
Part 1: 25 true/false questions (1 point each)	25	25%	15
Part 2: 5 short-answer questions (5 points each)	25	25%	15
Part 3: 2 essay questions (25 points each)	50	50%	30
Total	100	100%	60

Test 1: Mathematics Total Time: 60 minutes; possible points: 100	Points available for this section	Percent of total possible points	Minutes for this section
Part 1: 25 true/false questions (1 point each)			
Part 2: 5 word problems (15 points each)			
Total			

Test 2: Literature Total Time: 60 minutes; possible points: 100	Points available for this section	Percent of total possible points	Minutes for this section
Part 1: 30 matching questions (1 point each)			
Part 2: 5 short-answer questions (10 points each)			
Part 3: 2 essay questions (10 points each)			
Total			

Test 3: Biology Total Time: 80 minutes; possible points: 100	Points available for this section	Percent of total possible points	Minutes for this section
Part 1: 10 fill-in-the-blank questions (5 points each)			
Part 2: 10 short-answer questions (4 points each)			
Part 3: 1 essay question (10 points)			
Total			

Test 4: Sociology Total Time: 100 minutes; possible points: 250	Points available for this section	Percent of total possible points	Minutes for this section
Part 1: 1 essay questions (85 points)			
Part 2: 15 matching questions (3 points each)			
Part 3: 5 short-answer questions (5 points each)			
Part 4: 20 multiple-choice questions (4 points each)			
Part 5: 15 true/false questions (1 point each)			
Total			

Creating a Test-Smart Plan (Answers)

Test: History (example) Total Time: 60 minutes; possible points: 100	Points available for this section	Percent of total possible points	Minutes for this section
Part 1: 25 true/false questions (1 point each)	25	25%	15
Part 2: 5 short-answer questions (5 points each)	25	25%	15
Part 3: 2 essay questions (25 points each)	50	50%	30
Total	100	100%	60

Test 1: Mathematics Total Time: 60 minutes; possible points: 100	Points available for this section	Percent of total possible points	Minutes for this section
Part 1: 25 true/false questions (1 point each)	25	25%	15
Part 2: 5 word problems (15 points each)	75	75%	45
Total	100	100%	60

Test 2: Literature Total Time: 60 minutes; possible points: 100	Points available for this section	Percent of total possible points	Minutes for this section
Part 1: 30 matching questions (1 point each)	30	30%	18
Part 2: 5 short-answer questions (10 points each)	50	50%	30
Part 3: 2 essay questions (10 points each)	20	20%	12
Total	100	100%	60

Test 3: Biology Test Total Time: 80 minutes; possible points: 100	Points available for this section	Percent of total possible points	Minutes for this section
Part 1: 10 fill-in-the-blank questions (5 points each)	50	50%	40
Part 2: 10 short-answer questions (4 points each)	40	40%	32
Part 3: 1 essay questions (10 points)	10	10%	8
Total	100	100%	80

Test 4: Sociology Total Time: 100 minutes; possible points: 250	Points available for this section	Percent of total possible points	Minutes for this section
Part 1: 1 essay questions (85 points)	85	34%	34
Part 2: 15 matching questions (3 points each)	45	18%	18
Part 3: 5 short-answer questions (5 points each)	25	10%	10
Part 4: 20 multiple-choice questions (4 points each)	80	32%	32
Part 5: 15 true/false questions (1 point each)	15	6%	6
Total	250	100%	100

TAKING TESTS EXERCISE 2: TEST DEBRIEF

Purpose

To have students practice analyzing a past test to determine where points were lost and to make a test-smart plan for improving their score on future tests.

Supplies and Setup

Assign students to bring a copy of a graded test they have taken during the semester. If they have more than one to choose from, they should choose the one on which they got the lowest score. Have students open to the Test Debrief in *On Course* (in Chapter 6 Wise Choices in College sections). Students sitting in pairs.

Directions

1. *Decide who will be Partner A and who will be Partner B. Partner A will be the interviewer in the first round. Partner A, your role as the interviewer is to use your very best questioning and listening skills to help Partner B honestly and accurately fill in the Points Lost on the Test Debrief sheet. Be sure all points lost total the number of points lost on the actual test. You'll have five minutes.* [5 minutes]
2. *Switch roles. Partner B, interview Partner A and help him or her honestly and accurately fill in the Points Lost on the Test Debrief sheet. Once again, be sure all points lost total the same number of points lost on the actual test. You'll have five minutes.* [5 minutes]
3. *Partner A, now help Partner B identify the test-taking problems that cost him or her the most points and make a list of three things to do differently to improve the score on the next test. You'll have 10 minutes.* [10 minutes]
4. *Switch roles. Partner B, now help Partner A identify the test-taking problems that cost him or her the most points and make a list of three things to do differently to improve the score on the next test. You'll have 10 minutes.* [10 minutes]
5. *[Discussion] What were the problems that cost you the most points on the test? Did you uncover any problems that cost you points on the test but are not one of the seven listed on the Test Debrief? What will you do differently to improve your score on the next test?* [10–20 minutes]

Approximate Time: 40–50 Minutes

Instructor Notes

1. Consider listing on the board the test-taking problems and solutions the students identify during the discussion.
2. Consider asking students to report on the results they create on their next tests, discussing what they did differently and how well their new skills worked to improve their test scores.

TAKING TESTS EXERCISE 3: MARKING UP EXAMS

Purpose

Students learn that paying close attention to key words within questions can help them feel confident in the answers they choose.

Supplies and Setup

Document camera, copies of the list of questions on page 196.

Directions

1. Prior to class, assign the Wise Choices in College: Taking Tests part of Chapter 6 as a reading.
2. Divide students into groups (two to three students per group works best). Give each group a test question from the list of questions. Ask the groups to read Strategy 7 "Answer Multiple Choice Questions," then decide which strategy/strategies would apply to the test question they were given. Then, they discuss how they would mark up this test question to help them reach the answer.

3. When all students have an answer, one student from each group comes forward with the group's question and places it on the document camera. Then, after reading the question out loud to the class, they mark up the test question as their group discussed, explaining to the class *why* they are marking up the test question in the manner that they are.

Approximate Time: 25–45 minutes (depending on the length of discussion time)

Instructor Notes

1. The questions included are the ones I use because they show very common examples of "types" of questions (question 1 has absolute words in three of the responses, all incorrect; question 2, uses the word *conclusively*, which students forget is an absolute word; question 3 is a good example of "choose the *best* answer" as well as "treat the question as a short answer and see if an option matches"; question 4 shows that you only need to prove two things are correct in an "all of the above" question (and that "none of the above" is typically a distracter); and question 5 is perfect for using the "true/false" technique.
2. Ideally, if all your students are enrolled in a different class together, asking the instructor to give you an old exam and choose examples from that exam would be most meaningful. The key is to ask the students to explain *why* a particular option is incorrect.

Source: Submitted by Melanie Marine, University of Wisconsin–Oshkosh, WI.

Sample Multiple-Choice Test Questions

1. Most psychologists agree that

   A. children who grow up in institutions have no chance of succeeding in life.

   B. domestic violence is a behavior that is always found in boys from fatherless homes.

   C. those who receive little love and caring during infancy usually have personality difficulties.

   D. those who were not abused as children never abuse their children.

2. At the present time, there are relatively few women in positions of corporate management. One reason for this is

   A. until five years ago, no women had completed an MBA program.

   B. research has proven conclusively that women do not possess the skills required for corporate leadership.

   C. women have no interest in pursuing careers in management.

   D. there has been a general lack of formal and informal corporate programs for development of women as managers.

3. Milk is considered an excellent food because it

   A. tastes very good to many people.

   B. is relatively cheap considering that it is a superior food product.

   C. contains many vitamins and minerals.

   D. is used in the preparation of a variety of food products.

4. Which of the following cities is (are) in the state of New York?

   A. Syracuse

   B. Rome

   C. Albany

   D. All of the above

   E. None of the above

5. Among the causes of slow reading are

   A. lack of comprehension.

   B. reading word by word rather than in phrases.

   C. poorly developed vocabulary.

   D. too few fixations per line.

   E. A and B.

   F. A, B, and C.

   G. all of the above.

Embracing Change: Do One Different Thing This Week

Creators do all they can to become aware of the habits of thought, emotion, and behavior that sabotage their success. With this awareness, they take steps to revise any self-sabotaging habit patterns or beliefs, empowering them to create greater success. Experiment with being more self-aware by picking ONE of the following new beliefs or behaviors and trying it for one week:

1. Think: "I am choosing habit patterns and core beliefs that support my success."
2. Identify a "strange choice" that someone else makes and consider what belief about themselves, other people, or life would generate such a choice.
3. Identify a choice I make that someone else might think is "strange" and consider what belief about myself, other people, or life would cause me to make such a choice.
4. Identify an area of my life in which I am off course (even a little).
5. Identify a behavior that gets me off course and replace it with one that is more self-supporting.
6. Identify a thought that gets me off course and replace it with one that is more self-supporting.
7. Identify an emotion that gets me off course and replace it with one that is more self-supporting.
8. Identify a belief that gets me off course and replace it with one that is more self-supporting.
9. Identify the experience that I most enjoyed this week and identify careers that would provide similar experiences on a regular basis.
10. Review my personal rules (Journal Entry 25) and identify which ones I kept that day.
11. Do a self-assessment of my hard skills, soft skills, and preferences for work.
12. Your choice: A different belief or behavior you learned in this chapter with which you would like to experiment.

Now, write the one you chose under "My Commitment" in the following chart. Then, track yourself for one week, putting a check in the appropriate box when you keep your commitment. After seven days, assess your results. If your outcomes and experiences improve, you now have a tool you can use to improve your self-awareness for the rest of your life.

My Commitment						
Day 1	Day 2	Day 3	Day 4	Day 5	Day 6	Day 7

During my seven-day experiment, what happened?

As a result of what happened, what did I learn or relearn?

Chapter 6: Quiz Questions

(Please visit the Instructor Companion website for *On Course* at login.cengage.com or contact your local Cengage Learning sales representative to find electronic versions of the Quiz Questions.)

31. Recognizing When You Are Off Course

1. Leverrier predicted that an invisible planet was pulling the planet Uranus off its predicted course around the sun. Likewise, human beings are pulled off course by the invisible forces of their

   A. conscious minds.

   B. unconscious minds.

   C. Inner Guides.

2. Some people sabotage their goals and dreams by unconsciously choosing actions, thoughts, and/or emotions that get them off course from their goals and dreams.   TRUE   FALSE

3. When Creators are off course, they tend to deny it, make excuses, blame others, or give up.   TRUE   FALSE

4. One characteristic of Creators is that they are able to recognize and acknowledge when they are off course.   TRUE   FALSE

5. The story of Jerome, the accounting student, illustrates that once a person has a clear goal, he or she will not get off course.   TRUE   FALSE

32. Identifying Your Scripts

1. Eric Berne, the creator of a mode of counseling called Transactional Analysis, referred to our invisible inner forces as

   A. defense mechanisms.

   B. patterns.

   C. habits.

   D. scripts.

2. As part of our individual script, each of us has developed three kinds of habit patterns: behaviors, thoughts, and emotions.   TRUE   FALSE

3. Our habit patterns are motivated by our unconscious core _____.

4. We seem to create our scripts as a result of

   A. how others responded to us.

   B. what significant adults said to us.

   C. observing the behavior of significant adults in our lives.

   D. all of the above.

5. The purpose of our scripts is to maximize our pain and minimize our pleasure.   TRUE   FALSE

33. Rewriting Your Outdated Scripts

1. Diana, the student in the author's writing course, had a script from her childhood that said her brain didn't work well.   TRUE   FALSE

2. When our core beliefs about ourselves, about other people, or about the world are inaccurate, they can sabotage our success.   TRUE   FALSE

3. Diana's core beliefs about her inability to think caused her to hear what she expected to hear rather than what her teacher actually said.   TRUE   FALSE

4. Although it is not easy, human beings can revise their limiting beliefs and change their self-defeating habit patterns.   TRUE   FALSE

5. The parts of our scripts that are available to our conscious minds are our patterns of self-defeating actions, thoughts, and emotions. By revising these three patterns we can help revise our limiting core _____.

34. On Course at Work: Self-Awareness at Work

1. "Hard skills" are the special-knowledge skills that you've learned to do throughout your life—for example, swimming, writing, solving math problems, building a house, creating a budget, backpacking, playing chess, and reading.   TRUE   FALSE

2. "Soft skills" are the ones you have developed to cope with life—for example, making choices as a Creator, motivating yourself, being persistent, developing mutually supportive relationships, and believing in yourself.   TRUE   FALSE

3. The Holland Code is an inventory of personal preferences that can assist you in understanding your outdated scripts.   TRUE   FALSE

4. If you have not yet declared a major, where can you go on campus to take one of the inventories recommended in *On Course*?

   A. Your advisor's office

   B. The Registrar's office

   C. The Student Union

   D. The Career Center

5. Becoming aware of the match between _____ improves your chances of finding a satisfying career match.

   A. your desired income level and your preferred location

   B. your interests and your personality

   C. your family's plans and your need to work near them

   D. your personality and your desired income level

35. Believing in Yourself: Write Your Own Rules

1. According to psychologist Virginia Satir, we are all living by rules, although we may not be aware of them.   TRUE   FALSE

2. All of the unconscious rules that we live by need to be revised.   TRUE   FALSE

3. The author of *On Course* has polled thousands of college instructors who identify three behaviors that their most successful students do consistently. Which of the following is NOT one of these top three behaviors of successful students (though it may be a good rule nonetheless)?

   A. Attend every class from beginning to end.

   B. Seek help from tutors.

   C. Do their best work on all assignments.

   D. Participate actively in class.

4. At Baltimore City Community College, a study found that, on average, the more classes that students *missed*, the higher their grades were, especially in introductory courses.   TRUE   FALSE

5. A personal rule is your conscious intention. You may need to break one of your rules if something of a higher _____ conflicts with it.

36. Wise Choices in College: Taking Tests

1. Factors that determine how well you score on tests include preparation for the test, test-taking skills, and use of feedback on prior tests.   TRUE   FALSE

2. Test scores are not a good way of determining if you are off course in college.   TRUE   FALSE

3. Visualizing yourself successfully taking a test prepares you to think, feel, and act positively during that test.   TRUE   FALSE

4. It's a good idea to stay up all night studying before a test and use every available minute for preparation.   TRUE   FALSE

5. Before you begin answering questions on a test, take a few minutes to preview it.   TRUE   FALSE

Chapter 6: Essay Topics

1. One of the most valuable skills of successful people is their ability to identify the life roles in which they are off course and design a plan to get back on course. Write an essay in which you identify the life role in which you are the most off course. Discuss what you believe is the underlying cause (self-defeating patterns and limiting core beliefs) of your being off course in this role, and present a detailed plan of action for getting back on course. Let your plan contain both outer steps (changes in behaviors) and inner steps (changes in beliefs and attitudes).

2. We human beings are creatures of habit. Some of our habits (or patterns) support our success, whereas others get us off course from our goals and dreams. Write an essay in which you thoroughly explore one of your limiting patterns of behaviors, thoughts, or feelings. Then discuss how you may have come to adopt this pattern, and explain how this pattern hinders you in the pursuit of a rich, personally fulfilling life. Finally, discuss a plan for changing this pattern so that you can stay on course to your goals and dreams.

3. We adopted many of our present beliefs during our childhoods. We learned these beliefs from our parents and other significant adults. These beliefs—some empowering, some disempowering—often remain unconscious, and they control what we do, think, and feel. Identify one or more of your limiting beliefs, discuss how you may have come to believe it, and explain how it has limited you in the past. Finally, explain what you plan to do to revise this belief so that you can change the outcome of your future.

4. Too many people set goals for themselves that are below what they are capable of achieving. Examine your present goals and consider if you have undershot your true potential. If you now believe that you have chosen goals that are too modest, write an essay in which you explore your belief system to uncover the limiting core beliefs that are holding you back. Explore where these beliefs may have come from, and suggest what you plan to do to raise your goals in line with your true abilities.

5. Olympic gold medalist Jesse Owens said, "The battles that count aren't the ones for gold medals. The struggles within yourself—the invisible, inevitable battles inside all of us—that's where it's at." In an essay to be read by your classmates in this course, explore your own inner struggles. What inner forces have you done battle with, what has the battle been about, which side is presently winning, and what do you plan to do to triumph?

6. Children learn many of their inner rules from parents, other significant adults, and from others in their culture. Identify a child who is important to you (perhaps even one not yet born) and write a formal essay that you will present on his or her 21st birthday. In this essay, inform him or her about the most important rules you have chosen to create a rich, personally fulfilling life.

7. Using the student essays in *On Course* as a model, write an essay about how you used a strategy from Chapter 6 to overcome a problem in your life—academic, personal, or even at work. First explain the problem; then discuss the strategy you used and how; finally, identify what happened. Your instructor may submit your essay for possible publication in the next edition of *On Course*. Additional directions for writing and submitting these essays can be found at http://oncourseworkshop.com.

Answer Key to Chapter 6 Quiz Questions

31. Recognizing When You Are Off Course

Answers: 1. B   2. TRUE   3. FALSE   4. TRUE   5. FALSE

32. Identifying Your Scripts

Answers: 1. D   2. TRUE   3. beliefs   4. D   5. FALSE (The opposite is true.)

33. Rewriting Your Outdated Scripts

Answers: 1. TRUE   2. TRUE   3. TRUE   4. TRUE   5. beliefs

34. On Course at Work: Self-Awareness at Work

Answers: 1. TRUE   2. TRUE   3. FALSE (the Holland Code helps you match your interests with career choices.)
4. D   5. B

35. Believing in Yourself: Write Your Own Rules

Answers: 1. TRUE   2. FALSE (Some of our unconscious rules are helpful.)   3. B   4. FALSE (The more classes students missed, the lower their grades were.)   5. value

36. Wise Choices in College: Taking Tests

Answers: 1. TRUE   2. FALSE   3. TRUE   4. FALSE   5. TRUE

Adopting Lifelong Learning

Concept

Many students have lost the insatiable curiosity and effective learning strategies that served them so well as young children. For them, exciting forays into the mysteries of the unknown have been replaced by boredom, anxiety, and/or self-doubt. By (re)familiarizing struggling students with the skills of effective learners, we offer them the opportunity to replace their ineffective choices with more effective choices that can enable them to reach their potential. Additionally, by helping struggling students replace a fixed mindset (in which they believe there's little they can do to improve their academic success) with a growth mindset (in which they believe that hard work and persistence will improve their academic success), we empower them to make choices that improve their learning and academic success. In other words, in addition to teaching academic content, we need to help struggling students regain a learner's mindset and master the study skills they need to be a success in college . . . and a lifelong learner in the years beyond graduation.

EMPOWERS STUDENTS TO . . .

1. Adopt a learning orientation to life, willingly changing approaches that get them off course and actively learning new approaches that keep them on course.
2. Exchange a fixed mindset for a growth mindset.
3. Discover their preferred way of learning.
4. Become critical thinkers.
5. Learn what they need to know to accomplish their greatest goals and dreams.

Remember also to use the all-purpose exercises mentioned in the Introduction, actively engaging students in the exploration of JOURNAL ENTRIES, CASE STUDIES, ONE STUDENT'S STORY, ON COURSE AT WORK, QUOTATIONS, CARTOONS, FOCUS QUESTIONS, CHAPTER-OPENING CHARTS, and STUDY SKILLS. Remind students to use letters to label any in-class writing they do in their journals.

Case Study in Critical Thinking: A Fish Story

Purpose

To use critical thinking skills and a growth mindset to practice extracting valuable lessons from every experience, thus developing into effective lifelong learners.

Supplies and Setup

"A Fish Story" in *On Course;* journals; chime.

Directions

1. [Have students read "A Fish Story." One way to be sure everyone has read the selection before taking the next step is to have one student read the first paragraph aloud, another student read the second, and so on until the reading is complete.] [5 minutes]
2. *In your journal, quick-write an answer to the question at the bottom of the story: "If you had been in this biology lab class, what lessons about college and life would you have learned from the experience?"* [5 minutes]
3. [Put students in pairs.] *Partner A, read to your partner the lessons you learned about college and life. Partner B, respond with your best active listening skills, reflecting what you heard and asking for clarification or expansion. When I ring the chime, change roles: B reads, and A is the active listener.* [5 minutes]
4. [Have A's switch partners, creating new pairs, and repeat step 3 with their new partners. Switch and repeat step 3 as often as time allows.] [5–25 minutes]
5. *Look at what you wrote originally and take a few minutes to see if you can now dive deeper. Write new insights you think you could have learned from the experience with the fish.* [5 minutes]
6. [Quick-Write and/or Class Discussion] *What is the most important lesson that you drew from the experience in the biology lab? What lessons did others draw from the experience that you didn't think of? What did you learn from this discussion about how people create meaning from experience? What is the life lesson for you?* [e.g., "The deeper I dive, the richer are the learning rewards."] [5–10 minutes]

Approximate Time: 30–55 minutes

Instructor Notes

1. Point worth making: Human beings are "meaning makers." When we have an experience, we invent what it means to us. We see a present experience through the lens of our past experiences, and that shapes the meaning we make. Many "meanings" are embedded in any one experience, and Creators seek the meaning that best supports their success. This will occasionally require them to revise their answers or beliefs about themselves, other people, or the world.
2. A variation is to have students write new insights and discoveries (step 5) in their journals after each pair discussion.
3. See Exercise 4-3 for another use of "A Fish Story."

Journal Entry 25 Developing a Learning Orientation to Life

EXERCISE 25-1: The Choice Evaluation Process

Purpose

To gain important life lessons from a past mistake or a broken commitment.

Supplies and Setup

Handouts listing the six steps of the Choice Evaluation Process (in the Instructor Notes section), one for each student; students sitting in pairs (Partner A and Partner B); journals.

Directions

1. *What is a mistake?* [Guide the discussion to the idea that a mistake is a choice that gets us off course.] *Everyone makes mistakes. Victims rarely learn anything from their mistakes, so they keep making them over and over. Creators, on the other hand, learn from their mistakes, so they seldom repeat the same mistake. Their course corrections typically get Creators quickly back on course and teach them important life lessons.* [To illustrate this perspective on mistakes, consider sharing a mistake that you have made in your life, especially as an undergraduate, to get students thinking about the mistakes they have made. An alternative is to remind students about the mistakes that the authors of the One Student's Story essays report making.] [5 minutes]

2. *Now I'd like you to describe briefly in writing a mistake that you have made in your life. If possible, choose a mistake you made this semester in college. You will be sharing your mistake with one other person.* [5 minutes]

3. *In a moment you and your partner will use the Choice Evaluation Process to explore a mistake that one of you made. If you are the person asking the questions of the Choice Evaluation Process, use your active listening skills to help your partner dive deep into exploring the mistake. Here's what this might look like.* [Do a DEMO of the Choice Evaluation Process, perhaps using one of your own mistakes.] *You'll have 20 minutes with your partner, which may be only enough time to explore one person's mistake. However, if you get through quickly, feel free to switch roles and examine the other person's mistake. Any questions? Ready, begin.* [20 minutes]

4. [Quick-Write and/or Class Discussion] *What was your experience of doing the Choice Evaluation Process? What lesson did you learn from your mistake?* [e.g., "Sometimes I make choices based on what is convenient at the time rather than on what is best for accomplishing my goals."] [10–20 minutes]

Approximate Time: 40–50 minutes

Instructor Notes

1. Here are the six steps of the Choice Evaluation Process:
   1. What mistake did you make?
   2. What other choices could you have made?
   3. What's the likely outcome of each other choice?
   4. What choice(s) will you make if you face a similar situation in the future?
   5. Have you ever made a similar choice in the past? In other words, is this choice part of a pattern in your life?
   6. What's the life lesson for you?

2. You'll notice that the Choice Evaluation Process is similar to the Wise Choice Process from Chapter 2. Whereas the Wise Choice Process helps students make a wise choice in the *future*, the Choice Evaluation Process helps them examine a *past* choice and (A) discover more positive options, and (B) learn an important life lesson (so they don't repeat a self-sabotaging choice in the future). If students have difficulty coming up with an answer for step 1 (a mistake they made), they may be able to find one by revisiting their answers to "Making Academic Course Corrections" in Exercise 23-3. Or you might suggest a questionable choice that you have seen the student make: "I notice you've been absent five times already this semester. Could that be a mistake?"

3. A variation of the Choice Evaluation Process creates valuable lessons from a broken commitment. This is particularly appropriate if you had your students create course commitments earlier in the semester. The only change is in step 1.
   1. What commitment did you break?
   2. (Continue with steps 2–6 above.)

4. Another variation of the Choice Evaluation Process can be used to debrief the One Student's Story essays. Thanks to June Poman of Union County College (NJ) for this suggestion:
   1. What mistake did the student in the essay make?
   2. What other choices could he or she have made?
   3. What would be the likely outcome of each of these other choices?
   4. Have you ever made a choice like the one the student in the essay made? Is this choice part of a pattern in your life?
   5. What choice would you make if you face a similar situation in your life?
   6. What's the life lesson for you?

EXERCISE 25-2: The Failure Toss

Purpose

To gain valuable insights from a failure.

Supplies and Setup

Pen and paper for each student; trash can; students in groups of five.

Directions

1. *Everyone has failed at something. Victims rarely learn anything from their failures; worse, they may develop a fixed mindset—a belief that their learning ability is fixed and cannot grow. Creators, on the other hand, learn from their failures and develop a growth mindset—a belief that hard work and perseverance will help them learn nearly anything they need to know.* [1 minute]

2. *Before we do this activity, let's define a "failure." What do you think a failure is?* [A definition I like is "A failure is what your Inner Critic calls those times when you didn't create a goal or dream exactly on schedule." This definition keeps the Inner Critic at bay. After discussing the definition of a failure, consider sharing a failure of your own and what you learned from it. This will DEMO for students what they are about to do.] [5 minutes]

3. *Please fold your sheet of paper in half vertically, creating two columns. At the top of the left-hand column, write the word FAILURES. Below that, write a list of your failures in school and in life. No one else is going to see your failures, so you can be totally honest with yourself. Number each failure.* [5 minutes]

4. *At the top of the right-hand column, write the word LIFE LESSONS. In that column, write the valuable life lesson you learned from each of your failures. For example, maybe failure 1 was "My first marriage ended after only eight months." Next to that you might write that life lesson 1 was "I learned that I can never depend on someone else to create my sense of security." Maybe failure 2 was "I flunked out of college the first time I enrolled five years ago." Next to that you might write that life lesson 2 was "I need to choose friends who have the same goals that I do." Add as many life lessons as you learned from each failure.* [5–10 minutes]

5. *Choose someone in your group to read one life lesson . . . but not the failure. Then keep going around your group clockwise, with each person reading one life lesson. Remember, don't mention how you learned the life lesson; just state it. Keep going around your group until all in your group have presented all of their life lessons or until I call time.* [5 minutes]

6. *Now tear your paper in half along the fold. This leaves you with your FAILURES in one hand and your LIFE LESSONS in the other. Now make a choice. You can:*
   1. *Keep both your FAILURES and your LIFE LESSONS.*
   2. *Throw away your FAILURES and keep your LIFE LESSONS.*
   3. *Keep your FAILURES and throw away your LIFE LESSONS.*
   4. *Throw away both your FAILURES and your LIFE LESSONS.*
   Make that choice and do it now. If you choose to throw anything away, toss it into the trash can. [3 minutes]

7. *[Quick-Write and/or Class Discussion] What choice did you make? Why? What is the life lesson here for you?* [e.g., "Every failure can be a powerful teacher, and I want to hang on to my hard-earned life lessons."] [10–20 minutes]

Approximate Time: 25–35 minutes

Instructor Notes

As a variation, you can have students title the left-hand column with any or all of these: Failures, Mistakes, Challenges, Obstacles, Adversities.

EXERCISE 25-3: Lessons from Your Obstacle

Purpose

To gain wisdom from an obstacle.

Supplies and Setup

Journals; chime. You may wish to play relaxing instrumental music during this activity.

Directions

1. *First, we're going to do a relaxation. Then, I am going to take you on a journey in your minds. So get comfortable in your chairs, close your eyes, and prepare to relax.* [Do a progressive relaxation technique. One of my favorites is to

ask students to breathe deeply and rhythmically while you invite them to tighten muscle groups one by one from the tips of their toes to the tops of their heads.] [5 minutes]

2. [After the relaxation, begin reading the following guided visualization, waiting about 10 seconds for any ellipses . . . and waiting about 20–30 seconds at a PAUSE.] *Now, in your mind, imagine that you are walking along a path at the foot of a majestic mountain . . . notice all the natural beauty that is around you . . . See the tall, green trees . . . Hear the birds singing . . . Smell the wonderful piney odor . . . Feel the soft grass beneath your feet . . . Now look up at the top of the mountain. There in the distance at the top of the mountain you see one of your most important goals. Get a clear picture of your goal waiting for you at the top of this beautiful mountain. Picture it clearly and exactly as it will look when you have achieved it. [PAUSE] Now notice that there is a path that leads from where you are now, a path that goes all the way up the mountain to your goal . . . As your eyes follow the path up, notice any challenging obstacle on your path to your goal: perhaps the obstacle is a person in your way . . . perhaps it is a health problem . . . or not enough time . . . or lack of money . . . Perhaps your obstacle is a self-defeating behavior pattern like procrastination, or substance abuse, or watching too much television . . . Perhaps it is a self-defeating thought pattern like negative self-talk, self-judgments, or self-criticism . . . Perhaps it is self-defeating emotional pattern like constant anger or sadness or depression . . . Or perhaps it is a limiting belief about yourself, about other people, or about the world . . . What is the biggest, most challenging obstacle standing in the way of reaching your goal? What does it look like? Picture it clearly now. [PAUSE] What if your obstacle were actually a great teacher that is in your life to teach you an important lesson? What would this teacher say to you? Take time right now to really listen to your obstacle . . . Listen for one sentence of advice from your obstacle . . . What lesson does your obstacle have to teach you? Listen now. [PAUSE] When you are ready, bring your awareness back to this room and open your eyes. In your journals, write any advice that your obstacle gave you.* [10 minutes]

3. [Have half of the students stand and move their chairs/desks to the edges of the room. This will leave half of the students sitting down with enough space between their chairs for the others to walk.]

4. *In a moment, those of you who are standing are going to whisper the wise advice your obstacle gave you to the people sitting. As soon as you have whispered your obstacle's advice to one person, move on to another person and whisper it again, and then move to another and another.* [DEMO] *For example, suppose your obstacle told you, "You would be happier and more successful if you stayed away from people who constantly criticize you."* [Whisper this advice into one student's ear, and then, modeling what the students will do, move on and repeat the same advice to another student, and another.] *Try to get to everyone, and if you do, then keep going, whispering to people a second time.* [5 minutes]

5. *When you hear the chime, reverse places. Those of you sitting will stand and move behind the chair you were sitting in, and those of you standing will sit in the first empty chair you see. The people now standing will immediately begin whispering their obstacle's wise advice in the ears of the people now sitting. Keep whispering the same advice to different people until you hear the chime a second time. Then find a seat and take a few moments think about the wisdom you've just heard from your obstacle and the obstacles of others. Feel free to write any of this wisdom in your journal. Are there any questions?* [The success of this activity requires that everyone understand the directions before beginning, so be extra sure everyone is ready.] *Ready, begin.* [3 minutes]

6. [Let the first round of whispered advice go for about three or four minutes. Ring the chime to signal reversing roles and allow another three or four minutes for the second round. Then ring the chime a last time and give students a few minutes to relax and reflect on the wisdom they have heard. [8 minutes]

7. [Quick-Write and/or Class Discussion] *What was that experience like for you? What wisdom did you hear from your obstacle? From other people's obstacles? What is the life lesson here for you?* [e.g., "I have a powerful Inner Guide, but I need to take the time to listen to its wisdom."] [10–20 minutes]

Approximate Time: 45–50 minutes

Instructor Notes

This activity sets up the "Affirmation Whisper" activity later in the course. The Affirmation Whisper—one of my students' favorites—will be even more powerful with this preparation.

Journal Entry 26 Discovering Your Preferred Learning Style

EXERCISE 26-1: My Favorite Teacher

Purpose

To discover ways of learning effectively when an instructor does not teach to the student's preferred way(s) of learning.

Supplies and Setup

Students take the *On Course* Learning Preference Self-Assessment in Chapter 7. This self-assessment is also available online in the College Success CourseMate website for *On Course*; optional: a DVD or video of the film *Ferris Bueller's Day Off* and equipment to play it. As of this writing, the scene to show can be found at YouTube.com by searching for "Boring Economics Teacher." The length of the scene is 1:13 minutes.

Directions

1. *Think of your favorite teacher of all time and make a list of what you specifically liked about his or her teaching. For example, maybe you liked that this teacher had you do group projects or maybe you liked that the teacher would eat lunch with students in the cafeteria and showed a personal interest in you.* [5 minutes]
2. *Now think of your least favorite teacher of all time and make a list of what you specifically disliked about his or her teaching. For example, maybe you disliked that this teacher lectured for the entire class period in a boring monotone voice or you disliked that this teacher made the class do too much group work.* [Optional: Here you might show the very brief and funny scene from *Ferris Bueller's Day Off* in which a teacher, played by Ben Stein, is lecturing badly on voodoo economics.] [5 minutes]
3. [Place students in four groups according to their preferred way of learning, as determined by their scores on the self-assessment.] *As a group, combine your lists of what you liked about your favorite teachers' classes and create one list. Then combine your lists of what you disliked about your least favorite teachers' classes and create a second list.* [10 minutes]
4. *Now, imagine that you are taking a class with an instructor who exhibits some or all of the characteristics of your least favorite teachers. Being Creators and using what you know about preferred ways of learning, come up with a list of what you could do in this class to learn the subject well and get a good grade in the course, despite the instructor.* [10 minutes]
5. [Group reports: Have volunteers from each group present a summary of their preferred way of learning and one strategy for learning when an instructor isn't teaching to that preferred way of learning. If there is time, have each group present a second strategy for how to learn when an instructor isn't teaching to their preferred way of learning.] [10–20 minutes]
6. [Quick-Write and/or Class Discussion] *Which of these ideas will you try? Why?* [5–15 minutes]

Approximate Time: 45–65 minutes

Instructor Notes

In step 5, you may wish to point out those instances when one group says it doesn't like a teaching approach, but another group says that it does.

EXERCISE 26-2: Fine-Tuning Study Methods

Purpose

To discover new and appealing study strategies for maximizing learning in college.

Supplies and Setup

Students in groups of four to five, each with pen and paper; whiteboard or easel pad and markers

Directions

1. *Most students have developed at least some strategies to help them study effectively. In your group, discuss your favorite study strategies. Later, one person will share some of your group's best ideas with the whole class. You won't know who the group reporter is until I call on you, so everyone needs to record all suggestions. This is a good time to practice your best note-taking techniques.* [10–15 minutes]
2. *Now let's have a spokesperson report each group's best ideas.* [Choose a spokesperson from each group to report. As you record the ideas on the whiteboard or on an easel pad, you may want to have a student recorder make a copy that could later be copied and distributed. Consider grouping strategies into categories of *before*, *while*, and *after* studying.] [10–15 minutes]
3. [Quick-Write and/or Class Discussion] *Which of these study strategies will you try? What appeals to you about this strategy? How well does this study strategy complement your preferred ways of learning?* [10–15 minutes]

Approximate Time: 30–45 minutes

Journal Entry 27 Employing Critical Thinking

EXERCISE 27-1: The Logic of Advertising

Purpose

To practice analyzing a persuasive argument.

Supplies and Setup

A handout for each student with a copy of a magazine or newspaper advertisement duplicated on the upper half of the page. On the bottom half of the page, create three stacked rectangles (like a triple-layer cake) labeled REASONS (top rectangle), EVIDENCE (middle rectangle), and CONCLUSION (bottom rectangle). Place students in groups of three or four. Before this activity, they should have completed reading and writing Journal Entry 27.

Directions

1. [Distribute the handout.] *You'll recall from your reading in* On Course *that an argument is made up of Reasons, Evidence, and Conclusions. To what conclusion does this advertisement want you to come?* [Buy the particular product or service in the advertisement.] *Go ahead and write that in the box labeled "Conclusion." Now we're going to see how well the logic of this advertisement stands up to critical thinking.* [5 minutes]
2. *In your groups, fill in the boxes for Reasons and Evidence. In other words, in the advertisement, what reasons are given for buying this product or service? And what evidence is offered that the product or service will address those reasons?*

After you have filled in the Reasons and Evidence boxes, see if the conclusion is logical. [A DEMO here is very helpful. For example, you could offer another advertisement—perhaps projected on a PowerPoint slide—and explain the reasons, evidence, and conclusions presented or not presented in it.] [15 minutes]

3. [Lead a discussion regarding the logic of the advertisement. Keep emphasizing the importance of finding the unstated reasons, of identifying and assessing the evidence offered, and of evaluating the logic of the argument. Be sure that students consider both the verbal (text) and nonverbal (visual) elements of the advertisement. Help students see how the advertisement may appeal more to emotion than to logic. (e.g., If you buy this car, you'll be more popular.)] [10–20 minutes]

4. [Quick-Write and/or Class Discussion] *What is the life lesson here for you?* [e.g., "Much advertising is not logical at all. Instead it seeks to create a positive experience and have consumers associate that positive experience with the product."] [5–15 minutes]

Approximate Time: 35–55 minutes

Instructor Notes

1. After having students analyze the logic of print ads, you can have them do the same thing with television commercials. You can either play a recorded commercial or show one found on www.YouTube.com. You may need to play the advertisement a couple of times to help students see the subtle and quick-moving persuasive strategies used in commercials. One commercial available on YouTube that I like for this purpose is titled "Six Flags 'It's Playtime' commercial" (1:28 minutes).

2. Another option is to show a scene from a television show or Hollywood film in which an argument is presented. For example, www.YouTube.com has a number of scenes from the classic film *Twelve Angry Men*, in which jurors present one argument after another to persuade others of the guilt or innocence of a boy accused of killing his father. It makes a fascinating case study for critical thinking.

EXERCISE 27-2: RateMyProfessors.com

Purpose

To practice asking probing questions.

Supplies and Setup

"RateMyProfessors.com" handout (p. 210). Before this activity, students should have completed Journal Entry 27.

Directions

1. *How many of you are familiar with the website RateMyProfessors.com? Who'll tell us about this site?* [Have a volunteer explain that this website offers students the opportunity to rate professors on a scale of 1 (low) to 5 (high) for the following criteria: Easiness, Helpfulness, Clarity, Rater Interest, Hotness, and Overall Quality. Students can then add any comments they wish in order to explain their ratings.] [5 minutes]

2. [Place students in pairs and provide the handout.] *By way of example, here are ratings and comments posted on RateMyProfessors.com for two professors. Professor 1 received an average rating of 5 for Overall Quality, the highest score possible. Professor 2 received an average rating of 1 for Overall Quality, the lowest score possible. Let's take a look at the comments that students said about these professors.* [Have volunteers read the six comments aloud.] *It might appear easy to decide to take a course with Professor 1 and to avoid a course taught by Professor 2. However, a critical thinker would want additional information and would employ probing questions to gather that information.* [5 minutes]

3. *You'll recall from your reading assignment that arguments are made up of reasons, evidence, and conclusions.* [Write these three terms on the whiteboard for reference.] *With your partner, brainstorm a list of probing questions that you might ask the students who wrote these comments. The goal of your questions is to uncover any information that would provide a reason to reject the conclusions of the raters. In other words, you are seeking to uncover a hidden truth.* [10 minutes]

4. *Now, we're going to make a list on the board of your probing questions.* [As students offer questions, ask them to explain what they are after—are they questioning the reasons, evidence, and/or conclusions? What do they hope to

discover that might contradict the high or low scores? For example, a question might be "What grade did you get in the course?" What the question may be designed to determine is whether the student is praising the teacher because of a high grade or criticizing the teacher because of a low grade. In other words, the reason for the student's comment is the grade, not the professor's ability to teach.] [10–20 minutes]

5. [Quick-Write and/or Class Discussion] *What is the life lesson here for you?* [e.g., "Probing questions can poke holes in what appears to be the truth."] [5–15 minutes]

Approximate Time: 35–55 minutes

Instructor Notes

If you have Internet access in your classroom, you may want to take (or send) students to the **www.RateMyProfessor .com** website and look for and question reasons that students give for their ratings. Also, at the time of this writing, there is a link on the right side of the RateMyProfessor.com home page that says, "Professors Strike Back." On this web page, you'll find videos of professors responding to their students' comments. Some of the professors offer interesting "rebuttals" to students' criticisms, rebuttals that, too, can be scrutinized for their logic.

RateMyProfessor.com

With your partner, brainstorm a list of probing questions that you might ask the students who wrote the comments below. The goal of your questions is to uncover any information that would provide a reason to reject the conclusions of the raters. In other words, you are seeking to uncover a hidden truth.

Professor 1. This professor's average rating for Overall Quality (13 votes) is 5.0, the *highest* score possible. Here are comments from three of the raters (all grammar and spelling mistakes are in the original):

1. Very fun class. She is very clear about her expectations and expects you to do your best. Assignments were fun. Tests are multiple choice with no surprises. Final was not cumulative. I would definitely recommend her!

2. [She] is an awesome teacher. She kept the class interesting for us. She grades fairly and doesn't ask too much of her students. The class was very fun. She is good at what she does, and is very helpful and knowledgeable in her chosen field. I would take her class over and over again.

3. Take her class she is a hottie. I probably wouldn't have stayed awake if it weren't for that.

Professor 2. This professor's average rating for Overall Quality (3 votes) is 1.0, the *lowest* score possible. Here are comments from the three raters (all grammar and spelling mistakes are in the original):

1. HORRIBLE- possibly the worst professor I have EVER had! Presents—doesn't teach. He skips around and doesn't really make clear what you really need to know. Assumes that students should be able to understand right away as he doesn't dwell long on any one topic. Save yourself the headache and DON'T take this class!

2. Barely got a c last sem. he sucke

3. accuses the class of not studying. assumes that we don't because the class is failing. out of about 25, only a handful are passing. he's not helpful and grades too hard.

Diving Deeper: Would it make any difference to you if you knew what subjects each of these instructors teaches? Why or why not?

Comments are from www.RateMyProfessor.com.

EXERCISE 27-3: Timeless Wisdom Quotes

Purpose

Encourage students to think critically and make connections to specific course concepts and their lives through the use of Timeless Wisdom quotations.

Supplies and Setup

A list of quotations on one topic—for an example, see "Timeless Wisdom—Diversity" quotes handout (p. 212); electronic discussion board/blog/wiki

Directions

1. *There are two parts to this online assignment. Part 1 is the electronic discussion board, and Part 2 is a personal reflection paper. You will have seven days to complete this assignment, five days to post your chosen quote and analysis, and then two additional days to reply to three of your classmates' postings. You are required to read 10 of your classmates' postings. You will have three days after the discussion board closes to dropbox (or turn in) your personal reflection paper.*

2. ONLINE ACTIVITY:
   - *Read the Timeless Wisdom quotations. Choose the quote that most resonates with you. In other words, which quote did you most agree with or make a connection to? If you did not find a quote that made you say "Wow!" you can find your own quote about the topic. If you chose your own quote, you will need to check with your instructor first before posting.*
   - *Open the discussion board entitled Timeless Wisdom.*
   - *Type your chosen quote, including the author's name. Then, state why you chose the quote—what personal connections did you make to the quote, what does the quote remind you of, and/or why do you think this quote is significant? Submit your posting.*
   - *Read at least 10 of your classmates' postings. Then reply to three of your classmates' postings. Indicate whether you agree, disagree, or made a similar connection to each student's posting. All replies must be respectful and well thought out.*

3. PERSONAL REFLECTION PAPER: *How did this online assignment make you think about the topic of the quotations? What insights did you learn from the online discussion with your classmates? What connections did you make between this topic and the On Course principles we have been exploring in class?*

Approximate Time: 50–60 minutes for online discussion board

Source: Cris Davis and LuAnn Wood, Century College, MN.

Instructor Notes

Any of the Timeless Wisdom quotes from the *On Course* I Workshop or from the margins of the *On Course* text can be used for this activity. This activity could be easily altered to use as an in-class exercise.

Timeless Wisdom—Diversity

1. "We may have different religions, different languages, different colored skin, but we all belong to one human race." Kofi Annan

2. "What we have to do . . . is to find a way to celebrate our diversity and debate our differences without fracturing our communities." Hilary Clinton

3. "It is time for parents to teach young people early on that in diversity there is beauty and strength." Maya Angelou

4. "Diversity may be the hardest thing for a society to live with, and perhaps the most dangerous thing for a society to be without." William Sloane Coffin, Jr.

5. "Toward no crimes have men shown themselves so cold-bloodedly cruel as in punishing differences of belief." James Russell Lowell

6. "Human diversity makes tolerance more than a virtue; it makes it a requirement for survival." Rene Dubos

7. "We have become not a melting pot but a beautiful mosaic. Different people, different beliefs, different yearnings, different hopes, different dreams." Jimmy Carter

8. "Differences challenge assumptions." Anne Wilson Schaef

9. "Since when do you have to agree with people to defend them from injustice?" Lillian Hellman

10. "Tolerance is the positive and cordial effort to understand another's beliefs, practices, and habits without necessarily sharing or accepting them." Joshua Liebman

11. "Every human being, of whatever origin, of whatever station, deserves respect. We must each respect others even as we respect ourselves." U. Thant

12. "Don't ever let them pull you down so low as to hate them." Booker T. Washington

13. "I swore never to be silent whenever human beings endure suffering and humiliation. We must always take sides. Neutrality helps the oppressor, never the victim. Silence encourages the tormentor, never the tormented." Elie Weisel

14. "Let all bear in mind that a society is judged not so much by the standards attained by its more affluent and privileged members as by the quality of life which it is able to assure for its weakest members." H. E. Javier Perez de Cuellar

15. "No single tradition monopolizes the truth. We must glean the best values of all traditions and work together to remove the tensions between traditions in order to give peace a chance." Thich Nhat Hanh

Journal Entry 28 Developing Self-Respect

EXERCISE 28-1: Claiming Respect

Purpose

To identify qualities that students respect in someone else and to own these projections.

Supplies and Setup

Journals; students sitting in pairs (Student A and Student B). Write the following sentence stem on the board or project it on a PowerPoint slide: **I respect ___ because . . .**

Directions

1. *In your journal, write the name of a person for whom you have great respect. This person can be a family member, a coworker, a friend, someone here at college, someone famous you haven't ever met . . . absolutely anyone you respect.* [2 minutes]

2. *Below the person's name, copy the sentence stem from the chalkboard:* **I respect (person's name) because . . .** *Then complete the sentence five or more times, giving a different reason each time for why you respect that person. Focus on HOW the person lives his or her life rather than his or her accomplishments. For example, I might write, "I respect my sister Holly because she has experienced a great deal of physical and emotional pain in her life, yet she remains one of the most positive, loving, and caring people I know." [5–8 minutes]*

3. *Partner A, read your sentences to Partner B. But when you read the sentence, you're going to substitute* **yourself** *for the person about whom you originally wrote. So, I would say, "*I *respect* **myself** *because* I *have experienced a great deal of physical and emotional pain in* **my** *life, yet* I *remain one of the most positive, loving, and caring people I know." Partner B, when your partner has read all the sentences, reflect what you heard him or her say. Partner A, be aware of any thoughts or feelings you have as you read or listen to feedback from your partner. [8–10 minutes]*

4. *Switch roles. Partner B, you read now, and remember to substitute yourself for the person about whom you originally wrote. Afterward, Partner A, reflect what you heard your partner say. And Partner B, remember to be aware of any thoughts or feelings you have as you read or listen to feedback from your partner. [8–10 minutes]*

5. [Quick-Write and/or Class Discussion] *Did you find that what you respect in the other person is a quality you have as well? What was it like to claim the quality for yourself that you respect in the other person? Did your Inner Critic have anything to say? How about your Inner Guide? How do you feel right now? What would it do for your self-confidence if you acknowledged respect for* **how** *you live your life? What is the life lesson here for you?* [e.g., "My level of self-respect is determined not only by the goals I achieve but also by how I achieve them."] [10–20 minutes]

Approximate Time: 40–50 minutes

Instructor Notes

You may wish to point out that we often project our own thoughts onto others. So respecting someone for a particular quality may suggest that we either have or want to have that same quality. Emphasize that self-respect is about having admiration for HOW we or others live life.

EXERCISE 28-2: Symbol of Self-Respect

Purpose

To acknowledge and express self-respect.

Supplies and Setup

Set up this activity in a previous class by requesting that students bring in an item of which they're proud. This item might be a sports trophy, a grade report, a scholarship letter, a wedding ring, a picture they painted, and so on. If they can't bring in the item, they can bring a photo or a sketch of it, or they can describe it to the class. Whatever it is, it should be a tangible object. Write two sentence stems on a whiteboard or project them on a PowerPoint slide: **I am proud of this item because . . . What this item reveals about how I live my life is . . .** Have students form groups of three.

Directions

1. *The people who go first in each group will show the item they brought and (if necessary) explain what it is. Next, speaking to your group, complete the two sentence stems on the chalkboard. After the first person has gone, move clockwise around your group until everyone has finished.* [5–10 minutes]

2. *Now we are going to do the same exercise again. This time, go to your very deepest level of honesty. Let your Inner Guide suggest the deepest truth about why you are proud of this item and what it reveals about you. If you are proud of this item, it suggests a very deep self-respect. Honor yourself by expressing that deep self-respect. Don't worry about bragging. Bragging is encouraged, even required, in this activity.* [5–10 minutes]

3. [Quick-Write and/or Class Discussion] *What was it like to tell about what you deeply respect about yourself? What thoughts or feelings did you have as you explained yourself each time? Did your Inner Critic try to interfere? How do you feel right now? What would it do for your self-esteem if you fully acknowledge what you respect about yourself? What is the life lesson here for you?* [e.g., "All of my accomplishments are a window into my soul, revealing not only what is important to me but also how I live my life."] [10–20 minutes]

Approximate Time: 20–40 minutes

Instructor Notes

Emphasize that self-respect is about having admiration and pride for HOW we live our lives.

Writing

WRITING EXERCISE 1: BEAUTIFUL QUESTIONS/BEAUTIFUL OUTLINES

Purpose

To have students experience the value of using their readers' likely questions to organize writing.

Supplies and Setup

Envelopes, one for each student; index cards, 20 for each student; whiteboard and markers. In a previous class, assign students to bring with them a one-sentence thesis statement for an upcoming essay. It is wise to illustrate how a thesis is composed of topic and a claim. For more on this skill, see "Define Your Thesis" in the "Before Writing" section of Wise Choices in College: Writing (Chapter 7).

Directions

1. [Put students in groups of six or seven, sitting in a circle. Give each student an envelope and 20 index cards. Going around the room, have each student say his or her thesis statement aloud. If needed, help students revise their thesis

statements so that they contain a topic and a claim. Once all students have a workable thesis statement, ask them to write theirs on the outside of their envelopes.] [5–10 minutes]

2. *Pass your envelope to the person on your left. When you receive an envelope, read the thesis statement written on it. Then pause and think about beautiful questions that you might ask about that statement. The term "beautiful questions" comes from a line in a poem by e. e. cummings, who wrote: "Always the beautiful answer who asks a more beautiful question." What do you think he means by a "beautiful question?"* [Elicit some answers, such as "A beautiful question is one that causes someone to see something in an entirely new way." or "A beautiful question is one that causes someone to dig much deeper into a complex topic."] [5 minutes]

3. *Okay, let's practice asking beautiful questions. Suppose the thesis statement on the envelop reads, "A college degree is essential for success in the 21st century." The topic is "a college degree," and the claim is that "a college degree is essential for success in the 21st century." What beautiful questions would you want to ask the author about this claim?* [Elicit a large number of questions and record them on the whiteboard.] [5 minutes]

4. *Now turn to the thesis statement written on the envelope you're holding. What "beautiful question" comes to your mind about it? Write it on an index card and put it in the envelope. Now think of another beautiful question, write it on a card, and put it in the envelope. And finally, add a third card with a beautiful question. When you've added three questions, pass the envelope to the person on your left. Keep going around your small group until you get your envelope back.* [Completed envelopes should have 15–18 cards in them.] [10–15 minutes]

5. *Now that you have your envelope back, take out the cards and organize them in related piles. Perhaps two questions are almost the same, so you put them in the same pile.* [5 minutes]

6. *Now look over your questions and pick your three or four favorites. These are the three or four questions that you think are the most important to answer in your essay. Place them in the order you think they should be answered.* [5 minutes]

7. *Now, on a blank sheet of paper, write your thesis statement and under it, on separate lines, write the three or four questions in the order you think they should be answered. Below the last question, write, "Conclusion."* [5 minutes]

8. [Journal Writing and/or Class Discussion] *What you have created is a question outline. How have you organized your writing assignments in the past? How helpful do you think this question outline would be in organizing your ideas for an essay? How could you generate a list of questions on your own? What is the advantage of getting questions directly from your potential readers? If you didn't know the answer to a question, where could you find it? What did you learn/ relearn about organizing an essay? Could you use a question outline on an essay test? How will you use/or adapt this approach in your other classes?* [10–20 minutes]

Approximate Time: 40–65 minutes

Instructor Notes

You might ask each student to nominate the "most beautiful question" he or she received. Then ask the student to explain why the question is the most beautiful. What criteria did he or she use to award that distinction?

WRITING EXERCISE 2: PLAYING WITH STYLE

Purpose

To provide students with an experience of revising the style of their writing. This activity will also help students become more proficient at writing on a computer.

Supplies and Setup

"Playing with Style" handout (p. 217). Homework is assigned in class 1. Discussion is held in class 2. Students need access to a computer and the *On Course* text.

Directions

1. [Class 1: Distribute and review the handout. Answer questions and assign the activity for homework. Be sure students understand what is meant by "reading level" and how they can use a word-processing program to determine the reading level of prose writing.] [10 minutes]

2. [Class 2:] *What is the reading level of the original essay?* [The original essay has a Flesch-Kincaid reading grade level of 9.4, according to Word.] *So the reading level is at about the middle of the first year in high school. Does the reading level of the essay surprise you? Did you think it would be higher or lower than grade 9.4? What do you think is the average reading level of most U.S. newspapers?* [Answer: "about eighth grade," according to Philip Meyer in his book *The Vanishing Newspaper* (2009).] *Does that surprise you? Why do you suppose the reading level of most newspapers is so low?* [5 minutes]

3. [Place students in pairs.] *Read to each other the essay you revised to have a reading level two grades* below *that of the original essay. If you were successful, the reading level of your revision is grade 7.4 or below. Discuss the changes you made to lower the reading level.* [10 minutes]

4. *Now, read to each other the essay you revised to have a reading level two grades* above *the original essay. If you were successful, the reading level is grade 11.4 or above. Discuss the changes you made to raise the reading level.* [10 minutes]

5. [Class Discussion:] *What did you discover about how to lower or raise the reading level of your writing?* [e.g., change the number of sentences/paragraphs, the number of words/sentences, the number of characters/words, the number of passive sentences] *Who would like to nominate their partner to read an essay that has a reading level below grade 7.4?* [Discuss the style of the essay.] *Who would like to nominate their partner to read an essay that has a reading level above grade 11.4?* [Discuss the style of the essay.] *What did you learn or relearn? How will you use this knowledge when you write?* [20–30 minutes, depending on how many essays you discuss.]

Approximate Time: **Class 1**: 10 minutes; **class 2:** 45–55 minutes

Instructor Notes

1. To save students the time of typing the essay that they will be modifying, you could type it and send it to all students via email or post on a course management system.

2. When assigning the homework, consider pairing students who are computer savvy with students who are not. The computer-savvy students can help their partners with technical problems.

3. When pairing students in the second class, confirm that each has completed the homework. For students without completed homework, consider asking them to leave the room, do the work, and bring it to you by the end of the day. When students learn that your homework assignments have a "no escape" policy, they are more likely to complete them on time.

4. If your course meets in a smart classroom or you have access to a computer lab, it is possible to do the writing part of this activity during class time. However, this approach is less desirable because students finish the initial writing at very different times. If doing the writing part of the activity in class, circulate and help students who are having challenges with either the technology or the writing.

Playing with Style

1. Use the index in the back of *On Course* to find the One Student's Story essay by student Jason Matthew Loden. Type his essay into a word-processing program on a computer. Then determine the reading level of Jason's essay and write that number at the end of the essay.

   To determine the reading level of a piece of writing using Word 2010:

   > Click the **File** tab, and then click **Options.**

   > Click **Proofing**.

   > Under **When correcting spelling and grammar in Word**, make sure **Check grammar with spelling** is selected.

   > Select **Show readability statistics**.

   > After enabling this feature, open the file you want to check and check the spelling. After checking the spelling, Word will provide the document's reading level.

2. Make two more copies of Jason's essay.

   To make copies using Word 2010:

   > Place the cursor at the beginning of the essay.

   > Left-click the mouse, drag the cursor to the bottom of the essay, and release the left-click. (The entire essay will now be highlighted.)

   > Left-click the "copy" icon on the home tab. (You have now created a copy of the essay in the computer's memory.)

   > Now place the cursor where you want to insert a copy of the essay.

   > Left-click the "paste" icon on the home tab. (A copy of the essay will appear.)

   > Repeat this process to create a total of three copies of the essay.

3. Without changing the meaning of Jason's essay, revise the first copy until the reading level is at least two whole grades *lower* than the original. For example, if the original essay has a reading level of 9.4, your revision should have a reading level of 7.4 or lower. At the end of the essay, type the reading level of your revised copy.

4. Without changing the meaning of Jason's essay, revise the second copy until the reading level is at least two whole grades *higher* than the original. For example, if the original essay has a reading level of 9.4, your revision should have a reading level of 11.4 or higher. At the end of the essay, type the reading level of your revised copy. Then print each essay on a separate piece of paper.

5. Bring completed copies of the three essays to our next class. They are your tickets to *enter* and you must have all three tickets to attend.

Embracing Change: Do One Different Thing This Week

Being a lifelong learner will enhance the quality of your outcomes and experiences through your years in higher education and far beyond. Victims handicap their future success by focusing on "getting out" of college. If they do earn a degree, their learning experience is often so shallow that they haven't created a strong foundation on which to build their success. Creators, on the other hand, participate actively in the learning process, and thus have the information and skills (not to mention the neural networks) that will enhance their success for years to come. Here's your chance to develop one lifelong learning strategy. From the following actions, pick ONE new belief or behavior and experiment.

1. Think: "I learn valuable lessons from every experience I have."
2. Remind myself that, like a muscle, the more I exercise my brain, the stronger it grows.
3. Set a learning goal for each of my classes.
4. Find someone in my class with the same preferred way(s) of learning as my own and ask about his or her most effective learning strategies.
5. Make an educated guess about the preferred way of learning of one of my present instructors, and then determine a new learning strategy I could use to improve my outcomes in that class.
6. Make an effort to persuade someone to think or do something that I believe is important.
7. Ask probing questions about an argument that someone else presents.
8. Identify one piece of feedback I received that day and determine what course correction, if any, I will make as a result of that feedback.
9. Identify one choice I am making that does not support my goal to get a college degree and change it.
10. Find and study my college's academic honesty code, and make a commitment to live up to it.
11. Your choice: A different belief or behavior you learned in this chapter with which you would like to experiment.

Now, write the one you chose under "My Commitment" in the following chart. Then, track yourself for one week, putting a check in the appropriate box when you keep your commitment. After seven days, assess your results. If your outcomes and experiences improve, you now have a tool you can use for the rest of your life. Psychologist Carl Rogers reminds us that "The only person who is educated is the one who has learned how to learn and change."

My Commitment						
Day 1	Day 2	Day 3	Day 4	Day 5	Day 6	Day 7

During my seven-day experiment, what happened?

As a result of what happened, what did I learn or relearn?

Chapter 7: Quiz Questions

(Please visit the Instructor companion website for *On Course* at login.cengage.com or contact your local Cengage Learning sales representative to find electronic versions of the Quiz Questions.)

37. Developing a Learning Orientation to Life

1. Learners with a _____ **mindset** believe people are either born intelligent or they are not. They avoid a challenge because they fear their intelligence may not be up to the task.

2. Learners with a _____ **mindset** believe that intelligence is like a muscle—it gets stronger the more it's used. They accept challenges, work hard, learn from mistakes, change course if needed, and keep going despite setbacks and failures.

3. According to psychologist Carol Dweck, which of the following statements would be more likely to help someone develop a growth mindset?

   A. *You did so well in math. You're obviously very smart!*

   B. *You did so well in math. You're obviously a hard worker!*

   C. *You did so well in math. I'm so proud of you!*

   D. *You did so well in math. You obviously cheated!*

4. A *learning* goal would be to earn an A in a writing course. A *performance* goal would be to learn three ways to write an effective introductory paragraph.   TRUE   FALSE

5. Which of the following would NOT help you develop a growth mindset?

   A. Think of your brain as a muscle.

   B. Set performance goals (rather than learning goals).

   C. Seek feedback.

   D. Change course when needed.

38. Discovering Your Preferred Ways of Learning

1. Our preferred ways of learning are the only ways we can learn new information or skills.   TRUE   FALSE

2. Traditional college teaching—characterized by lectures and textbook assignments—MOST favors the learning preference of

   A. Thinkers.

   B. Doers.

   C. Feelers.

   D. Innovators.

3. Traditional college teaching—characterized by lectures and textbook assignments—LEAST favors the learning preference of

   A. Thinkers and Doers.

   B. Doers and Feelers.

C. Feelers and Innovators.

D. Innovators and Thinkers.

4. If an instructor does not teach to our preferred ways of learning, we cannot expect to learn the subject.   TRUE   FALSE

5. Knowing our preferred ways of learning suggests the kind of deep-processing strategies that might be best for us in creating strong neural networks in our brains and therefore, more deep and lasting learning.   TRUE   FALSE

39. Employing Critical Thinking

1. Critical thinking helps with making wise choices as well as constructing and analyzing persuasive arguments.   TRUE   FALSE

2. Which of the following is NOT one of the components of a logical argument?

    A. Reasons

    B. Evidence

    C. Probing Questions

    D. Conclusions

3. Probing questions can be helpful for challenging a conclusion.   TRUE   FALSE

4. If someone tells you that a movie is great and you ask why, you are asking the person to provide you with a logical conclusion.   TRUE   FALSE

5. A characteristic of evidence is that, if true, its accuracy can be verified.   TRUE   FALSE

40. On Course at Work: Lifelong Learning at Work

1. After graduation, when you have secured a job, you will finally be able to stop studying and learning.   TRUE   FALSE

2. Soft skills, like those you are learning in *On Course*, are in such high demand in the workplace that some training consultants charge many thousands of dollars *per day* to teach these skills to employees of American businesses.   TRUE   FALSE

3. Studies suggest that company executives who failed and did not learn from their mistakes and shortcomings rebounded and resumed successful careers.   TRUE   FALSE

4. Your college provides many resources for learning about careers. One such source on your campus is ___.

5. Ned Herrmann, creator of the Brain Dominance Inventory, suggests that alignment of what two things is predictive of success and satisfaction in a job?

    A. Your learning preferences and compatible careers

    B. Desired careers and income levels

    C. Enjoyable hobbies and time off from work

    D. Your learning preferences and level of self-esteem

41. Developing Self-Respect

1. If self-confidence is the result of *what* I do, then self-respect is the result of ___ I do it.

2. Once we have a foundation of personal values, we create integrity by choosing words and actions consistent with those values.   TRUE   FALSE

3. Each time you make a choice that goes against your own values, you make a deposit in your self-respect account.   TRUE   FALSE

4. When you break a promise (especially to yourself), you make a withdrawal from your self-respect account.   TRUE   FALSE

5. Which of the following does NOT help you to keep commitments?

   A. Make your agreements unconsciously.

   B. Make your agreements important—write them down.

   C. Create a plan; then do everything in your power to carry it out!

   D. If a problem arises or you change your mind, renegotiate.

42. Wise Choices in College: Writing

1. Most experts recognize three components in the writing process: writing, revising, and editing.   TRUE   FALSE

2. Effective writing enhances learning because it incorporates all the elements of the CORE learning system: Collecting, Organizing, Rehearsing, and Evaluating.   TRUE   FALSE

3. A ___ states the most important idea you want to convey to your audience.

4. The two most common kinds of writing in college courses are informative and

   A. entertaining.

   B. persuasive.

   C. philosophical.

   D. personal.

5. Which of the following is NOT one of the 4Es that are supporting details as described in this chapter?

   A. Can you give EVIDENCE to support that?

   B. Can you EVALUATE your support?

   C. Can you give an EXPERIENCE to illustrate that?

   D. Can you EXPLAIN that further?

Chapter 7: Essay Topics

1. Psychologist Carol Dweck and her colleagues have studied the causes and effects of two mindsets: growth and fixed. In an essay for college students, compare and contrast these two mindsets. Then explain which mindset you think you have and how you came to have it. Finally, explain any actions you plan to take to develop or strengthen a growth mindset.

2. Recall your favorite teacher or subject. With what you now know about preferred ways of learning, write an essay in which you explain why you liked this teacher or subject so much.

3. Students new to college are often stuck in old habit patterns that sabotage their academic success. In an essay for first-year college students, offer your suggestions for the most important behaviors, beliefs, and attitudes necessary for academic success. Suggest ways your readers could make a course correction if they need to. Use your own experience wherever possible.

4. In a letter to the board of education members where you went to high school, persuade them to make one significant change to help future students. Use your critical thinking skills to make a logical case for the change you suggest. Consider using your understanding of how the human brain learns best and your knowledge of individual learning preferences to develop your argument.

5. Educational philosopher John Dewey wrote, "The most important attitude that can be formed is that of the desire to go on learning." In an essay for new parents, discuss what they can do to preserve and nurture their children's love of learning. Use your understanding of how the human brain learns best and your knowledge of personal learning preferences.

6. Taking a personal inventory is often the first step toward improving an area of one's life. Write an essay in which you explore your strengths and weaknesses as a learner (both in school and out of school). End your essay by proposing changes that you could make to become a more effective learner.

7. Psychologist Mihaly Csikszentmihalyi wrote, "The ability to persevere despite obstacles and setbacks is the quality people most admire in others. . . ." Your perseverance through difficulties not only causes others to respect you, it raises your own self-respect. In an essay for a general audience, describe a time in your life when you persevered against inner and/or outer obstacles to reach a goal or dream of great importance to you. Conclude by telling what you learned from your experience and how it affected your sense of self-respect.

8. Using the student essays in *On Course* as a model, write an essay about how you used a strategy from Chapter 7 to overcome a problem in your life—academic, personal, or even at work. First explain the problem; then discuss the strategy you used and how; finally, identify what happened. Your instructor may submit your essay for possible publication in the next edition of *On Course*. Additional directions for writing and submitting these essays can be found at http://oncourseworkshop.com.

9. Using the "One Student's Story" essays in *On Course* as models, write an essay about how you used one or more new learning strategies (reading, taking notes, organizing study materials, rehearsing and memorizing study materials, taking tests, or writing) to overcome an academic challenge in college. First explain the academic challenge; then discuss what strategy or strategies you used; finally identify the outcome of your efforts. Your instructor may submit your essay for possible publication in the next edition of *On Course*, where it could inspire tens of thousands of your fellow students. Additional directions for writing and submitting these essays can be found at http://oncourseworkshop.com.

Answer Key to Chapter 7 Quiz Questions

37. Developing a Learning Orientation to Life

Answers: 1. fixed 2. growth 3. B 4. FALSE (It's the other way around.) 5. B

38. Discovering Your Preferred Ways of Learning

Answers: 1. FALSE 2. A 3. C 4. FALSE 5. TRUE

39. Employing Critical Thinking

Answers: 1. TRUE 2. C 3. TRUE 4. FALSE (You are asking for a reason.) 5. TRUE

40. On Course at Work: Lifelong Learning at Work

Answers: 1. FALSE 2. TRUE 3. FALSE 4. the career center; the library (Answers may vary or be very specific by campus, such as the Donaghey Center for Career Excellence.) 5. A

41. Developing Self-Respect

Answers: 1. how 2. TRUE 3. FALSE 4. TRUE 5. A

42. Wise Choices in College: Writing

Answers: 1. FALSE (also prewriting) 2. TRUE 3. thesis or main idea 4. B 5. B

Developing Emotional Intelligence

Chapter
8

Concept

People in the grip of overwhelming emotions are seldom effective. Consequently, one of the most essential components of success—by some accounts more important than academic intelligence—is emotional intelligence. Emotional intelligence is the ability to manage one's emotions and stay on course even when navigating life's most challenging storms. Just as we are responsible for the quality of our outer lives, we are responsible for the quality of our inner lives as well. In fact, cognitive psychologists suggest that we can only perceive what is going on outside of us through the lens of what is going on inside of us. Belief systems and inner conversations create our interpretation of the events going on around us, and in this way, our thoughts actually create our "reality." People who are emotionally intelligent are skilled at controlling the content of their consciousness. This skill allows them to make wise choices in the throes of emotional storms, while others struggle merely to survive. When we assist students to gain greater emotional intelligence, we empower them not only to be more effective in the pursuit of their dreams, but also to experience happiness, joy, and peace of mind on their journey.

EMPOWERS STUDENTS TO . . .

1. Take responsibility for the quality of their inner experience of life.
2. Honor their emotions, seeing both pleasant and unpleasant emotions as important feedback for keeping them on course.
3. More consciously choose the content of their consciousness, thinking and speaking more positively about themselves, others, and their world, thus creating an experience of greater optimism, joy, and happiness.
4. Avoid emotional hijackings, thus persisting in the face of challenges and setbacks.
5. Learn how to create more "flow" or peak experiences in their lives.
6. Improve relationships through empathy for and an understanding of the emotions of others.
7. Postpone instant gratification for future rewards.

Remember also to use the all-purpose exercises mentioned in the Introduction, actively engaging students in the exploration of JOURNAL ENTRIES, CASE STUDIES, ONE STUDENT'S STORY, ON COURSE AT WORK, QUOTATIONS, CARTOONS, FOCUS QUESTIONS, CHAPTER-OPENING CHARTS, and STUDY SKILLS. Remind students to use letters to label any in-class writing they do in their journals.

Case Study in Critical Thinking: After Math

Purpose

To develop critical thinking skills by exploring a real-life situation concerning emotional intelligence.

Supplies and Setup

"After Math" in *On Course*.

227

Directions

1. [Have students read "After Math." One way to be sure everyone has read the selection before taking the next step is to have one student read the first paragraph aloud, another student read the second, and so on until the reading is complete. Alternately, have six volunteers play the roles of the five characters and a narrator; then present the case study as a play.] [5–10 minutes]

2. [Before students score the characters, have them turn to the next section after the case study titled "Understanding Emotional Intelligence," and read about the four components of emotional intelligence. Again, you may want to have volunteers read the four components aloud. This information enables your students to make more informed choices.] [5 minutes]

3. [Here is an alternative to having students rank all of the characters from 1–5 on their emotional intelligence as the directions in the case study suggest. Divide your students into five groups, and assign one character to each group.] *Your task is to rate your character's emotional intelligence on a score from 1 (low) to 10 (high emotional intelligence). When your spokesperson reports on the number you have chosen for your character, I'll ask him or her to provide specific evidence from the story that justifies your group's score.* [10–15 minutes]

4. [Have each group's spokesperson give the group's emotional intelligence score for its character while you write the five characters' names and scores on the board or easel pad. Now, return to each group one by one and ask the spokesperson to offer specific evidence from the case study that led to each character's score. The key is to elicit specific behaviors that explain scores based on the four components of emotional intelligence. Thus, the explanations are far more important than the scores. For example, Professor Bishop may get a low score because he demonstrated poor relationship management when he announced Scott's low test score in front of the entire class.] [15 minutes]

5. [Quick-Write and/or Class Discussion] *What did you learn from this discussion about emotional intelligence and its importance for achieving your goals and dreams? What is the life lesson here for you?* [e.g., "If I manage my emotions, I will have a far better life than if I let my emotions manage me."] [5–10 minutes]

Approximate Time: 35–55 minutes

Instructor Notes

1. So as not to stifle discussion, I don't tell students what my scores are.

2. This class discussion is an excellent prewriting activity to be followed by students writing a persuasion essay supporting their opinions in the debate. Because students are now sharply aware of views opposed to their own, they often write much more thorough and persuasive essays than would be the case without the debate.

3. You might ask students to relate an experience they have witnessed in which someone (perhaps themselves) became hijacked by emotions and tell what happened as a result. Afterward, ask, "What could this person have done that would have been more emotionally intelligent?"

4. An optional step for this activity is to ask students to do a quick-write about and then a discussion of the Diving Deeper question: Imagine that you have been asked to mentor the person whom you ranked number 5 (least emotionally intelligent). Other than recommending a counselor, how would you suggest that this person handle his or her upset in a more emotionally intelligent manner?

5. An optional follow-up is to ask students to rewrite the case study; in their rewrite, they are to have all of the characters make emotionally wise choices.

Journal Entry 29 Understanding Emotional Intelligence

EXERCISE 29-1: I'm Willing to Feel . . .

Purpose

To help students become more conscious of the emotions they accept and those they reject.

Supplies and Setup

Students in pairs (Student A and Student B). Post the list of "I'm willing . . ." statements on a PowerPoint slide, whiteboard, or easel pad. (See Instructor Notes for list.)

Directions

1. *Healthy emotions tell us when we're on course or off course. Most people were raised to be comfortable with some emotions but uncomfortable with others. This exercise is designed to help you become more conscious of how comfortable you are with various emotions.* [2 minutes]

2. *Partner A will read one of the "I'm willing . . ." statements. Use your best acting skills to display the emotion you are mentioning. Partner B will respond, "I can accept you when you are feeling ____."* [Fill in the emotion that Partner A has just mentioned.] *Be conscious of how you feel as you say your part.* [DEMO the process, demonstrating the appropriate emotion.] *You may find that you feel comfortable when you express anger but uncomfortable when your partner expresses anger. There is no "right" or "wrong" way to feel. Just be sensitive to how you feel as you say or hear each of these statements about feeling your emotions. Watch for any feedback from your body, like a flutter in your stomach. If you finish before I call time, go back to the top of the list and repeat the list. Any questions? Okay, Partner A, begin.* [5 minutes]

3. *Now switch roles. Partner B, you read the statement, and Partner A responds, "I can accept you when you are feeling ____." Again, the key here is to be aware of how you feel as you express these ideas.* [5 minutes]

4. [Quick-Write and/or Class Discussion] *Did you notice emotions that you are more comfortable with feeling? Less comfortable with feeling? What emotions are you comfortable with others feeling? Uncomfortable with others feeling? What do you suppose is the value for you of this awareness? What is the life lesson here for you?* [e.g., "My emotions show up in my body long before they show up in my mind."] [5–20 minutes]

Approximate Time: 15–35 minutes

Source: This is a variation of an exercise by Gay and Kathlyn Hendricks.

Instructor Notes

Here are the statements to put on the whiteboard or PowerPoint slide:

I'm willing to feel all of my anger.

I'm willing to feel all of my anxiety.

I'm willing to feel all of my fear.

I'm willing to feel all of my sadness.

I'm willing to feel all of my guilt.

I'm willing to feel all of my resentment.

I'm willing to feel all of my depression.

I'm willing to feel all of my love.

I'm willing to feel all of my joy.

EXERCISE 29-2: Right Now I Feel . . .

Purpose

To improve students' ability to be aware of their emotions and to dramatize how the words that we think affect how we feel.

Supplies and Setup

Students in groups of three. Write the list of sentence stems on the board or project with a PowerPoint slide. (See Instructor Notes for the sentence stems.)

Directions

1. *For many people, staying in touch with their feelings is a great challenge. This exercise is designed to assist us to become more aware of our feelings.*

2. *Before we start, let's list as many feelings as we can think of. Call them out.* [Record the list of emotions on the chalkboard, further exploring suggestions that are not really feelings, such as "stupid." "Stupid" is not a feeling, but you may feel "embarrassed" when you think that you did something stupid.] *What's the difference between fear and anxiety? Between sadness and depression? Between anger and fury?* [10 minutes]

3. *The person in your group who has the next birthday goes first. That person will read and complete the first sentence stem. Moving clockwise, the other two people also read and complete the first sentence stem. Then the first person will read and complete the second sentence stem, and so on until all the sentences have been read and completed by each person. Be very conscious of how you feel as you say how you feel.* [DEMO the process.] *Any questions? Okay, decide who will go first, and begin.* [5–10 minutes]

4. [Quick-Write and/or Class Discussion] *What did you learn about your relationship to the various emotions you discussed? Did you notice your emotions changing as you said you feel a particular emotion? What does this suggest about how we can manage our emotions? What is the life lesson here for you?* [e.g., "The thoughts that I allow to linger in my mind create emotions that show up in my heart."] [10–20 minutes]

Approximate Time: 25–40 minutes

Instructor Notes

1. Here are the statements to put on the board or PowerPoint slide:

   Right now I feel . . .

   I feel angry when . . .

   I feel afraid when . . .

   I feel sad when . . .

   Right now I feel . . .

   I feel calm when . . .

   I feel peaceful when . . .

   I feel contented when . . .

   Right now I feel . . .

   I feel happy when . . .

   I feel joyful when . . .

   I feel loved when . . .

   Right now I feel . . .

2. An important point to bring out in the discussion is that the thoughts we allow in our consciousness greatly influence how we feel. Typically, recalling a past event that generated an emotion causes the emotion in the present. (This is a method many actors use to generate emotions for a part they are playing.) The stems in this activity are set up to move students from negative emotions to tranquil emotions to positive emotions.

3. A variation is to have students complete the sentence stems in writing (instead of speaking them). In this way they will create a kind of poem about their emotions. If you have them both speak and write these sentences, you can explore whether they experienced a difference emotionally in the two mediums.

Journal Entry 30 Reducing Stress

EXERCISE 30-1: Up on the Roof

Purpose

To experience how changing the content of one's consciousness changes the quality of one's experience.

Directions

1. *I'd like you to stand up and position yourself so you can spread your arms without touching anyone else. In a moment, I'm going to invite you to close your eyes, and I'm going to guide you through a mental experience with words. If you involve yourself totally in the experience, you may discover a powerful way to reduce stress in your life. When you're ready, close your eyes, take a deep breath, and here we go.* [1 minute]

2. *Picture yourself walking along a sidewalk in a large city. Above you, tall buildings tower as you weave your way through the crowd on the sidewalk. Now see yourself walking up to a huge building with a revolving door. As you push on the glass door, it glides open, and you find yourself entering an expansive lobby. Walk across the smooth marble floor to the elevator and push the UP button. The doors open, and once inside the empty elevator, you push the top button marked "ROOF." Hear the elevator music, and then feel the light sensation in your stomach as the elevator begins rushing you upward. After a long ride, the elevator doors open, and you step out into a deserted hallway. Look down at the end of the hall . . . notice a door down there. Walk over to the door, turn the handle, and push the door open. Now step into the dimly lit stairway. Take the stairs up until you come to another door. Push on the horizontal bar and feel the latch opening and the door swinging open. The brightness of the sun causes you to squint your eyes, and the breeze blows across your face as you step out onto the crunchy gravel of the roof. Birds are flying overhead, and the sky is dotted with a few white clouds. Notice that the edge of the building has a little parapet, a one-foot-high cement wall that runs around the entire edge of the roof. Walk over to the parapet, once again feeling the strong breeze nudging you forward. As you reach the parapet, step up on it. That's right—lift your foot and step right up on that little wall that runs around the very edge of the roof. Look over into the canyon between the buildings . . . notice the tiny people way down below . . . listen to the far-off sounds of automobile horns honking in the city . . . . Now, see how far out over the edge you can lean, and be aware of how you are feeling as you lean over that open space below you. . . . Be careful! That wind is blowing harder now. Don't let it blow you over the edge. . . . Okay, now step back down to the roof, feeling the gravel crunch beneath your shoes once again.* [5 minutes]

3. *Now as you stand on the roof, an amazing thing begins to happen. You feel a tingle on your back. Something is growing out of each of your shoulder blades. In a moment you realize that wings are coming right through your clothing, and they keep growing until they are large and strong. Strangely, these wings feel very familiar to you, as if you have had them all of your life. Flap your wings a few times. Notice that you have full control of them. Feel yourself confidently lift off of the roof a few feet, then settle back down. Now that you have your wings, and you feel confident in their use, step back up on the little parapet, the cement wall running around the edge of the roof. Once again, feel the wind blowing at your back, see the birds flying overhead, and look down at the tiny people and cars far below. Try leaning out again, and this time, if you want, let yourself soar off of the roof and fly around with the birds high into the white clouds. Soar around as high as you wish to go, then, after an exhilarating flight, come back and land once again on the roof. Step off the parapet and feel the gravel again beneath your shoes. In a moment, I'll be inviting you to open your eyes and return to this room, but before you do, you have something to decide. You need to decide if you will bring your wings back here with you or leave them behind. So, when you have decided whether or not to keep your wings, take a deep breath, let your eyes come open, and have a seat.* [5 minutes]

4. [Quick-Write and/or Class Discussion] *What did you experience when you stepped up on the parapet for the first time?* [Some people will report fear or concern about being on the roof.] *Was your experience different when you got your wings?* [Many people will report a much more positive experience once they got their wings.] *How many of*

you had a more positive experience on the roof after you got your wings? Where did your wings come from? [They created them with their thoughts.] *What is the life lesson about how to create a more positive experience of life?* [By consciously choosing to occupy the content of our consciousness with positive thoughts, we change our experience of life for the better. We can reduce stress by changing our thoughts.] *What is an area of your life where you could apply this wisdom?* [10–20 minutes]

Approximate Time: 20–30 minutes

Instructor Notes

This visualization can lead to some great discoveries. After this visualization, one participant said, "Thanks for reminding me that I have wings and that I can fly." You could follow the activity by playing the song "I Believe I Can Fly" by R. Kelly.

EXERCISE 30-2: Resolving Incompletions

Purpose

To give participants the stress-reducing experience of an outer world completion.

Supplies and Setup

Step 1 is done in one class period; step 2 is done in the following class period.

Directions

1. *Open your journal to a blank page. Make a list of incompletions that exist in your outer world—things you have been meaning to do but keep putting off. For example, you might include incompletions such as (1) make a dentist appointment, (2) get my car tuned up, (3) tell my boyfriend that I am upset with him, (4) complete term paper for history. Circle one of these incompletions that you are willing to complete before our next class meeting. Now I'd like each person to announce what he or she is going to complete. You'll get to report your results in our next class.* [Allow students to "pass" and not announce what they plan to complete.] [10 minutes]

2. [Next class period] [Quick-Write and/or Class Discussion] *What did you promise yourself to complete? How successful were you? How do you feel right now about completing or not completing it? If you did complete it, does your Inner Guide have anything to say about your success? If you didn't complete the action, what did you make more important than doing it? Does your Inner Critic or Inner Defender have anything to say about your failure to complete it? What does your Inner Guide have to say? Are you willing to recommit to doing it? What is the life lesson here for you?* [e.g., "Resolving incompletions is a great way to reduce stress that is caused by feeling overwhelmed by my to-do list."] [10–30 minutes]

Approximate Time: 20–40 minutes [spread over two classes]

EXERCISE 30-3: Happy Music

Purpose

To demonstrate that what we choose as the content of our consciousness influences the quality of our experience.

Supplies and Setup

Compact disc player. In the previous class, ask students to bring a song on a CD that inspires them or makes them feel happy, or the instructor can bring a variety of songs.

Directions

1. [Invite volunteers to play their songs.] [3–5 minutes for each song]
2. [Quick-Write and/or Class Discussion] *How do you feel right now? Do you feel better or worse than before you heard the music? What is it about the music that created this feeling? How can you apply this idea in other ways besides music? What is the life lesson about changing your emotional state?* [e.g., "I can manage my emotions by making wise choices about the music I listen to . . . and the books I read . . . and the friends I have . . . and by all that I allow into my mind."] [5–10 minutes]

Approximate Time: 5–45 minutes [depending on how many songs you play]

Instructor Notes

1. This is a good exercise to carry over to other class periods. You can begin and/or end a class with one or two uplifting songs.
2. This exercise can also be a good diversity exercise. Invite students to bring in music that represents the very best of their culture, music that inspires them or generates positive feelings.
3. After playing a number of songs (either in one class or over a number of classes), have students nominate and then vote on a "class song," one that inspires them to do their very best in the quest for their academic goals.

Journal Entry 31 Creating Flow

EXERCISE 31-1: Clump

Purpose

To offer participants an opportunity to explore their relationship with play. (Note: This is a great energizer and mood lightener, too.)

Supplies and Setup

Chairs pushed to the sides of the room; students standing in the middle of the room

Directions

1. *We're going to play a very silly child's game called Clump. Be aware of what you tell yourself and how you feel both as I describe the game and as you play it. Here's the way to play Clump. First, everyone walks randomly around the room. As you walk, I'll call out "Clump" plus a number, such as "Clump 4." As soon as you hear "Clump 4," your goal is to grab hold of three others to form a clump of four people, no more, no less. Any questions? Okay, let the Clumping begin.* [Vary the Clump number each time: Clump 2, Clump 6, Clump 3, and so on.] [5–10 minutes, depending on size of the group]
2. [Quick-Write and/or Class Discussion] *What did you tell yourself when you heard how to play Clump? What did you tell yourself while you were playing? How did you feel while playing? How do you feel right now? Do you like to play? What kind of play do you like? Why do you suppose some people lose the urge to play as they grow older? What gets in their way? What might their Inner Critics or Inner Defenders have to say? Is there any change you'd like to make in your life regarding play? What is the life lesson here for you?* [e.g., "Playing keeps me young at heart."] [5–10 minutes]

Approximate Time: 10–20 minutes

Instructor Notes

1. Optional: Video record a group of children playing Clump. Show the video and talk about the difference between the way the children and the adults played. Explore: Why the difference?
2. Be particularly sensitive to the people who don't want to participate in this playful activity. Without judgment, ask them to become aware of what their Inner Critic or Inner Defender is telling them. Note also that some people

confuse play with competition: If there's no competition, there's no play. Help them tease these two concepts apart. Also, you may need to adapt the game to the physical limitations of some of your students.

3. To add a level of challenge, you can change the directions so that you offer only a hint about how many people should clump. For example, "Clump the number of blind mice" (3) or "Clump the number of basketball players from one team who play at one time" (5). You can invite students to offer their own "Clump" directions.

EXERCISE 31-2: Work Becomes Play

Purpose

To explore how we can bring more of the advantages of play into our work.

Supplies and Setup

Whiteboard or easel pad; students in groups of four to five

Directions

1. *What are the positive characteristics of play? What makes play fun and enjoyable?* [Make a list of answers on the whiteboard or easel pad. For example, ideas might include "Games allow you to start over often"; "You get to choose your teammates"; "You decide when to play"; "There are immediate rewards for your skills"; "Rules keep the players honest"; "It's exciting to compete"; "Winning is fun"; "Each time you play, you improve your skills."] [5–10 minutes]

2. [Assign each group a small number of the listed items to discuss.] *Your goal is to figure out how to have your present or future work take on the characteristics of play that are on your list. For example, if play offers immediate rewards for your skills, think of how you could experience that same characteristic in your work.* [10–15 minutes]

3. *Let's have a report from each group on some of your best ideas.* [10–15 minutes]

4. [Quick-Write and/or Class Discussion] *What did you learn about enjoying work? Why do you suppose some people hate the work they do? How do you feel about the work you do now or plan to do in the future? Is there any change you'd like to make in your life regarding work? What is the life lesson here for you?* [e.g., "I can make choices that make my work more like play."] [10–20 minutes]

Approximate Time: 25–35 minutes

EXERCISE 31-3: Instructors Who Create Flow

Purpose

To have students develop a list of instructors who create "flow," so that they can make wiser choices when registering for future semesters. Students should have completed Journal Entry 31, so they can understand the concept of "flow."

Supplies and Setup

"Instructors Who Create Flow" handout (see page 236); students sitting in pairs; chime (or other way to signal a change of partners)

Directions

1. *Many students sign up for classes based only on college requirements and times that courses are offered. Often a more important criterion is who is teaching the course. We're going to do an activity that will enable you to learn about some of the outstanding instructors at our college. The next time you register, you will have more information with which to make wiser choices about your course selection. I'd like five different volunteers to each read aloud one of the qualities of "Instructors Who Create Flow." As you hear these qualities, think of the instructors you have had here at this college who rate high in these qualities.* [5 minutes]

2. *Fill in Line 1 with your nomination of one instructor who creates flow for you. Next you will be sharing your nomination with other students. If by any chance you can't think of an instructor who creates flow, then leave the line blank.* [5 minutes]

3. [Put students in pairs.] *You will now have a few minutes to exchange nominations with your partner. On your own form, write down your partner's nomination, both the instructor's name and courses taught. If you have time, go on to share more about how these instructors create flow for you. After a couple of minutes, I'll ring a chime and you will find a new partner and exchange instructors again. You'll get to meet with a number of partners so you'll learn about a number of instructors.* [10–25 minutes, depending upon how many partner exchanges you create]

4. [Quick-Write and/or Class Discussion] *Were there any instructors whose names you encountered a number of times? What is it about them that your classmates appreciated? What is the life lesson here for you?* [e.g., "I can better control the quality of my educational experience by making wiser choices about my classes."] [5–10 minutes]

Approximate Time: 25–45 minutes

Instructor Notes

Some students may want to talk about their "lousy" instructors. I recommend that you keep them focused on the best instructors, the ones who create flow for their students.

Instructors Who Create Flow . . .

1. Demonstrate a deep knowledge of their subject.
2. Show great enthusiasm for the value of their subject.
3. Set challenging but reasonable learning goals for their students.
4. Offer learning experiences that appeal to a variety of learning preferences.
5. Provide a combination of academic and emotional support that gives their students high expectations of success.

Instructor's Name	Courses This Instructor Teaches
1.	
2.	
3.	
4.	
5.	
6.	
7.	
8.	
9.	
10.	
11.	
12.	

Journal Entry **32** Believing in Yourself: Develop Self-Love

EXERCISE 32-1: Ways to Love Myself

Purpose

To create dozens of options for treating oneself with love.

Supplies and Setup

Journals or writing paper; "32-Day Commitment Form" handout (see page 238). Four easel pad markers and four easel pad pages, each entitled with one of the following words: PHYSICAL, MENTAL, EMOTIONAL, SPIRITUAL. Post these pages in various places in the room.

Directions

1. *Some of us are better at loving other people than we are at loving ourselves. Sometimes that's because we're just not sure how to love ourselves; nobody ever taught us. So, today we're going to create a list of ways we can be loving to ourselves. Notice the four topics posted around the room: Physical, Mental, Emotional, and Spiritual. Go to whichever one you choose.* [Give each group one of the markers.] [3 minutes]

2. *Your group's goal is to come up with a list of as many ways as possible to be loving to yourself in the realm you've chosen. For example, what ways can you be loving to yourself **physically**?* [Elicit examples, such as get a massage, eat a healthy meal, etc.] *What ways can you be loving to yourself **mentally**?* [e.g., listen to my Inner Guide and not my Inner Critic, read a good book, etc.] *What ways can you be loving to yourself **emotionally**?* [e.g., spend time with people I love, express anger in a healthy way, etc.] *What ways can you be loving to yourself **spiritually**?* [e.g., say a prayer, spend time in nature, etc.] *Write your ideas on the easel pad page. Remember, the goal here is quantity. As many as possible—ready, go!* [During the activity, you may want to assist a group that gets stuck.] [10 minutes]

3. *Now we're going to hear some of your ideas for showing love to ourselves. In your journal or on a sheet of paper, title a page WAYS TO LOVE MYSELF. I suggest that you make a list of all the suggestions, even the ones you don't think you'll ever do. Maybe you'll read this list five years from now and find a suggestion that will be just perfect for you then. Now, let's have a reporter present each group's suggestions.* [20 minutes]

4. [Quick-Write and/or Class Discussion] *What would your life be like if you treated yourself with these loving actions when you are going through a challenge or a crisis in your life? What would it do for your self-esteem if you treated yourself better every day? What is the life lesson here for you?* [e.g., "If I consistently treat myself with love, I'll have plenty of overflow for the important people in my life."] [10–20 minutes]

5. *Here's a 32-Day Commitment Form. Consider making a commitment to do one of these loving things for yourself every day for 32 days.* [Pause for students to write a commitment.] *Is there anyone who would like to publicly announce a 32-day commitment?* [5 minutes]

Approximate Time: 45–55 minutes

Instructor Notes

Students may disagree about where to place some ideas for loving oneself (for example, does "Meditate" belong under Mental or Spiritual?). I allow all suggestions to stay wherever they are placed; if an item comes up in two or more realms, that's fine, too. (Thus, "Meditate" might be in the list for Mental *and* Spiritual.) The point is that students leave class with a menu of options for self-care.

32-Day Commitment

Because I know that this commitment will keep me on course to my goals, I promise myself that every day for the next 32 days I will take the following action: _____

Day 1	Day 17
Day 2	Day 18
Day 3	Day 19
Day 4	Day 20
Day 5	Day 21
Day 6	Day 22
Day 7	Day 23
Day 8	Day 24
Day 9	Day 25
Day 10	Day 26
Day 11	Day 27
Day 12	Day 28
Day 13	Day 29
Day 14	Day 30
Day 15	Day 31
Day 16	Day 32

By making and keeping promises to ourselves and others, little by little, our honor becomes greater than our moods. Stephen Covey

Success is . . . the long-term consequence of making and keeping promises—promises to others . . . and promises to yourself . . . the more you exercise your self-discipline, the stronger it gets. Harvey Cook

EXERCISE 32-2: Affirmation Whisper

Purpose

To demonstrate the power of self-affirming statements and give students' self-worth a boost.

Supplies and Setup

Chime. Students need to know their personal affirmation (Journal Entry 12) by heart or have it written on an index card. Arrange the room so that half of the students are sitting in chairs (randomly placed about the room), and half of the students are standing behind the chairs in which students are sitting. Be sure there is enough space between the sitting students for the standing students to walk among them without bumping into anyone. I recommend soothing instrumental music as background; "Angelic Music" by Iasos is my choice.

Directions

1. [Give all directions—steps 1 to 3—before starting the activity. You may want to project abbreviated directions on a PowerPoint slide for students to reference throughout the activity.] *In a moment, those of you who are standing are going to whisper your affirmation in the ears of the people sitting down. But instead of saying, "**I** am a bold, happy, loving man," you will say "**You** are a bold, happy, loving . . . **man or woman**," whichever gender is appropriate. It helps also to say the person's name first.* [DEMO by whispering your affirmation into one student's ear and then moving on and repeating it.] *As soon as you have whispered your affirmation to one person, move on to another person and whisper your affirmation again. Keep whispering until you hear the chime ring, even if that means you repeat your affirmation for some people. And here's a last thought for those of you sitting down—it seems to enrich the experience if you close your eyes.* [Make sure that everyone knows how to pronounce everyone's name correctly. You may also wish to determine if there is a student with a hearing challenge who would prefer to have the affirmations spoken in a particular ear.]

2. *When you hear the chime, reverse roles. Those of you sitting will stand and walk behind your chair, and those of you standing will sit in the first empty chair you see. As before, the standing people will immediately begin whispering their affirmations to the sitting people. Start whispering as soon as someone sits in the chair in front of you and keep moving around the room whispering to other people until you hear the chime ring, even if that means you repeat your affirmation for some people.*

3. *When the chime rings a second time, simply relax. Find a comfortable position anywhere in the room, sitting or lying down, and take a few minutes to think about what that experience was like for you. Are there any questions?* [The success of this activity requires that everyone understands the directions before beginning, so be extra sure everyone is clear.] *Ready, begin.* [Steps 1–3 will take about 10 minutes.]

4. [Let the first round of whispered affirmations go for about two to four minutes. Ring the chime to signal reversing roles and allow about three to four more minutes for the second round (allow a little extra time for the second group to switch roles). Then ring the chime a last time and give students about two or three minutes in silence to relax and take in and think about the affirmations they have just heard.] [10 minutes]

5. [Quick-Write and/or Class Discussion] *What was that experience like for you? How do you feel right now? What can you do to feel like this more often? What did you hear? What is the life lesson here for you?* [e.g., I'll never forget one of my students saying, "How different, warmer, sweeter this life might have been, if only once each day I might have heard these loving words so gently spoken."] [10–20 minutes]

Approximate Time: 30–40 minutes

Instructor Notes

This powerful activity is one of my students' all-time favorites. It often creates an experience for some students that is nothing short of sacred. I take great precautions that no one ruins that experience for the class. Occasionally, there is someone who gets uncomfortable and wants to make a joke of the activity. If you sense there is someone in your class who might do this, give everyone the opportunity to opt out.

EXERCISE 32-3: What I Appreciate About Myself

Purpose

To acknowledge positive characteristics about oneself.

Supplies and Setup

Students sitting in pairs (Student A and Student B)

Directions

1. *For the next little while, you're going to have an exchange with your partner about self-love. Whoever starts will say, "What I appreciate about myself is . . ." and finish the sentence. Then the other person will say, "What I appreciate about myself is . . ." and finish the sentence. Go back and forth. Take your time. Think deeply and feel deeply. Trust your Inner Guide and don't hold back.* [You might want to do a DEMO by sharing some of the things you appreciate about yourself. If you sense that some students are uncomfortable, encourage them by saying that truthful bragging is definitely encouraged in this activity. Of course, as always, allow students to choose to not participate.] [5 minutes]

2. [Quick-Write and/or Class Discussion] *What was that experience like for you? What was it like to hear your partner expressing appreciation for him- or herself? What was it like to say what you appreciate about yourself? What thoughts or feelings did you have as you expressed yourself each time? Did your Inner Critic try to interfere? How do you feel right now? What would it do for your self-esteem if you fully acknowledged all your positive traits? What is the life lesson here for you?* [e.g., "Loving and appreciating myself are the secret ingredients of my success."] [10–20 minutes]

Approximate Time: 15–25 minutes

Instructor Notes

In pairing students for this activity, you might want to suggest that students choose a partner with whom they have felt a close connection during the semester. This closeness can free people to be more expressive of their appreciation for themselves.

Embracing Change: Do One Different Thing This Week

Strong emotions are part of the human experience, but what we do with them is up to us. Victims often let strong emotions become their excuse for making choices that promote immediate pleasure or escape from discomfort while sabotaging future goals and dreams. Creators, however, have learned to weather the storms of strong emotions and refuse to be blown off course. From the following actions, pick ONE new belief or behavior.

1. Think: "I create my own happiness and peace of mind."
2. Write a list of eight emotions and add eight more emotions to the list each day. Afterward, circle which of the 56 emotions I experienced during that week.
3. Identify and record a "strong emotion" as I experience it. Note at the end of the week if I see a pattern in the kind of strong emotions that I experience.
4. Identify a "strong emotion" as someone else is experiencing it, and note how I respond.
5. Talk to someone about emotions, mine or theirs.
6. Take the following new action to reduce stress in my life: ___.
7. Notice when I experience "flow," and observe what I am doing at the time.
8. Show fellow students the list of five instructor qualities that create "flow," and ask them to name the instructor they have had who most demonstrates these qualities. I will consider enrolling in a class taught by one of these instructors.
9. Do the following to nurture myself: ___.
10. Your choice: A different belief or behavior you learned in this chapter with which you would like to experiment.

Now, write the one you chose under "My Commitment" in the following chart. Then, track yourself for one week, putting a check in the appropriate box when you keep your commitment. After seven days, assess your results. If your outcomes and experiences improve, you now have a tool you can use for the rest of your life. Consider the insight of Confucius, the ancient Chinese philosopher, who said, "They must often change, who would be constant in happiness or wisdom."

My Commitment						
Day 1	Day 2	Day 3	Day 4	Day 5	Day 6	Day 7

During my seven-day experiment, what happened?

As a result of what happened, what did I learn or relearn?

Chapter 8: Quiz Questions

(Please visit the publisher's *On Course* website at login.cengage.com or contact your local Cengage Learning sales representative to find electronic versions of the Quiz Questions.)

43. Understanding Emotional Intelligence

1. Having mental intelligence (a high IQ) is all one needs to create great success in college and in life.   TRUE   FALSE

2. In an experiment during the 1960s, young children were divided into two groups on their ability (or lack of ability) to postpone the immediate gratification of eating one marshmallow in order to get two marshmallows later. Years later the group that was able to postpone gratification scored, on average, 210 points higher on the SAT (Scholastic Aptitude Test) than did the group that chose immediate gratification.   TRUE   FALSE

3. Writing a term paper instead of attending a party that you'd love to go to is an example of

   A. emotional self-awareness (knowing your feelings in the moment).

   B. emotional self-management (managing strong feelings).

   C. social awareness (empathizing accurately with other people's emotions).

   D. relationship management (handling emotions in relationship with skill and harmony).

4. Making an effort to help someone feel comfortable in a situation that is new to him or her is an example of

   A. emotional self-awareness (knowing your feelings in the moment).

   B. emotional self-management (managing strong feelings).

   C. social awareness (empathizing accurately with other people's emotions).

   D. relationship management (handling emotions in relationship with skill and harmony).

5. Noticing when someone else is experiencing sadness or anxiety is an example of

   A. emotional self-awareness (knowing your feelings in the moment).

   B. emotional self-management (managing strong feelings).

   C. social awareness (empathizing accurately with other people's emotions).

   D. relationship management (handling emotions in relationship with skill and harmony).

44. Reducing Stress

1. Creators accept responsibility not only for the results they create in their outer world but also for the emotions they experience in their inner world.   TRUE   FALSE

2. When stress persists, stress hormones (cortisol and epinephrine) remain active in the body's systems, damaging almost every part of the body.   TRUE   FALSE

3. To reduce stress of many kinds, you can choose new behaviors and/or new thoughts.   TRUE   FALSE

4. Feeling overwhelmed is probably the most common stressor for college students. To begin reducing this feeling, you can use the following self-management tool to list and prioritize everything you need to do in each of your life roles (then you can begin doing the high-priority tasks one by one).

   A. Next actions list

   B. Tracking form

   C. 32-day commitment

   D. Calendar

5. High stress has a positive impact on memory and other mental skills such as creativity, concentration, and attention to details.   TRUE   FALSE

45. Creating Flow

1. When our perceived skill level is high and our perceived challenge level is low, our inner experience is one of

   A. anxiety.

   B. flow.

   C. boredom.

   D. none of the above.

2. When our perceived skill level is low and our perceived challenge level is high, our inner experience is one of

   A. anxiety.

   B. flow.

   C. boredom.

   D. none of the above.

3. When our perceived skill level and our perceived challenge level are about the same, our inner experience is one of

   A. anxiety.

   B. flow.

   C. boredom.

   D. none of the above.

4. Psychologist Mihaly Csikszentmihalyi found that typical working Americans experience the most flow

   A. while watching television.

   B. over the weekend.

   C. on vacations.

   D. on their jobs.

5. Each time you create flow by testing your present skills against a new challenge, your skills improve. Thus, over time, by creating flow again and again, your skills continue to improve.   TRUE   FALSE

46. On Course at Work: Emotional Intelligence at Work

1. Responding impulsively to the actions of bosses or coworkers shows a lack of the emotional intelligence component called emotional self-management.   TRUE   FALSE

2. Embarrassing a coworker by pointing out his or her poor performance to others shows a lack of the emotional intelligence component called emotional self-awareness.   TRUE   FALSE

3. In fields such as engineering, medicine, computer science, or the law, emotional intelligence has little importance in getting and keeping the job.   TRUE   FALSE

4. To be an outstanding leader, one must be able to resolve conflicts that happen in the workplace. In emotional intelligence terms, this skill is called

   A. emotional self-awareness.

   B. emotional self-management.

   C. social awareness.

   D. relationship management.

5. Imagine that you are the leader of a team at work. One member of the team is always late, never meets deadlines, and angers her teammates. You feel your temper rising with this person's poor work habits. Which of the following choices demonstrates the most professional behavior?

   A. In the next team meeting, confront the offending team member with the evidence of her poor teamwork.

   B. While you are still motivated by your anger, send an e-mail about this coworker's lack of motivation to your boss.

   C. When calm, meet with the offending team member alone, share your feelings about her behaviors, and make a request for a change in behavior that will help the team function more effectively.

   D. Stop sending her notices of when and where your team is meeting.

47. Believing in Yourself: Develop Self-Love

1. Self-love is the core belief that I AM LOVABLE.   TRUE   FALSE

2. The way to develop self-love is through achieving bigger and better accomplishments.   TRUE   FALSE

3. Now that we are adults, we are responsible for continuing (or beginning) our own nurturing.   TRUE   FALSE

4. Exercising, eating healthy foods, and avoiding dangerous drugs are ways to nurture ourselves

   A. mentally.

   B. emotionally.

   C. physically.

5. Compassion for yourself is an emotional antidote for toxic self-judgments.   TRUE   FALSE

48. Wise Choices in College: Managing Money

1. Managing money is a skill as important and challenging as reading and writing.   TRUE   FALSE

2. According to a source at the University of Indiana, credit card debt is more dangerous to your college success than academic failure.   TRUE   FALSE

3. The benefit of qualifying for grants and student loans is that you don't need to pay them back.   TRUE   FALSE

4. If you make poor choices with your credit card in college, what consequences could result?

    A. You could have trouble purchasing a home or a car.

    B. You could lose out on a job.

    C. You could be charged higher interest rates on future credit cards.

    D. All of the above.

5. Which of the following typically offers lower costs for financial services (checking accounts or loans, for example)?

    A. Banks

    B. Credit unions

Chapter 8: Essay Topics

1. Misfortune happens to every human being. Victims often get overwhelmed by their distressing emotions, whereas Creators move on to more positive futures. Using your knowledge of emotional intelligence and strategies for reducing stress, write an essay comparing how you dealt with a misfortune in your past with how you might deal with that same misfortune today.

2. Much research has been done on "flow" experiences, in which time seems to stop and the participant is totally and positively absorbed in the activity. In an essay intended to contribute to a better understanding of "flow," offer a description of one of your own "flow" experiences at school, work, or play.

3. Few people are fully conscious of the chatter of their inner aspects such as their Inner Defender, Inner Critic, and Inner Guide. In an essay for college students, explain how these inner aspects impact the quality of their inner experience. Present your readers with methods for dealing positively with their inner voices.

4. Author William Saroyan advised, "Try as much as possible to be wholly alive. . . . You will be dead soon enough." In an essay for a general audience, explain what specific steps one can take to create the experience of feeling "wholly alive."

5. Many people focus on what is wrong in their lives, whereas a rare few seem to radiate a positive outlook on life. In an essay for a mass-circulation magazine (such as *Reader's Digest*), tell about the most positive person you have ever known.

6. We sense how much a person loves us by how he or she treats us, especially in times of challenge or pain. Similarly, we can know how much we love ourselves by how we treat ourselves both in good times and in bad times. Write an essay for teenagers who are addicted to drugs. In this essay describe the importance of self-love, offer ways to assess the level of one's self-love, and help these teenagers develop a self-care plan for increasing their self-love.

7. Using the student essays in *On Course* as a model, write an essay about how you used a strategy from Chapter 8 to overcome a problem in your life—academic, personal, or even at work. First explain the problem; then discuss the strategy you used and how; finally, identify what happened. Your instructor may submit your essay for possible publication in the next edition of *On Course*. Additional directions for writing and submitting these essays can be found at http://oncourseworkshop.com.

8. Using the "One Student's Story" essays in *On Course* as models, write an essay about how you used one or more new learning strategies (reading, taking notes, organizing study materials, rehearsing and memorizing study materials, taking tests, or writing) to overcome an academic challenge in college. First explain the academic challenge; then discuss what strategy or strategies you used; finally identify the outcome of your efforts. Your instructor may submit your essay for possible publication in the next edition of *On Course*, where it could inspire tens of thousands of your fellow students. Additional directions for writing and submitting these essays can be found at http://oncourseworkshop.com.

Answer Key to Chapter 8 Quiz Questions

43. Understanding Emotional Intelligence

Answers: 1. FALSE   2. TRUE   3. B   4. D   5. C

44. Reducing Stress

Answers: 1. TRUE   2. TRUE   3. TRUE   4. A   5. FALSE

45. Creating Flow

Answers: 1. C   2. A   3. B   4. D   5. TRUE

46. On Course at Work: Emotional Intelligence at Work

Answers: 1. TRUE   2. FALSE (emotional self-management)   3. FALSE   4. D   5. C

47. Believing in Yourself: Develop Self-Love

Answers: 1. TRUE   2. FALSE   3. TRUE   4. C   5. TRUE

48. Wise Choices in College: Managing Money

Answers: 1. TRUE   2. TRUE   3. FALSE (student loan must be paid back)   4. D   5. B

Staying On Course to Your Success

Concept

Staying on course to a rich, personally fulfilling life is one of a human being's greatest challenges. Forces both outside of us and inside of us constantly conspire to divert us from this achievement. By assisting students to plan and take their next steps, we not only remind them of the changes they have made to better their lives, we help them keep their sights on both a positive future and the wise choices that will guide them there. As we bid our students farewell for now, we give them the momentum to head off into a great life of their own creation.

EMPOWERS STUDENTS TO . . .

1. Review what they have learned about themselves in this course.
2. Assess the changes they have made to improve the outcomes of their lives.
3. Identify additional changes they wish to make in the near and distant future.
4. Plan their next steps toward living a rich, personally fulfilling life.

Journal Entry **33** Planning Your Next Step

EXERCISE 33-1: Self-Assessment Revisited

Purpose

To have students acknowledge the changes they have created in their lives during this course and to decide what additional changes they want to make.

Supplies and Setup

Journal Entry 33 completed; students sitting in pairs (Student A and Student B)

Directions

1. *Partner A, read to your partner what you wrote for Step 2 of Journal Entry 33. When Partner A is finished, Partner B will respond, "What I heard you saying in this entry is . . . ." Partner B can then add any other comments or observations that come to mind. [5 minutes]*
2. *Now, Partner B, you read Step 2 of your Journal Entry 33. Afterward, Partner A will respond, "What I heard you saying in this entry is . . ." and then add any other comments or observations that seem appropriate. [5 minutes]*

3. [Repeat steps 1 and 2 above for Step 3 of Journal Entry 33.] [10 minutes for both partners to read and respond]
4. [Repeat steps 1 and 2 above for Step 4 of Journal 33.] [10 minutes for both partners to read and respond]
5. [Repeat steps 1 and 2 for Step 5 of Journal 33.] [10 minutes for both partners to read and respond.]
6. [Quick-Write and/or Class Discussion] *What important discoveries have you made in this course? What changes have you made in your life? What additional changes do you plan to make in the future? What life lessons do you want to remember from this course?* [e.g., I will remember to pause before important choices I make and ask, "Which choice will help me create my goals and dreams?"] [10–20 minutes]

Approximate Time: 50–60 minutes

EXERCISE 33-2: Commencement

Purpose
To offer an opportunity for students to review and reflect on what they have learned in this course.

Supplies and Setup
A beach ball (or other light ball) with key terms written on it with a permanent marker: SELF-RESPONSIBILITY, SELF-MOTIVATION, SELF-MANAGEMENT, INTERDEPENDENCE, SELF-AWARENESS, LIFELONG LEARNING, EMOTIONAL INTELLIGENCE, BELIEVE IN YOURSELF, WISE CHOICES, CRITICAL THINKING, CORE (and any other concepts you want to review). Write four sentence stems on the board or project them on a PowerPoint slide. (See Instructor Notes for the sentence stems.) Paper and pens. Optional: video recorder.

Directions
1. [You may wish to have students standing in a circle for this step.] *Let's take a few minutes to review where we've been this semester. I'm going to toss this ball to someone. When you catch it, read the first word or words that you see and tell us the most important thing you have learned or relearned about that topic. You can tell us what the concept means to you or about a strategy you learned, an experience you had that illustrates this concept, or whatever feels appropriate to you. There is no right or wrong answer. When you're done, toss the ball to another person, and that person will do the same thing. It's fine if you talk about the same topic that someone else discussed. Each topic will probably be discussed a number of times in different ways.* [10–15 minutes, or until you sense that the key points of the course have been adequately reviewed]
2. *On a sheet of paper, complete the four sentence stems you see written on the whiteboard. I will be collecting this as feedback to me about your experience in the course. Be as complete as possible.* [Collect what the students have written. Collecting these forms prevents students from merely reading from them in the next part.] [10–15 minutes]
3. *Now we're going to have a commencement exercise for our class. To commence means to "begin." So this exercise is the beginning of the rest of your lives. I invite you to come to the front of the room and talk to us from your heart for a couple of minutes. Tell us the most important things you've learned in this course; tell us what you want in your life; tell us what you know are the keys to your success; tell us anything else that you want us to know. When one person finishes, the next person can come right up. I'm just going to sit here and listen. Who would like to be first?* [There may be a couple of long periods where no one comes to the front to speak. If you are patient with the silence, most times someone will come forward.] [10–25 minutes]

Approximate Time: 30–55 minutes

Instructor Notes
1. Post the following four sentence stems:
   1. Important goals and dreams in my life include . . .
   2. The success strategies I will use to achieve them include . . .
   3. Changes I would make in this course include . . .
   4. Most of all from this course I want to remember . . .

2. I recommend video recording the commencement presentations. Students in your class will enjoy watching themselves later, and the video is great to show at the beginning of future classes to show new students the amazing journey they are about to undertake. You can also use the video for recruiting new students to take your course.

3. You might want to mention that some students' Inner Critics or Inner Defenders will give them all sorts of reasons why they should not go to the front of the room and speak. That's why doing so is such a great boost to their self-esteem: They get to show their Inner Critics and Inner Defenders who is making the choices that matter.

EXERCISE 33-3: Appreciations

Purpose

To experience an avalanche of affirming thoughts that can boost the students' sense of self-worth.

Supplies and Setup

Journals; chime; students sitting in circles of 8 to 10. Write the words APPRECIATE, ADMIRE, RESPECT on the board or project them on a PowerPoint slide.

Directions

1. *Open your journal to a clean page and write your name at the top of the page. Now pass your journal to the person on your right.* [1 minute] [For students who don't have their journal, a piece of paper will do.]

2. *When you get your neighbor's journal, write a short note telling what you **appreciate, admire,** and **respect** about him or her. You'll have only one minute, so get right to the heart of what you wish to say. When I ring the chime, sign your name and pass the journal to your right. Keep writing and passing until your journal comes back to you. Then read what people wrote to you.* [20–30 minutes]

3. [Quick-Write and/or Class Discussion] *What was it like to write appreciations to others? What was it like to read the appreciations written to you? How do you feel right now? What would it do for your success if you fully acknowledged all the aspects of yourself that others appreciate, admire, and respect? What is the life lesson here for you?* [e.g., "I am having more of an impact on other people's lives than my Inner Critic ever let me realize."] [10–20 minutes]

Approximate Time: 30–50 minutes

EXERCISE 33-4: *On Course* in the Movies

Purpose

For students to reflect on *On Course* concepts and see how they are applied in Hollywood films.

Supplies and Set up

Handout that lists films (p. 250)

Directions

1. *For this assignment, you will watch a movie and analyze how it illustrates concepts we have covered in our course this semester.*

2. *Don't simply give a plot summary of the movie; instead choose certain scenes and/or key themes that relate to any of the Eight Choices of Successful Students (found on the inside front cover of your* On Course *textbook) and/or related ideas presented in the book. Rather than try to tie in all eight choices, you might focus on two or three areas that you think stand out the most in the movie. You may choose to analyze one character in particular, or you may give examples of things that many characters in the movie did that demonstrated (or did not demonstrate) patterns of thought, emotion, and behavior consistent with a particular* On Course *principle.*

3. *Choose from the following films:*

The Blind Side	*Rain Man*
Any Star Wars movie	*Lean on Me*
For the Love of the Game	*Tuesdays with Morrie*
Rocky IV	*12 Angry Men*
Hoosiers	*Yes Man*
The Karate Kid	*Forrest Gump*
Dead Poet's Society	*Homeless to Harvard*
Mr. Holland's Opus	*The Bucket List*
Good Will Hunting	*Stand and Deliver*
Finding Forrester	*Pay It Forward*
Breakfast Club	*Slumdog Millionaire*
Dangerous Minds	*Patch Adams*
Antwone Fisher	*Any Harry Potter movie*
Akeelah and the Bee	*The King's Speech*
Tangled	*Coach Carter*

Approximate Time: 15 minutes to give assignment.

Source: Submitted by Lisa Marks, Ozarks Technical Community College, MO.

Chapter 9: Essay Topics

1. Almost everyone would agree that they want to live a rich, personally fulfilling life—yet few people know what they mean by the idea, let alone how to create such a life. In an essay for *Success Magazine,* define what you consider to be a rich, personally fulfilling life and explain how you plan to create such a life.

2. In an essay to be given to your children (or grandchildren) on their 21st birthdays, present your philosophy of living a successful life. Be specific about what defines a successful life for you and how you plan to create it.

3. In an essay for the author of our textbook, *On Course,* explain what parts of the book you found most valuable and any that you found less valuable. Please send a copy of your essay to Skip Downing, c/o Cengage Learning College Programs, 20 Channel Center, 6th Floor, Boston, MA 02210.

4. Using the "One Student's Story" essays in *On Course* as a model, write an essay about how you used any specific strategy, including study strategies, from this book to overcome a problem in your life—academic, personal, or even at work. First explain the problem; then discuss the strategy you used and how; finally, identify what happened. Your instructor may submit your essay for possible publication in the next edition of *On Course.* Additional directions for writing and submitting these essays can be found at http://oncourseworkshop.com.